EATS NYC

A GUIDE TO THE BEST, CHEAPEST, MOST INTERESTING RESTAURANTS IN BROOKLYN, QUEENS AND MANHATTAN

BY SYLVIA CARTER
WITH ADDITIONAL QUEENS REVIEWS BY
PETER M. GIANOTTI

NEWSDAY

ANDREWS AND McMEEL
A Universal Press Syndicate Company
Kansas City

MW00680084

In memory of my father, Charles Sylvester Carter,
a natural-born storyteller
who once ate 52 pancakes at a sitting

Additional copies of this book may be ordered by calling (800) 642-6480.

Library of Congress Cataloging-in-Publication Data

Carter, Sylvia, 1946–
    Eats NYC : a guide to the best, cheapest, most interesting restaurants in Brooklyn, Queens, and Manhattan / by Sylvia Carter ; with additional Queens reviews by Peter M. Gianotti.
        p. cm.
    ISBN 0-8362-0809-9 (pbk.)
    1. Restaurants—New York (N.Y.)—Guidebooks. I. Gianotti, Peter M. II. Title.
TX907.3.N72C37 1995
647.95747'1—dc   95-31157
                                                                           CIP

Book designed by Lisa Martin

CONTENTS

ACKNOWLEDGMENTS

My friends eat with me, so I won't have to order 20 things at once and try to eat them all myself. They also call me whenever a new place opens on their block. So do readers, bless them.

Kim Darrow shares my life and saves all my columns as a way of saying he loves me.

Thanks to former *Newsday* editor Anthony Insolia, who thought up the idea of "Eats," and to Donald Forst, *New York Newsday* editor, and Anthony Marro, *Newsday* editor, who continue to believe in the column. Thanks to all the *New York Newday* and *Newsday* folks who give me tips and other help: fellow reviewers Peter Gianotti and Jane Freiman, food editor Irene Sax and former food editor Peggy Katalinich, Herbie Wheeler, Marie Bianco, Cara de Silva, Bea Lewis and Carol Bennett. Liane Guenther, Larry Striegel and the rest of my friends on the copy desk caught a lot of typos before these reviews were published the first time, and I thank them.

Thanks especially to Ginny Dunleavy and Ellen Neary, who fact-checked the reviews and were always good-humored, and to Bob Heisler and Steve Schatt, who edited them for this book.

Jim Leff scouted out lots of good places and also helped update some. Lorie Brau helped me get organized—or tried—and updated information, too. Victor Nelson is always an alert scout. Jerry and Phyllis Morgan are loyal eaters and restaurant scouts. Suzanne Curley is my lookout in Brooklyn and subs for me in a pinch. Missy McKenna will take the subway to any restaurant, no matter how far. Donald Gardenier and Tom McGillis can be depended upon for several meals in one night, and so can Aytan Diamond. Every food critic is in desperate need of a good seamstress, and the talented Edith Pauly is mine. Thanks to Ken May and David Lehman, my good neighbors.

For always believing in me, thanks to David Black, my agent, and to Anne Raver, Beverly Hall Lawrence, Geraldine Shanahan and Tonice Sgrignoli.

To all the intrepid eaters who have sat down at tables with me, thank you, too. You know who you are.

INTRODUCTION

When I was thinking about taking a job in New York right after college, I asked Paul Myhre, a journalism professor, whether I should go to North Carolina instead. He said he wouldn't tell me what to do. But he did say that he would not trade his years living in New York "eating doughnuts under a bare light bulb" for anything. So of course I came to New York, intending to live on doughnuts and macaroni and cheese from the Automat if need be.

Instead, to borrow from the song, "I'll take Manhattan," with all its amazing and wonderful things to eat.

A souvenir T-shirt used to say, "New York, New York, a town so nice they named it twice." That sure is true when it comes to food. I've eaten sea urchins, cow cod soup (don't ask), halo-halo (a cold fruit and bean drink from the Philippines), falafel, tamales, arepas (corn cakes), custard ice cream, pizza at Coney Island, garlicky pastrami at Pastrami King, cheeseburgers at the Corner Bistro. From Sabrett hot dogs with cumin-laden onions on the street to the lush banana cream pies baked by Charlotte Bero at Anglers & Writers, the best of everything is here, and I try to find it for you.

When the "Eats" column began, I used to say I reviewed "dives, joints and roadhouses." This phrase had a catchy ring to it.

What I meant was that I'd go anywhere, no matter how out of the way, in search of a good meal.

Really, "New York Eats" and "BQ (Brooklyn Queens) Eats" are about all kinds of places to eat well without spending a lot. At some of the eateries in this book, you can get a bowl of soup or a blue plate special so hearty it's a meal for under $5. At some special occasion places you may spend $25 or even a little more, but you'll get your money's worth.

Don't look for stars. "Eats" restaurants don't get stars, which means you have to read the review to see what's good. I like that, because without the shorthand code I can tell you to have the cheeseburger and skip the desserts, or I can tell you the food is wonderful but the service is slow.

And I get help in Queens from Peter M. Gianotti, who reviews restaurants in Nassau and Suffolk counties for *Newsday* and is co-author of *Newsday*'s *Long Island Restaurant Guide 1995–96*. Peter has reviewed more than half the Queens restaurants in this collection. His recommendations carry his last name and the promise of good eats.

"Eats" restaurants are the comfortable sorts where men can loosen their ties and kick back, and where women won't need to wear stockings on a sultry summer day. Some of them don't look fancy, but you can't eat looks. They're my kind of places, and yours.

Gotta go now. So many restaurants, so little time.

NOTE

If a restaurant takes reservations, the review contains a Reservations category that reflects this. If a review contains no Reservations category, the restaurant does not take reservations.

Credit cards are listed under the Prices category.

AE = American Express
CB = Carte Blanche
DC = Diners Club
DS = Discover
MC = MasterCard
V = Visa

Since restaurants, hours, prices and locations change frequently, we recommend calling ahead to confirm the information in this book.

ANGLERS & WRITERS
420 Hudson St.
(212) 675-0810

HOURS: Monday–Thursday, 9 a.m.–11 p.m.; Friday–Saturday, 9 a.m.–midnight; Sunday, 10 a.m.–10 p.m.
PRICES: Entrées/lunch $6–$12.50; soup/salad $3.50–$4.50. Brunch Saturday–Sunday $5.50–$7.75.
RESERVATIONS: Accepted only for dinner.
ACCESS: Not wheelchair-accessible.
KIDS: No children's menu but will accommodate.
HOW TO FIND IT: At St. Luke's Place; subway line 1 to Houston Street/Varick Street station.

We midwesterners are famous for being stoic and undemonstrative. Words like sensual don't come up a lot when people are talking about the heartland.

That's just because New Yorkers don't know how to read us. In our own way, we are rash, hedonistic even. We celebrate summer with lush black raspberry pie, we eat two hefty slabs of mile-high pound cake and call it a meal. When I was small, my mother baked bread twice a week, and on those days our supper was bread, home-churned butter and honey. Then we had dessert: brown-sugar, sour-cream sweet rolls.

That's the sort of thing I recommend doing at Anglers & Writers. Just go whole hog, as we say in Missouri, where I'm from, and in Wisconsin, where Anglers & Writers owner Craig Bero is from.

A friend of mine, a New Yorker born and bred, got right into the spirit of things at Anglers & Writers. After sampling a wide range of baked goods, my chum said, "I'd have angel food for the appetizer, because it's light. If I were sharing, I'd have apple pie and Key Lime pie for the main course, and the cheesecake [cottage cheese] for dessert. That's the four basic food groups."

It is, when Charlotte Bero, Craig's mom, is in the kitchen. This tiny, white-haired dynamo's baked goods are a wonder: angel food cake smothered in Seven Minute icing, pound cake with a touch of mace and a delicacy of crumb, Black Cap wild raspberries (picked by two fishermen in Wisconsin's Nicolet National Forest) sweetened just enough and piled generously into a flaky pie crust (a secret recipe that represents the know-how of a lifetime of pie-making), pie made from Transparent August yellow apples, cinnamon-walnut crumb cake with a pat of butter on the side. Those tart summer apples, exulted Charlotte, are "truly the most wonderful apple for pie."

Once in a while, something is slightly off the mark—I'm thinking of chocolate frosting that was too sweet—but all is forgiven when I bite into a thick banana cream pie with a mellow custard that is just barely sweet. Whipped cream is the real thing here, and impossibly fluffy. "Ma," as Craig Bero calls his mother, cooked on a woodstove and learned to get by with as little sugar as possible, because it had to be bought in town; fruit could be gathered free, and Craig tagged after his father, who knew where to find all the wild berries. With less sweetening, the fruit flavors shine.

As they come in season, you may see thimbleberries, elderberries, mulberries and gooseberries. Some of the fruits for these purely divine desserts come from family in Wisconsin, a source that Craig Bero once described this way—"generations of our family working the rocky soil of the northern Wisconsin fields." The Montmorency pie cherries are from home.

What's more, eating at Anglers & Writers is a lot like eating at home, or a home you wish was yours. Doilies and vases of summer blooms grace the solid old oak tables, and iron pots and tackle boxes hang about the room. There's a collection of rolling pins and an old rolltop desk that would do any farmhouse proud. Cake may come on a slightly chipped plate sprigged with blue posies, too pretty to part with.

Of course, I can recommend some other good things at Anglers & Writers, if you're the sort of person who really insists on protein or vegetables. The luscious BLT came on lovely whole-grain semolina toast. An open-face roast turkey sandwich with nice brown gravy and a little compote of raisins was satisfying. We hope to get there some Friday to sample whitefish served "in the style of a Wisconsin Friday fish fry."

Next door is a winsome shop, The Bespeckled Trout, where chocolates, charming teapots and slices of the same pie are sold (for a dollar less than at Anglers & Writers). Up the block is Village Atelier, another Bero establishment.

Algoma, Wis., the Beros' hometown, is the native word for "the place where the wild flower grows." It is also the place where sweet wild berries grow, and the birthplace of this city's best pie baker.

THE ANGRY MONK
96 Second Ave.
(212) 979-9202

HOURS: Daily, 6 p.m.–midnight
PRICES: Entrées $8.50–$10.50. AE, DC, DS, MC, V.
RESERVATIONS: Usually not necessary.
ACCESS: Dining area/restrooms wheelchair-accessible.
HOW TO FIND IT: Between 5th and 6th Streets; subway line F to Second Avenue station (at Houston Street); bus line M15.

The 14th Dalai Lama has said, "My true religion is kindness." As Anne Lamott says in her excellent book on writing, Bird by Bird, that makes the exiled Dalai Lama "the sanest person currently on earth." Who could argue with that?

To get in the mood for kindness, you might start by eating at The Angry Monk, formerly known as Tibetan Restaurant. You will be doing yourself a kindness, and maybe this good food will even put you in a kindly frame of mind.

Contrary to the name, just sitting around at The Angry Monk is soothing. (There are a couple of couches perfect for lounging.) Sometimes it is a little troubling, too, for all around the walls are photographs of Tibet by Nancy Jo Johnson, who lived for four years in Katmandu. The images are wild and lonely, high and snowy, beautiful, and often sad.

These photographs are nourishment for the soul as surely as ngotse gonga thang, a cozy egg-drop soup with spinach, is food for the body.

Some of The Angry Monk's food must be much more sophisticated than it would be in Tibet, where, at least in the coldest areas, it is impossible to grow any vegetables or grain. At The Angry Monk, there are many vegetables, reflecting the variety available in New York. And while there are plenty of beef dishes (not yak, likely the most common Tibetan meat), it is also possible to order fried rice with cashews and chicken. (Tibetans generally slaughter only large animals, believing that if a life must be taken, it is morally better to take only one life instead of many. So traditionally, chickens, being on the small side, would not be killed for food.)

One thing that's not so different than what you might have in Tibet is bocha, the buttered, salted Tibetan tea. Don't knock it until you've tried it. It is rich, made with a bit of butter and some cream, but it is surprisingly delicious.

A rich, hearty tomato soup called thang was a serendipitous beginning one winter night, but another appetizer you have to try is tsong ngopa, which the menu translates as butter-fried onions. Actually, they must have meant batter-fried, for these tasty little morsels were battered and so crisp that not a hint of oil remained. Don't miss shogo-baley, endearingly translated on the menu as "potato chop," a big ball of fluffy potato studded with onion and other vegetables, battered and greaselessly fried. These were so irresistible that we ordered more on a second visit.

Meatballs, or shari ngopa, were well-seasoned, almost like sausage. Steamed dumplings known as sheymo were a bit thick-skinned but still tasty—savory potato-filled sheymo were our preference over milder vegetable dumplings. Shabaley was a big, flat sort of dumpling stuffed with zesty minced beef. Perky chick-pea salad was a good choice, too.

Lamb curry marinated in yogurt, called luksha shumdeh, was hot (chile-hot, I mean) and tender, with lots of good curry sauce for sopping up rice, served on the side. Chile-chicken, chasha khatsa, was slightly fatty but so flavorful that nobody minded. Chasha shumdeh, a yogurt-marinated curried chicken, was delectable, too.

Among the vegetarian dishes, we were partial to a cold dish of cauliflower, tofu and peas, with plenty of chile-powered oomph. Ask about fingtse, the 12-vegetable dish with bean-threads, a wonderful melange of mushrooms, potatoes, Chinese cabbage, more than one kind of mushroom, onions, tofu and other good things. "American chop suey" was a plate of prettily arranged noodles, vegetables and a fried egg with crisp edges. The word "cute" just had to be used to describe such a tidy little plate, the folks at our table agreed. But gyathuk, or noodles in soup, was a rather bland mixture of spaghettini-type noodles, raw mushrooms, peas, carrots carved into flowers, spinach and hard-boiled egg. The mushroom-based broth was nice enough but none of the ingredients seemed to add much to the dish. Adding a little of the peppy chile sauce, which is always brought to the table early in the meal, helped. A second sweet, deep maroon sauce made of beets is always offered, too.

For dessert, there is an ever-so-slightly sweet steamed rice dish called deysee, made with yogurt and plump golden raisins, and the chef often mixes peaches and other fruits into purchased ice cream.

The Angry Monk has an inviting, homey look, with an expanse of hardwood floor and, besides the smaller tables, a couple of big, sturdy tables to accommodate large groups. Unlike so many New York restaurants, a thought has been given to pegs for coats. (The restaurant workers hang their own jackets on a series of hooks beneath the yet-to-be-in-business bar.)

As you exit, notice the prayer shawls knotted in a row along the door handle. Perhaps it is not too farfetched to think of each wisp of fragile silk as a prayer, or a kind thought.

BABY JAKE'S
14 First Ave.
(212) 254-2229

HOURS: Sunday–Thursday, 6 p.m.–midnight; Friday–Saturday, 6 p.m.–4 a.m. Lunch daily, 10 a.m.–6 p.m. Sunday Brunch 11 a.m.–5 p.m.
PRICES: Entrées/sandwiches $6.95–$13.95; appetizers $3.50–$6.95. AE.
RESERVATIONS: Taken only for parties of eight or more.
ACCESS: Dining area/restrooms wheelchair-accessible.
KIDS: No children's menu but will accommodate.
PARKING: Commercial lot at Houston and Avenue A.
HOW TO FIND IT: Between 1st and 2nd Streets; subway line F to Second Avenue station; bus line M15.

In the Village, sleeping late is a tradition. Now, I hardly ever get to "sleep in," as the New York phrase goes, but I think back fondly to times past when I would get up at noon, or even 1 or 2 p.m.

Back then, after black coffee at home, the problem was where to eat. On Sunday, or even Saturday, plenty of places served brunch. On weekdays, a few reliable spots (the Pink Teacup comes to mind) served eggs all day long, bless them.

Baby Jake's is such a place. Breakfast stretches until 4 p.m., and lunch is served until 6 p.m. My kind of place.

Baby Jake's has an open kitchen, an open attitude, a few tables and some booths (my preferred seating) at the back. Service can range from good to scatter-brained (one waitress couldn't recall the specials for more than a minute and had to retreat often for a look at the specials blackboard), but Jake's is such a comfortable kind of place that it makes you feel tolerant. It's the kind of laid-back place where you can sit around and read for an hour, the kind of place where people at the next table call over and ask if you liked the Jazz beer. (Jazz is Dixie's contribution to the light beer scene, and it tastes more or less like bubbly water. Have Dixie, or Blackened Voodoo instead.)

When I met a friend for lunch at Baby Jake's, I made mine breakfast—a plate of eggs poached to order with savory, oniony home fries and spicy, perfectly grilled andouille sausages. We tucked into a small mountain of thin-cut sweet potato fries, so well-done we thought they might be overdone, but no, they were just right. And my friend braved a "Jake burger," even in these days when most burgers are made of turkey and other substitutes, and pronounced it one of the best she had had in a long while. The juicy meat was topped with melting peppered jack cheese and a pecan-maple barbecue sauce. The white-potato fries with the burger were dandy, too. Homemade iced tea washed it all down.

A few days later when we went for dinner, there was a major disappointment

—no sweet potatoes. No fries, no bourbon-spiked mashed sweet potatoes. We were able to bear up only because there were ample garlic mashed potatoes ($2.50 for a side order).

As an appetizer, cornmeal-dusted fried oysters were fresh as could be, morsels of pure goodness with smoked chile-cocktail sauce and some corn salsa on the side. Crab cakes were fine but not very spicy, even with chipotle-pepper tartar sauce.

A teenage friend got into the casual spirit of Jake's by mixing together the components of her grilled salmon fajitas—the fish, peppered jack cheese, black and white beans and a salsa made of green tomatillos. It tasted great that way. A monkfish special with a sauce of smoked tomatillos, garlic and basil, and a steak of the day with hefty mushrooms and frizzled onions were both expertly cooked by chef Shawn Knight and his energetic sidekicks, but wild mushroom ravioli came in a creamy basil sauce that was too rich for more than a few bites; plain pesto would have sufficed.

Delicious banana bread pudding, with nearly caramelized fruit, was huge, enough for two to share, or maybe four. But it's enough for four if one of them is me. There's a great sound track, too, with Patsy Cline and other oldies.

CAFFE LURE
169 Sullivan St.
473-2642

HOURS: Dinner Monday–Thursday, 6:30–11 p.m.; Friday–Saturday, 6:30 p.m.–midnight; Sunday, 6:30–10 p.m. Lunch daily, 9 a.m.–3:30 p.m.
PRICES: Entrées $12–$14; pizza $9. Lunch $4.50–$6.50
RESERVATIONS: Recommended for dinner.
ACCESS: Wheelchair-accessible; restrooms equipped for disabled.
HOW TO FIND IT: Between Bleecker and Houston Streets; subway lines A, D, E or F to West 4th Street/Washington Square station.

The first night Caffe Lure opened, I met a couple who make it a tradition to go to first nights of restaurants opened by Jean Claude Iacovelli. They were there when Jean Claude, the small, enormously popular restaurant a block south of Caffe Lure, opened 2½ years ago. Here they were.

You'll be there soon, too. Here's why: This kitchen puts a spin on the expected, usually without its coming off contrived. For French food, the prices are kind. A friend once dubbed Jean Claude "Bouley in blue jeans." The jeans fit, because Iacovelli and his chefs once worked at that fabled restaurant, Bouley. Now the team, with chefs William Prunty and Danforth Houle presiding, is setting out to improve on its own admirable record.

The atmosphere is decidedly French, from the haze of cigarette smoke to the bottles of water placed on each table for easy pouring. (Incidentally, there are few if any coffee bars in town that can beat the properly frothed cappuccino served here.) And service is professional.

With the basket of chewy, dark-crusted bread, faintly sour and utterly irresistible, order some wine from the short list (a 1993 Cotes-du-Rhone from Chateau d'Aigueville is much more drinkable than the too-new Bordeaux on the list), and let talk come easily. Take in the look of the place—a small brick pizza oven wedged into a corner, fishing lures that hang above the doorway to the kitchen, a big mirror that helps open up what could seem like a stiflingly cramped space. "Drink only the Monserrat," counsels the mirrored door to the unisex rest room.

Utilitarian brown paper covers the white linen tablecloths at Caffe Lure, but the napkins are of fabric, not those lamentable paper ones that shred apart before you're finished eating.

Who can say why the awning reads Caffe while the menu says Café? The latter would be the correct French. But perhaps the Italian spelling is a lucky one; it promises pizza and experimentation, both of which flourish here.

Margherita pizza makes a fine lunch all by itself or, when shared, a good beginning. It was divinely light, the mozzarella and tomatoes of exquisite quality. The crust could have been on the fire just a little longer, but they'll get it right, I know.

The menu you get may not be precisely the one I sampled. One night, gently cooked warm lobster was served over cellophane noodles fragrant with mint in a coconut sauce. In less talented hands, this dish could have been an awful mess; it was vivacious instead. A Napoleon of salmon tartare with crispy shreds of artichokes, shiitake mushrooms and a bit of sevruga caviar came close to being too fussy, but it got better the more we ate. There was a lovely salad of baby spinach dressed in a subtle sauce of Port and lemon and topped with more tender bits of warm lobster. A soup of pumpkin and black beans swirled like a painting and sweetened with caramelized apples was a mite sweet for me, yet its appeal was considerable.

We liked a tangle of squid with mildly peppery fettucine and a bit of sun-dried tomato. Beets worked surprisingly well with poached oysters and arugula, but the beef carpaccio beneath the mollusks was one ingredient too many.

As at Jean Claude, there are usually only five or six entrée choices. Trust me, trust Caffe Lure. Everything that didn't quite pan out will be perfection, or close, the next time, and if it isn't, it won't be on the menu quite the same way again.

Among the best of what we sampled was fresh halibut seared to a fine crustiness, moist within, served over a heap of whipped potato-black-olive puree, with a gorgeous slice of broiled red tomato and a pool of tomato-seed vinaigrette. Who else does that? I've not seen it elsewhere, and immediately I wanted to experiment at home.

The most sensational fish, though, was the tiny, succulent rouget, a fish seldom seen outside of France. The grilled eggplant with it might have been improved by a salting-down before cooking, to leach out some of the bitter edge that eggplant has, but the demiglace was well-made, tidbits of tomato and onion a welcome contrast to the fish.

Salt-baked purple fingerling potatoes, the slices scarcely bigger than a dime, tasted still of fresh earth and were scrumptious with poussin, a small chicken roasted whole in the brick oven. The oven imparted lots of flavor to the bird, but it was a little too pink at the joint and a bit dry in other spots. Duck was fatty beneath the skin, but the brown sauce that surrounded it was tasty enough. Beet risotto was the liveliest component of a venison plate with juniper-berry sauce.

Buttery tarte tatin and lavender crème brûlée of great delicacy were the only desserts earlier this week, but better to do just a few things and do them well.

I look back now at what I've said and think that it doesn't sound quite positive enough. Let me be clear; I love Caffe Lure and its daring, and I have great faith in this enterprise. *Je reviens, tout de suite.*

CASANIS
54 E. First St.
(212) 777-1589

HOURS: Dinner daily, 6 p.m. to varying closing hours. Brunch Saturday–Sunday, noon–4 p.m.
PRICES: Entrées $14–$16; appetizers $4.75–$6. Brunch $8–$10.
RESERVATIONS: Recommended.
ACCESS: Steps at entrance; small, tight area.
ENTERTAINMENT: Live jazz during Saturday brunch.
HOW TO FIND IT: Between First and Second Avenues; subway line F to Second Avenue; bus lines M15.

Slowly, softly French food ordinaire is returning to New York. I don't mean ordinary in the English sense of the word, but in the French sense. Just as a vin ordinaire is an everyday but often delicious French wine, I think of neighborhood French restaurants as affordable enough for a visit once a week, maybe oftener.

This new breed of restaurant is user-friendly French, not the kind of place you have to save for weeks to afford. You know the ones—Le Cirque, La Côte Basque, Lutèce.

If your neighborhood is the East Village, or anywhere near it, you can go to Casanis instead. (The name is that of a French pastis, or licorice-flavored drink. There's a deeply satisfying fish soup for $4.75 and roasted duck with fig sauce for $14.50. As French food goes, this is fairly easy on the wallet. Casanis is also one of the comeliest garden spaces in all New York right now.

There's got to be a downside, right? Well, yes.

Some nights you may have to wait an hour for a table. (You can reserve, so do. Or go early in the evening, when diners who go in for the late Downtown club scene aren't awake yet.) And one night we had to wait nearly an hour for dessert, seemingly only because the harried waitstaff could not find anyone in the kitchen to plate them.

The plus side is that after trying almost everything on the changing menu several nights, I can report that almost all of it is good, some of it better than that.

On summer nights, you can walk straight from the street into a walled garden spruced up with a few Romanesque ledges and some old mirrors, a tree or two, and a delightfully decorative cat who often sits in a window one story above the garden and looks down on the proceedings.

The restaurant proper will be cozy, too, come colder months; the premises could pass for a Parisian tabac and are decorated with water pitchers bearing the name Suze, a French aperitif, and American commercial artifacts from Camel cigarettes and Rolling Rock beer. The customers, too, supply a kind of decoration; they're good-looking, confident, stylish without trying too hard. These are people who come to eat, not to be seen.

They eat soup, and the ones at Casanis make lovely starters. Cold mushroom soup was mild and a bit thin, but refreshing on a sultry evening, and chilled asparagus soup was a cool treat. Chef Mono Rafael's Marseilles fish soup (he hails from there) had that deep, complex flavor that comes of simmering shells from lobster and other shellfish, and it was served with small toasts and rouille, a garlic mayonnaise spiked with chile peppers. Shredded cheese came on the side, but you'll do better swirling mayonnaise into the soup instead of Gruyère.

Perfect stems of steamed asparagus in a good vinaigrette were served with avocado, an inspired and tasty study in green. Tangy salmon tartare with lemony kiwi sauce was ideal hot-weather fare. Baked sardines in a tangy escabeche and handsome, moist grilled tuna over a tumble of greens were excellent choices, but mussels mariniere, though not the least bit gritty, were only adequate because of underseasoning. Even now-commonplace menu items such as the ubiquitous mesclun salad and warmed goat cheese salad were lifted above the ordinary because Rafael mixes an exquisite vinaigrette, with a light hand on the vinegar.

One of the best entrées borrowed from Thai cuisine to combine lemongrass with grilled salmon on spinach with a scattering of small, pungent olives. Just about the time sautéed codfish with garlic mashed potatoes arrived at our table, a breeze kicked up, making the robust dish just right for a summer's eve, after all. Some of the roasted duck was too chewy one night, but when we tried it again another time it was tender. Rabbit with fennel, olives and orange sauce was a good idea, but the lapin itself was dry and stringy. (To his credit, our waiter noticed that a friend didn't eat it, inquired about the dish and then took it off the bill.) Expertly roasted chicken with garlic mashed potatoes and excellent steak au poivre with a generous stack of thin-cut pommes frites were classics of their kind.

If dessert ever comes—and one night it was a bit like waiting for Godot—you'll be glad it did. Tarte tatin was almost startlingly good in a season when apples are not at their best, and cherry custard was a homey comfort, served slightly warm. Extremely tart lemon and passion fruit sorbets were costly ($5.50, $6 for the passion fruit) but worth it, superior to others about town

CI VEDIAMO
85 Avenue A
(212) 995-5300

HOURS: Daily, 5–11:30 p.m.
PRICES: Entrées $6.50–$9.95; appetizers $3.50–$4.50.
ACCESS: Dining room downstairs, not wheelchair-accessible.
HOW TO FIND IT: Between 5th and 6th Streets; subway line F to 2nd Avenue/Houston Street station; bus line M15.

Everyone at Ci Vediamo owns the restaurant. The person who is your waiter tonight will be the dishwasher next week. And from dishwasher through manager, everyone on the staff owns a piece of the action. They all have a vested interest in hoping you will come back; in Italian, "Ci vediamo" means "See you later."

Giorgio Penna, who consulted with or worked at such high-profile places as The Plaza Hotel, San Domenico and Café Society, is fond of quoting a line about Ci Vediamo's teamwork—"pulling off the impossible." It really does seem that way. The goal of the team, all of whom dress alike (red suspenders) and even smell the same (Versace scent), is "to feed the masses with class and decor," said Penna, who was born in Rome and grew up in Buenos Aires.

The busy downstairs dining room is done in sleek black, red and white, with a plaster bust here, a bronzed cherub there. Crisp napkins, folded to form a pocket for the silver at each place setting, are cloth, not paper. The way your plate looks when it is sent from the kitchen may well have been influenced by someone who learned the art of plating at Le Cirque. Chefs are the only staff members who do not rotate into a new position each week, so that table clearers understand firsthand what it is like to be managers, managers know well the tedium of washing dishes. This way, said Penna, "You will have a feeling to treat people nice."

There are three chefs: Dino Carulli, who worked at Palio and Parioli Romanissimo; Dante Faccepti, who worked at the 21 Club and Marcello Torucci, who worked at Primavera.

Uptown at these and other big-name restaurants, Penna said, he and his friends had observed the waste of ingredients, staff and money—and the way that inflated prices. They wanted to provide quality food and service at prices that reflected true costs. With their system, the team makes a living as thin as a shaving of Parmesan cheese. But, said Penna, they look ahead with confidence to the future when this brave experiment may expand into a chain.

At these prices, it's wonderful. Maybe the tomato ravioli special one night was better than the spinach ravioli in a sauce that was long on tarragon another night. But always, garlic-rubbed toast served in a pool of creamy pesto for mopping, is fabulous. You can count on it. Always, grilled polenta with sautéed mushrooms is a welcome starter. Spicy linguini alla puttanesca, rich with capers and both black and green olives, is zesty and dependable. Mushrooms—shiitake or Portobello—sautéed with olive oil and garlic are meaty and fresh. There are more complex salads, but we swear by a simple toss of greens, leeks, fennel and shaved Parmesan.

Caramelized onions, anchovies, olives and capers topped a lightweight crust for pissaladiera, a delightful choice from the pizza portion of the menu. And we are partial to the basic margherita, this one topped with rounds of cherry tomato, since those were what had looked best in the market.

When duck was a special, it could be ordered with either orange sauce or a more zingy black pepper sauce. On the regular menu, chicken breast sautéed with artichokes, mushrooms and a touch of Barolo wine was a splendid choice. For an $8.95 price tag, you won't do better than veal Milanese, pounded thin, lightly breaded and topped with chopped tomato and onion and a bouquet of arugula. Gorgeous spinach was beautifully sautéed with garlic for an irresistible side dish. Desserts were divine, especially tirami su.

Instead of working for tips, Penna said, Ci Vediamo's staff is earning goodwill, "so we can make another restaurant in the future." When they find out about the prices and service, people "will come in quantities," he said. "If you add all the breadcrumbs, that will be all the earnings." He's right; so far, Ci Vediamo is packed every night.

Could restaurants like this one be the way of the future? We hope so.

CITADEL
311 Church St.
(212) 941-0202

HOURS: Dinner Monday–Thursday, 5–11 p.m.; Friday–Saturday, 5 p.m.–midnight. Lunch 11 a.m.–3:30 p.m.
PRICES: Entrées $10–$12; fixed-price dinner $15; appetizers $3.50–$8.50, sample plate $16.50. Lunch $6–$7; price-fixed lunch $8.50. AE, DS, V.
RESERVATIONS: Recommended.
ACCESS: Two small steps at entrance; restrooms wheelchair-accessible.
HOW TO FIND IT: One block south of Canal Street near Lispenard Street; subway lines A, E or N to Canal Street station.

Citadel is a Russian-run boîte, with settees and couches up front and very reasonably priced French food in back. The young chef, Vladimir Gorevich, attended the Culinary Institute of America and has worked in Le Cirque's kitchen. Herman Rozenberg, the owner, said he wanted a place for his friends—and he knew a good chef. Voilà! A restaurant! When Rozenberg couldn't read a wine list scribbled on the back of the menu, he brought the bottles. "Here,'" he said. "It's heavy, but this is the wine list." You can get a steak with three-peppercorn glâcé for $12, kuliabiaka, or salmon wrapped in puff pastry, for $11.50, and a whole roasted chicken (a little rare near the bone) for $11. The best buy, though, is the endearingly titled spread of appetizers, "enough to everybody," $15. Included were roasted beet salad with walnuts, garlicky red potatoes, grilled zucchini and eggplant, an onion and apple salad, smoked chicken salad, roasted French green beans and much, much more. And it truly was enough for everybody.

CUB ROOM CAFÉ
183 Prince St.
(212) 777-0030

HOURS: Dinner Monday–Thursday and Sunday, 5:30–11 p.m.; Friday–Saturday, 5:30 p.m.–1 a.m. Lunch Monday–Friday, noon–5:30 p.m. Brunch Saturday, noon–5:30 p.m., and Sunday, 11 a.m.–5:30 p.m.
PRICES: Entrées $10–$16. Lunch $7–$12. Brunch $4–$12. AE.
RESERVATIONS: Recommended for groups of 6 or more.
ACCESS: Entrance ramps; restrooms equipped for disabled.
KIDS: No children's menus but will accommodate.
HOW TO FIND IT: At Sullivan Street; subway line E to Spring Street station, line 1 to Houston Street station or line N to Prince Street station.

You may have read in all the upscale-restaurant columns about the chi-chi Cub Room. Now read this: Next door to the Cub Room there's the unpretentious Cub Room Café. At the café, prices for mostly good food are nearly as friendly as those at your neighborhood coffee shop.

You can walk through a door that connects the two establishments to peek at the higher-priced Cub Room proper. Or if you're meeting friends—no reservations here—you could have a drink at the bar next door first.

The surroundings at Cub Room Café itself, however, are anything but shabby.

Bunches of chile peppers hang above the semi-open kitchen, and an array of fall squash and gourds festoons the blackboard of daily specials. People wear black, but they seem down-to-earth, intent on impressing.

They talk over wine, like the wonderful red Terrasses de Guilhem, 1993, from the Languedoc. One night we felt like having good, lightly sweetened lemonade instead. You can also get a beer—Bass ale, Warsteiner pilsner, Brooklyn lager. And if you want to go for a bit of glamour from next door, try a Negroni (the Italian martini made with Campari, vermouth and gin) or a Bobby Burns, made with Black Label Rob Roy, bitters and Drambuie. We didn't avoid these just because of the steep cost ($6.50 for the Negroni, $8 for the Bobby Burns) but because somehow they seemed too upscale to be imbibed before meat loaf or grilled cheese.

Salads are meal-sized or big enough to split. I'm thinking of the splendid spinach salad ($5.95), tossed with hard-cooked eggs, red onion and warm bacon vinaigrette; if I had the chance to become a regular, I'd eat it once a week. A Mediterranean sampler plate was terrific—garlicky hummus, the chickpea spread; wilted cucumber salad; lemony tabbouleh made with parsley and bulgur; and a grain salad made with rice and two kinds of wheat. One night Niçoise salad, a special, was made with fresh-grilled tuna.

Silky house-cured salmon and cured ham that was almost like prosciutto were draped over a big heap of romaine lettuce and a slather of sour cream with capers. A large wedge of well-seasoned potato-onion frittata ($5.95) came with a toss of house greens in a balsamic vinaigrette. Smooth potato-leek soup, a special, made a satisfying supper after a big plate of grilled-bread salad, combined with capers, tomatoes that were really red, black olives, mozzarella and balsamic vinaigrette. Another day chicken soup was based on good homemade broth and contained lots of homey root vegetables and roasted noodles, a good idea.

Because these things were so satisfying I never got around to trying the grilled cheese sandwich (honest!) or the Cub burger.

I did try a special sandwich of the day, focaccia stuffed with tomatoes (somebody at Cub Room Café has the good sense to use ripe plum tomatoes when others look anemic), basil and creamy mozzarella, came with gingery, colorful coleslaw made out of cabbage, red pepper, carrots and shavings of zucchini. What looked to be the same slaw but tasted tamer, less heavy on the ginger, came alongside crusty crab cakes. A handsome serving of moist, herb-roasted chicken came with polenta (this season's sub for mashed potatoes). Meat loaf was bland, but I could eat a whole plateful of the accompaniment, potatoes mashed with their red skins. Turkey pot pie was too mildly seasoned, and dryish macaroni and cheese made with smoked bacon and beer needed help from Tabasco. Salmon lasagna sauced with oven-roasted tomatoes didn't quite work, either. If your entrée is a little boring, order a huge heap of beautifully browned fries ($4) to pep it up. Every table needs at least one batch.

Desserts are a trifle high-priced, at $5 each, but they are absolutely worth it. My favorite, the fresh fruit crumble, is so large it could easily serve two. One day the crumble was apple and blueberry, another day it was raspberry, strawberry and blueberry. The sour-cream fudge cake was moist and old-fashioned, the carrot cake deeply flavorful and fresh. These are the kinds of cakes that could win a blue ribbon at a state fair. The ice-cream sandwich was tough to eat—two big oatmeal cookies and two scoops of ice cream slathered in fudge sauce. Another day simple, soft sugar cookies were a treat.

I've never eaten next door, but I don't feel the least bit deprived. Not as long as I can eat french fries, drink beer and gaze at a painting restful in its simplicity—a highway unfurling into a blue night. Not as long as I can have cookies for dessert.

FRANKLIN STATION CAFÉ

222 W. Broadway
(212) 274-8525

HOURS: Daily, 11 a.m.–10 p.m.
PRICES: Entrées $9.50–$12.50; appetizers $3–$6. AE, DC, MC, V.
RESERVATIONS: Recommended for groups of five or more.
ACCESS: Two steps at entrance.
ENTERTAINMENT: Artists' slide shows nightly 6–10 p.m. (changes every five weeks).
HOW TO FIND IT: Corner of Franklin Street and West Broadway; subway line 1 to Franklin Street station.

Franklin Station Café is one of those unlikely ideas that succeeds. In this case, the idea is Malaysian-French, in a hip Tribeca location.

The high-ceilinged space gives the impression of being carved out of granite, almost like a cave—but a light, airy one that's above ground, up a short flight of cast-iron steps. The dining room also functions as a gallery, displaying some of the work of Marc Kaczmarek, the French half of the ownership. (Changing photographs of work by Martine Tulet, projected on a screen in one corner, was the art on exhibit recently.) The Malaysian owner, Mei Chau, who is also an artist, calls their partnership "a New York story." He's the maître d' and sees to the sandwiches; she does much of the cooking.

"We like to eat, too," explained Chau. The two artists used to go to restaurants and lament, "This food is not good," she said. So, while waiting for their big breaks, Chau and Kaczmarek decided to open a noodle shop.

But what a noodle shop! The food itself is art, because it looks so beautiful, and it tastes great, too. The mood is happy, the prices are ridiculously low, the service friendly.

Satay chicken, marinated in a hearty, grainy peanut sauce and served with coconut rice was so good that a friend and I kept spooning peanut sauce over the rice and eating more of it long after the chicken was gone. Tender curried chicken in lots of cumin-rich broth that soaked into potatoes as well as the rice was equally good. Spicy shrimp soup made with thick, fresh noodles, Chinese watercress and an abundance of lemongrass and chile lived up to its name. Tom yam shrimp in a hot and sour broth was powerfully hot, and it lived up to the menu motto—"natural, healthy, tasty"—on a day when stuffed-up sinuses sought relief.

Sandwiches were spectacular, too. "Who is the lucky one of you who gets this beautiful smoked salmon sandwich?" cried our host as he carried it to the table. His enthusiasm was entirely justified. For $6.75, there's no better deal in town: silken Petrossian salmon, meltingly fresh mascarpone cheese, chives and a hint of lemon. To die.

When you read on a menu, "mozzarella, basil, tomato and extra-virgin olive oil," your hopes don't necessarily rise. In Manhattan of the '90s, the mozzarella could be dry, the basil not quite fresh, the tomatoes unripe and the olive oil of a quality that would suffice for cooking but is not really good enough to shine on its own. The wonder of Franklin Station is that every ingredient is pristine, chosen with care, and that a sandwich here is a glorious sum of its parts.

Even tuna salad is rethought here. Made with red onion, celery and just a hint of jalapeño pepper, it was just different enough to be interesting, just same enough to give meaning to the promise of "old-fashioned" on the menu. As with other sandwiches, the tuna came on rustic bread that was much more than an afterthought.

Café au lait came in big bowls, French-style, and you might want to try fish congee for a sustaining breakfast. Espresso was strong and hot, and iced tea was strong enough so that it didn't lose its flavor when the ice melted. Herbal tea and fresh juices were also on the menu. Or make your dessert an iced cappuccino.

The French part of the menu is at its finest in the coffee and the desserts—classic and delicious apple tart, pear tart, lush crème caramel.

This is the sort of place where you can feel comfortable sitting alone, sipping café au lait and reading.

HOME
20 Cornelia St.
(212) 243-9579

HOURS: Dinner Monday–Saturday, 6–11 p.m.; Sunday, 5:30–10 p.m. Lunch Monday–Friday, 11:30 a.m.–3 p.m. Brunch Saturday–Sunday, 11 a.m.–4 p.m. Breakfast Monday–Friday, 9 a.m.–11:30 a.m.
PRICES: Entrées $13–$16; appetizers $5–$8. Lunch $4–$9. Brunch $6–$10. AE.
RESERVATIONS: Recommended.
ACCESS: One step at entrance; restrooms on same level.
PARKING: Commercial lot on Seventh Avenue.
HOW TO FIND IT: Between Bleecker and West 4th Street; subway lines A, D, E or F to West 4th Street/Washington Square station or line 1 to Christopher Street station; bus line M8.

Home is where the heart is, the saying goes. By that criteria, the restaurant Home really is home.

Not that Home is like home; it isn't.

At home, people are always trying to get, or keep up, a matching set of dishes. At Home, the dishes are joyfully unmatched, some of the prettiest dishes in all New York, I think.

At Home, David Page and the staff do the cooking; at home, I do it. At home, you might get potatoes, but at Home, you get incredible sardine-potato cakes—mashed potatoes with the red skins on formed into patties and nicely browned—at brunch, and garlic potato cakes of a similar make for breakfast and as a side dish with the excellent peppered Newport steak at dinner.

At home, the cooking was never like this. But Home is like home—or at least the home you wish you'd had—in that when you go there, you trustingly eat what they serve. The foods are familiar, even if the preparation is inventive. The menu isn't long, but it is good.

"Home is the place that when you have to go there, they have to take you in," wrote Robert Frost. While they don't have to take you in at Home—except at brunch and breakfast, when they don't take reservations—we take another meaning from that poem. Home, or home, is the place you belong, by roots as deep and strong as grapevines and just as impossible to destroy. This restaurant, only here for a year, has the feel of a place that will last.

Barbara Shinn, Page's partner in life and in the restaurant, has an uncommon gift for making people welcome. When Shinn, an artist who is as graceful as Page is tall and gangly, says she's glad to see you, she really does seem to mean it. Sincerity is an attitude all too rare these days. And when you choose a wine—perhaps the 1992 Qupe Syrah from California's Centra Coast ($27), one of my favorites—Shinn makes you feel like the smartest person in the world, beaming and telling you how that was the very first wine she chose for the restaurant.

There are a million small, beautiful touches here. If I mention the cleverly built-in nook by the service bar for tossing corks into, I may neglect to mention the pleasant pale-yellow walls, reminiscent of those on a porch. If I mention the intriguing photographs, I might leave out the sweet little collection of cookbooks in the window. So just look around, and be pleased. I guarantee you will be.

It seems constricting, too, to have to stick to a recitation of the menu. After all, new ones will certainly be coming along, just as, at home, a newly worked-out recipe may come to hold sway over old favorites.

At lunch we sat beneath striped awnings in the garden to sip cold white wine and eat a salmon special done with fresh chives and thyme and an order of those wonderful garlic potato cakes, this time with a sauce that's essence of tomato with a bit of fresh rosemary. Page has a good feel for fresh produce, much of it from the greenmarkets. Who can resist his asparagus and roasted beet salad with goat cheese, or the beautiful tangle of "spring lettuces" with sunflower seeds for crunch and mustard-thyme dressing for pizzazz? Page loves oysters, and fixes them all sorts of ways—simple ways, to let them shine. A recent one I loved was a "po' boy" sandwich of crisp-fried oysters, served with a citrus-cucumber-red-onion salad that was sheer inspiration.

At brunch we were smitten by lovely fresh trout, but almost more so by a hash of wild mushrooms (we spotted a chanterelle), sweet pepper, bacon and sweet potatoes. With the potato cake of the moment, the one with sardines mixed into it and a poached egg on top, we ordered a side of home fries—really small, pan-roasted new potatoes. They were perfection, as was the side order of thick-sliced, well-cooked crunchy bacon. Thick, light French toast came with a smashing strawberry-rhubarb sauce, and our only complaint was that there could have been a mite more sauce. Even thick, chunky ketchup was homemade. Any lunch entrée and the dessert special of the day may be had for a reasonable $9.94.

Homemade corn muffins, moist and not crumbly, were a hit at breakfast with honey and cream cheese blended together, and hefty, satisfying slices of raisin toast didn't even need the homemade blackberry preserves that came with them. These choices, best with a cup of good, strong coffee, were $2 each, or for $4 you can get eggs and home fries; add a buck and a half and you can have them with sage sausage from Faicco's, the venerable Italian pork store just around the corner on Bleecker Street.

At dinner, there are always such possibilities as the trout (this time done with radish, cucumber and lime), served with an artichoke pancake, or the wonderful cumin-crusted pork chop with warm potato salad, or the roasted chicken with sautéed greens and spicy onion rings. There is cornmeal fried rabbit, and on Sunday nights, oyster stew. But next season, there will be a variation on these sturdy themes, and almost certainly it will be as good.

Chocolate pudding was truly a homey comfort, and biscuit-dough strawberry shortcake was the right idea but could have used a tad more berries to moisten up the biscuit.

We get letters from Home. Well, all right, they are newsletters, actually, but we like getting them. Barbara sent a postcard to let us know about her art show. This is not just something that happens to reviewers; everyone who eats there becomes a friend of Home.

Maybe I have a special fondness for Home because I ate one of the first plates of food they ever served when they opened. I watch Home flourish the way you watch your favorite children grow. I don't really want to write about it, all I really want to do is go Home again.

IPOH GARDEN MALAYSIA
13 Eldridge St.
(212) 431-3449

HOURS: Daily, dinner 4–10:30 p.m., lunch 10 a.m.–4 p.m., breakfast 8–10 a.m.
PRICES: Entrées $6–$22. Lunch $2.50–$7. Breakfast $1–$5.
RESERVATIONS: Recommended.
ACCESS: Two steps down at entrance.
HOW TO FIND IT: Between Forsyth and Kenmare Streets; subway line D to Grand Street/Chrystie Street station or lines F or J to Delancey/Essex Streets station; bus lines M14, M15, M101, M102.

In olden times, a dining companion who comes from Malaysia explained, captors would judge how much ransom they might be able to get from hostages' families by serving the prisoner fish.

If the captive ate the whole fish, they knew they were dealing with peasants. If the prisoner ate only the head of the fish, he was pegged as middle class. And if the hostage ate only the eye of the fish, the captors were overjoyed, for they knew they had captured someone possessed of great wealth.

Being democratic and having taken no prisoners when we went to Ipoh Garden Malaysia, we ate fish head in a mild coconut curry, with big clumps of tomatoes, okra, eggplant, zucchini and fried pork skin soaking up the flavor of the sauce. Then we ate a whole fish fried with soya beans, and we ate the two dishes with approximately equal enjoyment.

To find some of the best Malaysian food in New York, be it fish or noodles, head way down to where Eldridge Street begins, just south of Canal Street, almost under the Manhattan Bridge. The street is narrow, with scarcely enough space for both curbside garbage and passersby. But along Eldridge, inside a string of small Asian restaurants, people with elbows to tables are digging into noodle bowls with great gusto.

At Ipoh Garden Malaysia, at one table near us, workers in dusty blue shirts were eating noodles and drinking Guinness stout (a taste developed during Malaysia's British colonial days, perhaps?). Provisions were stowed in any spot where there was an inch or two of spare room. Signs bearing the Malaysian characters for special dishes were posted on the walls. Ipoh Garden was brightly lit and bustling, with virtually no decor to speak of, but we loved the whole scene, and we loved the food.

Maylasian food is not Chinese food. It is not Asian Indian food. These languages, as well as Bahasa Malaysia, are spoken there. Most Indians speak Tamil. But Malaysia's cuisine is not merely borrowed from other places. It is lively and distinct, robust with spices.

Some dishes on the menu will seem familiar, such as the noodles known as chow fun. Others, such as "strange taste crab," will seem offbeat. (We still don't know what it is.)

You might start with rojak, a refreshing Malaysian salad that included cucumbers and pineapple, seasoned with shrimp paste and palm sugar. Another zesty starter was squid with satay sauce. Then move on to noodles, either in soup or pan-fried. Laksa, noodles in a mild, thin coconut curry, came with garnishes of hard-cooked eggs and fish cakes.

The fashion designer Zang Toi eats here and swears by the Hock Kian home-fried noodles, which, back home in Malaysia, generally would be eaten for a late-night snack. A big bowlful costs a mere $4.25. (Hock Kian, by the way, is a province of southern China. Many Hock Kians, also known as Fu Kiens, live in Malaysia.)

Zang recommended okra with shrimp paste and sour shrimp, and while this unusual taste may not please everyone, we liked it. We also were partial to asam shrimp in a steaming pot of curried broth, made with eggplant and curry sauce, similar to the one on the laksa.

Hainan chicken rice, which a Malaysian friend, Chia Wong, thinks of as "a test," was served up with ginger and chile sauce, and we wouldn't mind testing this satisfying dish again and again.

With the help of our Malaysian guide, we abandoned the menu and consulted a friendly waitress. That was how we managed to order snow-pea pod leaves with crab sauce and fried bean-curd sheets. (Maybe this dish was on the menu, but by this time we weren't paying attention.)

Fu yei, a fermented bean, was mashed into kang kong, a luscious green vegetable sautéed with blachan, or fermented shrimp paste, a basic flavoring of Malaysian and some other cuisines. Our pal said this vegetable would be fed to pigs in Malaysia. The pigs, I fear, would not get to have it as we did, with a condiment of fresh chopped ginger, chile and soy, mixed in a tiny plate.

We ate chicken steamed with ginger and soy, with watercress over it. We ate until we could eat no more, and then we packed up a bit more food to take home. (After all, we needed an appetite for ice cream at the Chinatown Ice Cream Factory over on Bayard Street, a stop we hardly ever skip when we're in this part of town.)

"Almost everything was very typical," said Chia, our Malaysian friend, approvingly. "You will find it on every street, in any coffee shop."

JEAN CLAUDE CAFÉ & BAR
137 Sullivan St.
(212) 475-9232

HOURS: Sunday–Thursday, 6:30–11 p.m.; Friday–Saturday, 6:30–11:30 p.m.
PRICES: Entrées $10–$14; appetizers $5.50–$8.

RESERVATIONS: Taken only for parties of six or more.
ACCESS: Dining area/restrooms wheelchair-accessible.
KIDS: No children's menu but will accommodate.
HOW TO FIND IT: Between Prince and Houston Streets; subway line 1 to Houston/ Varick Streets station or line N to Prince Street station.

A few thin slices of good bread were soon demolished. The place was noisy and crowded, no reservations, no no-smoking section, no Edith Piaf for atmosphere. The plain truth is, we don't want you to go to Jean Claude.

My friends made me say all those things. That's because we adore Jean Claude, a find staffed by escapees from the acclaimed Bouley, and we want to be able to get in. If everyone else goes to this restaurant, we may find ourselves standing forlornly in the street, gazing in at happy eaters surrounded by walls of sheet copper and pale lemon-gold.

The reality is this: The skinny-sliced sourdough bread was soon replenished, and the lively atmosphere and curls of cigarette smoke gave Jean Claude an air as authentically French as a navy beret. Yet it is an original. After three visits, we remained as enamored as we had been at our first bite of delicate mushroom ravioli in leek sauce the first evening.

The charming Jean Claude Iacovelli (tres gentil, the French say), who works the front of the house, and Bernhard Gth and Frank Castronovo, the chefs, all had been at Bouley. (Gth, who is German, also worked at Tantris, a three-star Michelin restaurant in Munich, and Castronovo for Bocuse in France.) The food reflects Bouley's luster, but the prices are not at all like Bouley's. Even a flavorful sirloin steak with pink peppercorns, wonderful, creamy potatoes gratin Dauphinois and a tumble of watercress was a mere $12.50.

"We have food that usually you pay a lot of money for," said Gth. "Every second day, we go to the market. I bought me a small lamb. . . . This is the first restaurant, and we have a lot of energy. We are very happy now."

The brilliant blue spring water bottles that decorate one window—the other may feature a food mill filled with radishes, a bowl of beets that looked freshly dug—bear an unfamiliar Ty Nant label and may only be redeemed in California. It turns out this slightly bubbly water ($6 a large bottle) is from Wales. The cooking, like the choice of water, is not of a particular country so much as it is confidently the best of what it is.

Salad of organically grown varied lettuces that have come to be called mesclun was remarkable for its quality, for earthy, puckery black olives and for accompanying croutons topped with goat cheese of sublime freshness. Vinaigrette was a grace note, not too flashy on its own, on arugula salad with the thinnest of filet mignon carpaccio and mushrooms. Thin-sliced salmon carpaccio in a warm balsamic-radish vinaigrette was equally lovely. One night the spare, frequently changing menu offered ravioli filled with minced sweetbreads in a sauce that seemed a reduction of leeks. Always a smash hit, and always on the menu so far, was a mix of warm organically grown dandelions, crisp bacon and crumbled potatoes in vinaigrette.

Merely reading "linguine with ripe tomatoes, basil and garlic" does not convey a generous depth of flavor that is characteristic of the food here. Another night, there was fettucine with a delicate sauce of fresh artichokes, tomatoes and basil.

Salmon with savoy cabbage in a robust red wine sauce was spectacular, adding needed flavor to the mild fish. Radishes, beets and the greens of both in gingery citrus sauce formed a delicious, offbeat foundation for medallions of monkfish. Sautéed skate, which mimics the taste of scallops, was served on fennel confit and beet greens with mushroom-caper sauce. "We use everything," said Gth. "If not, we could never keep the prices."

One night freshly grilled pieces of chicken were served on spring vegetables in a luxurious sherry sauce called Xeres, after the Spanish town. Another night, sautéed chicken was served over tomato-fennel confit (a borrowing from the skate entrée) and eggplant in sherry sauce. Dinner-sized mesclun salad was topped with glazed "pearls" of tender sweetbread, about the size of the onions for which they were named.

Already, a good-looking, partly French-speaking crowd lines up at the bar, tended by Olivier, to wait for tables after 8 p.m. So go early, or wait until Jean Claude is old enough that some forsake it for a newer (surely not a better) place.

There were three perfect desserts. White chocolate went into a wisp of mousse that played perfectly against a splash of mocha sauce. Tart, cold orange parfait with candied endive (don't worry, you won't even recognize it as endive) and a breath of rosemary was refreshing. Crème brûlée beneath a whisper of crust made us remember why we loved this before it became hackneyed. We tipped back exemplary espresso from thick, brown cups. I know, I lay on superlatives too heavily. Let's just say not a morsel was left on any of our plates.

KUN PAW
39 Greenwich Ave.
(212) 989-4100

HOURS: Monday–Sunday, noon–midnight.
PRICES: Entrées $7.50–$13; appetizers $3.25–$4.95. Lunch $5.95–$6.95; appetizers $2.95–$4.95. MC, V.
RESERVATIONS: Taken only for dinner groups of five or more.
ACCESS: Dining area wheelchair-accessible, restrooms are not.
KIDS: No children's menu but will accommodate.
HOW TO FIND IT: Between Sixth and Seventh Avenues, at Charles Street; subway line E to 14th Street/8th Avenue station or lines L or F to Sixth Avenue/14th Street station; bus lines M7, M14.

Thai food is tops with me, so when Kun Paw opened just a few city blocks away from my house, I was happy-sad.

Happy because there might be a source of good, spicy Thai food so close to home and sad because I used to dote on the risotto primavera at the Italian restaurant that used to be in this corner storefront. After trying Kun Paw three times, happy is winning out.

The floor-to-ceiling windows make Kun Paw bright and airy but leave little space for wall decorations. A few festive trapunto hangings of elephants are enough, and they're pleasing to the eye. (Trapunto, I just learned from a friend in the Home section, is a stitchery pattern around a design that is padded, in this case, elephants.)

More important, the food is pleasing to the palate.

"This is my first love," said chef Arthur Chunton, who cooked Italian at Mezzaluna. (Relatives still run the Bangkok restaurant where he got his start.) We started with a slew of his appetizers—crisp, clean spring rolls filled with utterly fresh ground chicken (instead of the more usual pork), shrimp and glass noodles. Cold summer rolls—scallops, shrimp, tofu and bean sprouts bundled in egg-roll skins—were the perfect antidote for a hot night, along with a chilly Bangkok beer.

Kun Paw has both crisp and steamed Thai dumplings, not always available at other Thai places. The crisp ones were stuffed with a winning combination of minced chicken, scallion and cilantro, and the delicate steamed dumplings encased a filling of minced shrimp, mushrooms, water chestnuts, scallops and bits of carrot.

Mee krob, crisp noodles tossed with tangy tamarind sauce, shrimp, bean sprouts and yellow beans, were first-rate here, some of the best I have tasted. We wanted to have tod mun, or mixed fish salad, but it wasn't available. Tom yum, the Thai soup fragrant with lemongrass, lime juice, tree ear mushrooms and fresh shrimp was flavorful but light.

We favored a salad of green papaya, string beans, peanuts and tomatoes with chewy sun-dried shrimp and a spicy chile-fired dressing, and yum woon sen, glass noodles with ground chicken and fresh shrimp tossed with lime juice, onions and biting chile pepper. (Dried shrimp, by the way, is common in Thai cuisine, and though it may be an acquired taste, we prefer it when Thai cooks don't bend to American tastes and substitute fresh shrimp where dried ones are called for.) Ground chicken was combined with scallions, lime juice, red onion and chile for an uncommonly fine larb gai. For goong pla, whole grilled shrimps were tossed with onions, lemon, lime and chile.

Khao pad, the traditional Thai fried rice, was freshly made and not hot enough to try the patience of newcomers to the cuisine. Pad Thai—I always order it "not too sweet"—probably is one of the best-known Thai noodle dishes, and here it was a felicitous blending of stir-fried vermicelli noodles, hard-boiled egg, fish sauce, garlic, bean sprouts, tofu and peanuts, with either chicken or fresh shrimp, and a bit of dried shrimp ground up into the sauce. Kang ped puk, a mixed-vegetable dish, was a little heavy on baby corn for our taste but the coconut-and-red-curry sauce was delicious. Steamed vegetables with peanut sauce was too tame for me, but, hey, not everybody wants to set their taste buds on fire.

Moist, delectable gai yang, a grilled half-chicken marinated in Thai herbs and served with a chile dipping sauce, was a favorite at our table. Grilled salmon steak was a success, too, prepared with julienned kaffir lime leaf and green curry sauce. A whole fried fish, sea bass one night, snapper another, pla lard pik, was topped with sparkling chile and garlic sauce. Some nights, Chunton said, there's porgy, and sometimes there's sticky rice and sweet rice, made with fresh mango. Chunton's cold house noodle is made with slightly dried, cooked beef, yellow curry sauce and ground peanuts, and it seems to taste even better when it's a buck or two cheaper as a lunch special.

Homemade vanilla and mango ice creams were smooth and smashing the first time we tried Kun Paw, but on a later visit the mango, though still full of fruit flavor, had more ice crystals.

KWANZAA

19 Cleveland Pl.
(212) 941-6095

HOURS: Dinner Monday–Thursday, 5 p.m.–midnight; Friday, 5 p.m.–2 a.m.; Saturday, 4 p.m.–2 a.m.; Sunday 4 p.m.–midnight. Brunch Sunday, noon–4 p.m.
PRICES: Entrées $11.95–$15.95; appetizers $5.95–$8.95. Brunch $18.95–$23.95. AE, CB, DC, DS, MC, V.
RESERVATIONS: Recommended for weekends and brunch.
ACCESS: One step at entrance.
KIDS: No children's menu but will accommodate.
ENTERTAINMENT: Sunday brunch Gospel music; Wednesday–Thursday live music, occasionally Friday–Saturday, call ahead; Friday comedy night.
PARKING: Commercial lot near restaurant.
HOW TO FIND IT: Between Spring and Kenmare Streets; subway lines D or F to Broadway/Lafayette Street station; bus line M1.

Kwanzaa is a celebration, a statement of freedom from other holidays that have been imposed on the African-American consciousness. And now it's a restaurant.

The restaurant is a beautiful space filled with people who are gorgeous to look at. The mood was so festive one January night that if the servers and chefs were still getting their sea legs, the crowd seemed willing to make allowances. We were, at least.

You could get Jamaican patties (chicken, vegetable or beef) this good on Flatbush Avenue in Brooklyn, but you couldn't get this ambience. Jamaican-born designer Brian Goodin has created a luminous restaurant-gallery space for displaying artworks. Goodin has used African fabrics in simple, yet stunning ways; for example, narrow cloth runners hang from the ceiling here and there. A transparent organza printed in an African-inspired style is particularly fresh-looking. And arguably the best table in the house is the one in an alcove where a hanging lamp with a cutout pattern makes shadows on the wall and tablecloth. You can't, of course, eat good looks, but Kwanzaa is an exceedingly pleasant spot.

Chef John Cabbell's menu is said to include influences of the American South, the West Indies and Africa. In fact, truly African foods get short shrift right now, unless you count a nice, but not-startling Nguzo Saba salad, a "seven principle" combo of radicchio, arugula, apples, endive, plum raisins, almonds and baby corn, served with both curried yogurt dressing and a "jerk vinaigrette" spiced with Scotch bonnet peppers. Jerk vinaigrette is also dandy on Caribbean shrimp. Food of the American South was well represented by decent crab cakes, sticks of crisp-fried okra served with curried yogurt, and yummy, if slightly greasy, sweet-potato fries. Red beans and rice with andouille sausage were mysteriously bland, desperately seeking Tabasco.

In the entrée category, jerked pork ribs were flavorful and reasonably tender, and the popular Bahian shrimp, sautéed in white wine and fresh coconut, were nicely done though a little sweet for my taste. Curried chicken with potatoes, apples and raisins was mild but appealing in a homey way. There's dandy southern fried chicken, crisp outside and juicy within. We also liked kingfish escoveche marinated in a scallion-lemon vinaigrette and stuffed with a savory mixture of tomatoes, onions and chile peppers. Best side dishes were sweet-potato fries and spicy vegetarian collard greens.

Squares of peach cobbler and a delicate apple tart (no molasses in these) were originals in an age of mass-produced three-berry pies all over town.

LES DEUX GAMINS
70 Waverly Pl.
(212) 807-7047

HOURS: Monday–Saturday, 8 a.m.–midnight; Sunday, 10 a.m.–11 p.m.
PRICES: Entrées $12.50–$17; appetizers $3–$10; fixed-price lunch $15; sandwiches $6.50–$8.50; breakfast items $1.85–$2.75; continental breakfast $9. One menu. AE.
ACCESS: One level; restrooms not wheelchair-accessible.
RESERVATIONS: Taken only for groups of 10 or more.
HOW TO FIND IT: At Christopher Street between 6th and 7th Avenues; subway lines A, D, E, or F to West 4th Street/Washington Square station or line 1 to Christopher Street station; bus line M8.

L es Deux Gamins is just what this town needs—an easy-on-the-wallet, unpretentious French café.

The chairs and tables have a comfy, lived-in look, and the bathroom is papered in wine labels. There's a magazine rack, and if you want to sit around and read for a while, nobody bothers you. In the window there is a sign illustrating common French foods such as "steack frites" (the fractured spelling only adds to the charm) and cornichons, the perky little French pickles. The cornichons are said to cost extra—"supplement," as the sign says—but in fact they do not. We had scrumptious duck rillette—think of it as essence of duck—with a generous number of pickles, no extra charge.

I am leaping ahead in my story, though. To begin anew: one of the most pleasant things about Les Deux Gamins is that it opens at 8 a.m. for breakfast either French or American-style. In a part of town where some of MacDougal Street's Italian coffee houses do not open until 10 or later and the standard opening time for stores is 11 a.m., noon or even 1 p.m., this is especially to be commended. Merci beaucoup to Gamins' owners Robert Arbor and Herve Aussavis, who run Les Deux Gamins in a relaxed style. There's champagne by the glass, and a bottle of Cotes du Ventoux set us back only an easy $12.

My own favorite beginning to the day is a big white Pillivuyt bowl filled with perfect café au lait, a luxurious skiff of foamed milk decorating the excellent coffee. This coffee is so soulful that I forced a friend who doesn't even drink coffee to put his hands around the big, handleless cup and take a sip. "I can see why people would like it," he admitted grudgingly. If most of the coffee in these parts were as splendid as the coffee at Les Deux Gamins, perhaps my pal would drink it.

The coffee set a high standard, but the rest of the menu measured up. Orange juice was truly fresh-squeezed, when we asked for it that way, not what so often passes for fresh and is not. A pain au chocolat made a nice breakfast; so did a hearty omelet of tomatoes, goat cheese and mushrooms.

When it's a special, don't miss tender boeuf bourguignon, a tribute to chef Arbor's skill and the importance of carefully chosen ingredients. Steak frites were nicely done, too. We favor the thin, frizzled ham on a croque monsieur, a grilled ham and cheese sandwich the French way, and roasted potato salad, a heap of beautiful greens in a mustard-tinged vinaigrette surrounded by slices of crisply roasted potatoes. (Why is it that, at all too many restaurants, greens are not properly dried, vinaigrette not well-made and properly clingy the way it is here?) Or have the Gamin namesake salad with a tumble of greens and a grilled chicken breast.

For dessert, there was superb bread pudding with apricots, served with crème anglaise, a pleasant chocolate mousse and good apple tart. I, of course, could be content with just one more café au lait.

LUCKY CHENG'S
24 First Ave.
(212) 473-0516

HOURS: Sunday–Thursday, 6 p.m.–midnight; Friday–Saturday 6 p.m.–2 a.m.
PRICES: Entrées $5.75–$16.25; appetizers $3.75–$8.50. AE, DC, MC, V.
RESERVATIONS: Suggested.
ACCESS: Not wheelchair-accessible.
KIDS: Half portions available.
ENTERTAINMENT: Monday live acting performances, 9:30 p.m. and 10:30 p.m.; Friday–Saturday live DJ, 8 p.m.
HOW TO FIND IT: Between 1st and 2nd Streets; subway line F to Second Avenue/ Houston Street station; bus line M15.

How is Lucky Cheng's different? Let me count the ways.

This two-story location was built as a Turkish bathhouse in the late 1800s, and downstairs there's still the original tile and vaulted ceilings, plus a second bar. The Jacuzzi has become a pond for fish and turtles. Just ask the bartenders for fish food and then feed the fish.

So far, all this may sound light-years away from Uptown's elegant China Grill, but consultant Peter Klein, who had been chef at that very establishment, brought in Chris Genoversa, China Grill's former sous chef, as Cheng's chef. Gregory Wang, who had also worked at China Grill, is sous chef.

The most Downtown things about Lucky Cheng's, though, are the waiters. Or should we say waitresses? Wearing high-style drag, they provide attentive service and suggest favorite dishes. We especially liked the pale aqua see-through outfit with floating sleeves, though it is a bit of a worry to think of the possible conflagration should such a sleeve trail into one of the lighted candles.

Lucky Cheng, co-owned by former busboy M. Ching Cheng and Robert Jason, an MTV producer and director, follows the happy custom of making many wok stir-fries and side dishes available in small or large plates. This makes it possible to order a few small plates and call them a meal.

Calamari was good both times we tried it; once delicate rounds of it arrived "crackling" atop a bed of greens in a potent dressing of miso, lime juice and hot-chile oil. In another preparation on another night, the calamari was lightly fried and served with zesty tomato-ginger salsa. Spicy dragon noodles (one of the small/large items) came in a truly spicy Thai sauce, and the shrimp perched on top of it were fresh-tasting. But the red miso sauce that came with steamed fire-cracker dumplings was better than the flat shrimp filling.

If you still eat beef, order at least a small side taste or appetizer of Thai-style beef salad on a pile of dainty little lettuces with peanut dressing. Tasty Sichuan beef in hot oil came in only a large, but not overwhelming, size.

Time was when food the likes of Lucky Cheng's was strictly a West Coast affair, or maybe you could find it in Chinatown. But say hello, New York, to miso, peanut sauce and five-spice powder around every corner. One of the most dynamic ways of tasting that aromatic mixture (star anise, cloves, Sichaun peppercorns, fennel and cinnamon) is on chicken laquered with plum barbecue sauce and served with pineapple salsa. Crispy soy chicken, less zesty than five-spice, came with pancakes and apple salsa. Steamed whole fish (red snapper the night we ordered it) had plenty of oomph in a chile-cilantro sauce. A small piece of barbecued salmon was fine, too.

By now, you're getting the drift of this menu—bamboo-steamed vegetables with a sparkly miso-tahini dipping sauce, greens very lightly stir-fried (10 seconds or so on the fire), beautiful greens with a ginger-miso vinaigrette, fried spring rolls stuffed with chicken and peanuts with a sweet-mustard dipping sauce, and fried brown rice with five vegetables, eggs and scallions. There's even, shades of the '50s, a pu-pu platter. Jasmine or brown rice is $2 the bowl.

The wine list is short and a little too sweet, and desserts need work. So for the time being, go out for ice cream. But I figure it this way: If M. Ching Cheng has bused tables at Gotham Bar & Grill, Prix Fixe, Da Silvano and other such places for 18 years, he must have learned a thing or two about how to run a restaurant.

And if you take friends from Kansas, as I did—I swear; how could I make this up?—they will be sure to admit they're not in Kansas anymore.

MARUMI
546 LaGuardia Pl.
(212) 979-7055

HOURS: Dinner Sunday–Thursday, 5:30–10:30 p.m.; Friday–Saturday, 5:30–11 p.m. Lunch Monday–Friday, noon–3 p.m.
PRICES: Entrées $7.50–$13; sushi and sashimi $1.50–$3.50. Lunch box $5.50–$9. AE, MC, V.
ACCESS: Dining area/restrooms wheelchair-accessible with some manuevering.
HOW TO FIND IT: Between West 3rd and Bleecker Streets; subway lines A, B, D, E or F to West 4th Street/Washington Square station or lines D or F to Broadway/Lafayette Street station; bus lines M1, M8.

Potatoes are not a big part of Japanese cuisine. For example, you never see a piece of Idaho potato lurking in the vegetable tempura. And frankly, much as I love potatoes mashed and hashed, there's something unappealing about the idea of a batter-coated potato. Potatoes do very nicely fried on their own, without frills, thank you very much.

But when a friend reported that at Marumi he had been served wedges of roasted potatoes, skins on, with chicken katsu—a breaded, fried cutlet—it made perfect sense to us. It also made us eager to visit this bright, orderly little store-front, where the walls are just a shade lighter than the color of lush, green-tea ice cream. We discovered this happy addition to the Village scene in the deep of winter, when big bowls brimming with steaming broth and noodles are at their most alluring. (Remember the movie Tampopo? We think of that hilarious quest for the best noodles whenever we eat dishes such as these.)

On what was the coldest day of the year so far, we drank steaming mugs of green tea and ate niku udon, tender sliced beef with fat egg noodles in a sturdy beef broth. Another night, a friend who has lived in Japan was feeling peaked and she asked for tamago toji udon, although it was not on the menu. It was a homey bowlful of noodles mixed with scrambled eggs. "It warms you inside and out," our friend said. It was just the sort of thing we would adore eating snug in bed on a night when icy wind whips around city street corners. With udon dishes, a shaker of dried shichimi, sesame and orange peel), came for spiking up the hotness quotient.

Lemony salads were based on iceberg but sometimes containing asparagus, a floweret of broccoli or marinated tomato. Salad or a small bowl or miso soup came with many entrées, as is the custom.

We sampled the aforementioned chicken katsu with potatoes, carrots and per-fect out-of-season asparagus, and liked it well enough. Alongside it there was tonkatsu sauce, a kind of cross between Worcestershire and ketchup. On another day we had potatoes as part of a chicken teriyaki lunch box and likes them best of all that way, soaking up delicious juices.

Tasty green beans and watercress with sesame dressing, goma ae, served in a suribachi, the mortar used to grind the sesame seeds, were refreshing.

Yaki nasu was eggplant quickly broiled until the skin was crisp, the inside flesh a mellow contrast. It was so wonderful we ordered seconds.

Raw tuna and avocado was fanned out on lettuce leaves for another appealing appetizer. Cold eel with thin slices of cucumber had a lightly pickled taste. Sliced raw yellowtail salmon was exquisitely fresh in sashimi with thin sliced ginger and wasabi, that keen green horseradish condiment.

Sushi rolls we sampled also were fresh and good: California maki, avocado, crab, fish roe and cucumber; yasai, a roll of avocado, delicious asparagus, cucum-ber, pickles and black mushrooms; tempura roll, a piece of shrimp tempura ris-ing out of a seaweed-wrapped roll that also contained cucumber and something that was akin to mustard mayonnaise. Oyako maki, or "parent-and-child" roll, was salmon rolled with salmon roe and shiso, a leaf that tastes of lemon and mint. There also is a mini chirashi, or "scattered" sushi special, $4.50, vinegared sushi rice spread in a box with fish, egg and vegetables scattered over the top.

Broiled eel with kabayaki, a semi-sweet barbecue sauce that resembles teriyaki, was tender and delicious. Octopus with cucumber and thin-sliced lemon was another seafood delight. We also favored grilled, marinated eel and thin-sliced cucumber in rice vinegar. With grilled foods, another peppery condiment, san-sho, came in a shaker, to cut sweet and oily tastes.

A box lunch of chicken teriyaki, shrimp and vegetable tempura, pickles with sesame and potato salad (is this Japanese?) was a great deal for $9.

Sake, cold or hot, goes well with this food. And if you order two Suntory malt beers, the third is free, so it makes sense to go with a group of at least three people. For dessert, there's green-tea ice cream in pleasantly shaped green bowls, with a red-bean topping that is optional. We prefer red beans made into ice cream, and in our book, this topping will never beat hot-fudge sauce. Green-tea ice cream by itself is a smooth finish to the meal, and, like potatoes, it is best savored on its own.

MATCH
160 Mercer St.
(212) 343-0020; after 4 p.m. (212) 343-0830

HOURS: Dinner daily, 6 p.m.–midnight; late-night menu to 4 a.m. Lunch daily, 11:30 a.m.–4 p.m.
PRICES: Entrées $12.50–$18.50; appetizers $5.50. Lunch $8.50–$14.75; appetizers $4.75. Late-night menu is a limited dinner menu. AE, MC, V.
RESERVATIONS: Recommended.
ACCESS: Wheelchair-accessible; restrooms equipped for disabled.
ENTERTAINMENT: Live jazz Sunday–Monday.
PARKING: Commercial lot across from restaurant.
HOW TO FIND IT: Between Houston and Prince Streets; subway line N to Prince Street station or lines D or F to Lafayette Street station; bus line M1.

I loved the food at Match, one of Downtown's hottest scenes right now. Chef Chris Heyman, formerly at Casa La Femme and Jerry's 103, strikes just the right balance between inventive and familiar on the menu, and prices are fair.

Would I eat at Match again? Only if I could go at a time when the place was less noisy and crowded. (How about 3:30 p.m. on a weekend, a time friends of mine tried and told me about?) Or maybe I'd just eat at the bar and not bother waiting for a table.

The decor is industrial, but in a pleasant way, not too harsh. It's a bit like being inside an Edward Hopper painting, but more cheerful.

In fact, hanging at the bar and ordering a multitude of appetizers, $4.75 apiece, is not a bad option. Our crowd couldn't get enough of potato-chive dumplings, a starch-on-starch extravaganza of mashed potatoes inside dumpling skins, served with golden onion marmalade. Sparklingly fresh oysters were barely grilled with fresh corn and cilantro, and fried blue-corn ravioli came with a zippy black bean salsa. Mooshu duck roll and wild mushroom bruschetta were appetizers we would happily order again. To sample a lot of these tasty morsels, order a dim sum sampler of three appetizers, for two or more diners, $7 per person.

From the raw bar, there's osetra or sevruga caviar, freshly opened oysters, tuna and cucumber hand roll, grilled salmon skin daikon hand roll, tuna seviche, sushi or sashimi. It all looked gorgeous, but I had fallen in with a group of people, otherwise of sterling character, who wrinkled their noses when the subject of raw oysters came up, so I did without.

This is one "in" place, crowded and noisy, where the excellent service is without "attitude," and that's a small miracle. After we had eaten appetizers, known here as "8-inch plates," at the bar and had been seated, our waitress informed us that there would be a wait of 15 or 20 minutes for the main dishes, since we had already eaten the appetizers. Would we like to order a few salads to while away the time? (We were stunned. At other places, I've had many a longer kitchen-to-table time lag with nary an explanation.) So we nibbled on a nice enough organic mesclun salad (lots of commendably tender dandelion greens) with carrot-ginger dressing and a lively arugula salad with yellow wax beans and beets.

Instead of being labeled entrées, larger plates are called "10-inch plates." Vegetables for the obligatory grilled vegetable plate were billed as organically grown, and they were carefully cooked, served with a grain salad of quinoa and lentils. At the opposite extreme was perfectly medium-rare sirloin in lush red-wine sauce with a few tangy fresh currants, accompanied by a potato-shiitake mushroom cake and steamed snow peas and snap peas. Heaven.

Roasted chicken with garlic mashed potatoes is on nearly every menu these days, but Match's version was an outstanding one, the fowl juicy and flavorful.

Wok-seared bluefin tuna was really too rare on the first pass, but when my friend sent it back for more cooking there was no argument, no scornful attitude. It was moist even after more time on the fire. Wild-mushroom ravioli with a multi-herb pesto of basil, cilantro, dill and tarragon was a knockout. And tamarind-brushed lamb chops, expertly grilled, were perfection. The pear-mint chutney with the chops sounded as if it would be too weird, but it wasn't.

So tables don't get too crowded, the wait staff uses stacked plate racks to good advantage. It's a smart idea; in New York, where space is at a premium, there's no reason to restrict such racks to bakery displays.

Desserts may be ordered as sampler plates for $7.25 a person, but I have eyes for nothing but the wonderful frozen cappuccino sundae, really more like an Italian semifreddo. For the record, there was also fine crème brûlée lightly flavored with candied ginger, good lemon tart and an unusual banana-chocolate-cream "pie," more like an individual tart with a chocolate crust that clung stubbornly to the bottom of the small tart dish. Never mind, it was tasty even without the crust.

Along with chef Heyman, Bill Gilroy (owner of the wildly popular Lucky Strike nearby) and Peter Fay are partners in Match. They've got a winner.

MEKKA
14 Avenue A
(212) 475-8500

HOURS: Sunday–Tuesday, 6 p.m.–midnight; Wednesday, 6 p.m.–1 a.m.; Thursday, 6 p.m.–2 a.m.; Friday–Saturday, 6 p.m.–3 a.m. Brunch Saturday–Sunday, 11 a.m.–4 p.m.
PRICES: Entrées $7.95–$11.95; appetizers $2.95–$6.95. Brunch $1.95–$7.95. AE, MC, V.
ACCESS: Wheelchair-accessible; restrooms equipped for disabled.
KIDS: Half portions available at brunch.
ENTERTAINMENT: DJ Thursday 9 p.m., Friday–Saturday 10 p.m.
HOW TO FIND IT: Between Houston and 2nd Streets; subway line F to Second Avenue station.

In the East Village, where offbeat often seems the norm, Mekka seems comparatively tame—it's just slightly updated southern cooking, in a hip space, with Zambezi beer from Zimbabwe thrown in. (For beer aficionados, let it be known that there's also Tsing Tao from China, Chimay from Belgium, Red Stripe from Jamaica.) The prices are modest, the crowd handsome.

My favorite soup, on a night when I was coming down with the flu, was a nourishing bowl of blackeged pea soup with smoked turkey ($2.95). But a robust and zesty catfish chowder packed with vegetables was a good choice, too. The "soul roll" ($2.50), a name I love, consisted of flaky pastry wrapped around a bundle of savory red beans, rice and shreds of greens, homey brown gravy on the side. (This may be made of leftovers and could vary from day to day.) A tangy marinade had really soaked into Cajun grilled shrimp to give them lots of punch. (At $5.95, the shrimp are the priciest appetizer.)

If there hadn't been that party—for "On the Down Low Underground Hip Hop," with rapper Doug E. Fresh and Preacher Earl presenting Kay Superior— I'd have gone back to try the fried catfish dipped in corn meal, and maybe the pan-seared blackened catfish, too. As it was, I only got to nibble on a corner of a pal's spicy-grilled catfish, which was tender and flavorful. But I was raised on catfish, especially the cornmeal-dusted, pan-fried kind, and I'd been counting on trying some every possible way.

Dinners came with two vegetables, and peppery Creole corn that was a special was a clearcut winner. Macaroni and cheese—always a vegetable, mind you, in any southern joint worth a mess of collard greens—was good, too. Mashed potatoes with a touch of chedder cheese were delicious. But, speaking of greens, the collards had a slightly too-sweet taste, perhaps because sugar was added. Yams were cloyingly sweet, too, even sweeter than the sweet potato pie was had later for desert.

You could just have a whole plate of vegetables ($6.95), or you could have some meat with all those side dishes. I recommend a smothered pork chop with fried Granny Smith apples or chef Michael Franklin's smokin' shrimp etouffe. Baby back ribs were not quite tender enough, but I mean to try the chopped BBQ sandwich when I get back to Mekka. (And I was lusting for some "funky southern fried chicken," too.)

Desserts were predictable and pleasing southern-comfort food—peach cobbler, apple crunch and sweet potato pie. But judging by the room full of svelte figures, the crowd at Mekka, which is owned by the same folks as the Upper West Side's Shark Bar, never takes more than a bite or two of those calorie-laden sweets. Downtown, this is Mekka.

MIKA
349 W. Broadway
(212) 941-9537

HOURS: Dinner Sunday–Thursday, 6–11:30 p.m.; Friday–Saturday, 6 p.m.–1 a.m. Lunch Monday–Saturday, noon–3:30 p.m. Brunch Sunday, noon–5:30 p.m.
PRICES: Entrées $11–$19; appetizers $4.25–$9; sushi entrées $10–$16; sushi rolls about $3.75; sashimi about $2.50. AE, MC, V.
RESERVATIONS: Recommended weekends for large groups.
ACCESS: Dining area/restrooms wheelchair-accessible.
KIDS: Half portions available.
PARKING: Commercial lot across from restaurant offers patron discounts.
HOW TO FIND IT: Between Grand and Broome Streets; subway line N to Prince Street station or line A to Canal Street station.

Be prepared to spend a bit more at Mika than at some other "Eats" places. I promise you that, for the adventurous eater, this is a place that makes sacrifice worthwhile. Brown-bag a couple of lunches and spend what you save on Mika.

You'll be eating food prepared by Debra Aronoff, a chef who has worked in such highly regarded kitchens as Montrachet, Vong and Tribeca Grill.

And you won't be able to help liking Michaela Sharon, the tall, lean, elegant co-owner, known as Mica (Mika is the Japanese spelling). She brings to this enterprise a quirky background suited, perhaps, to a bistro that is Japanese, yet not Japanese. She was born in Hamburg, Germany, and raised in Israel before living (and cooking) in Paris, helping set up a Japanese sushi place in Tel Aviv and managing an elegant restaurant in Johannesburg. Her travels took her to other parts of the world, too, and her inclination took her to the French Culinary Institute. For the last two years, Sharon managed Tribeca Grill, where she met Aronoff. The rest is history—or soon will be. This is a very, very, good restaurant.

No small part of Mika's charm is that fresh, excellent sushi is relatively reasonably priced. (Good sushi is never cheap. Think about it: Would you want raw fish to be cheap?)

Sharon interviewed 25 sushi chefs and started with one who didn't work out. Then she found Ken Shimizu, an extremely skillful yet laid-back sushi chef. Shimizu is Japanese, as all sushi chefs worth their wasabi mustard are, but he has traveled a lot and is open to new ideas, to a fusion of different styles. Yet he cuts no corners. Shimizu's sushi is, as the current New York saying goes, "like buttah." It's flawless, it's classic, it's art. I dare you to find yellow tail sashimi that is more pristine.

A deluxe sushi assortment included salmon, mackerel, shrimp, flying fish roe and salmon roe, all velvety fresh. Soba-noodle and Napa cabbage house roll wrapped in seaweed came with a sesame dipping sauce. The roll was presented on end, with the vegetables sticking out almost like flowers in a beautiful presentation. And an eel hand roll moved one companion to say, "I would eat eel every day if I could have this eel!"

Almost every plate makes you feel that kind of enthusiasm. Scallops baked with mango could be just weird; instead, they're wonderful, with the fruit at just the right degree of doneness—and I don't mean raw—and scallops that were as fresh as the sushi fish. Wonton skins turned into Japanese quesadillas with the addition of goat cheese and a dollop of salsa were fun, a gift from the house when the batter for scallion pancakes we had ordered wasn't right and the kitchen declined to send them out.

Portobello and shiitake mushrooms were grilled and combined in inspired fashion with smoked tofu. Char-grilled squid in a sauce of soy and roasted-peanuts was another inventive idea that worked.

The entrées, in thoroughly non-Japanese style, were generous in size and that was a good thing—as we all swiped things from each other's plates so as not to miss a single taste thrill. The friend who had ordered a wasabi-crusted salmon attacked it so fast I could get no more than a forkful, and no wonder. It was a marvel of moist salmon inside a spicy crust, with roasted beets and potatoes and a citrus-soy vinaigrette sauce. Asahi ruby trout (morning sun ruby trout) was left whole and steamed in a basket, presented with near-caramelized grilled leeks, sautéed endive, bok choy and slender Japanese eggplant, all in a zesty black-bean vinaigrette. Slices of simply sautéed monkfish were served with molded couscous on a bed of bright salsa made of carrot, red pepper and shiso, a Japanese green.

Crisply sesame-crusted crab cakes were served with small ears of corn on the cob, sautéed baby bok choy and wasabi crème fraiche.

Two of the several sakes were Aramasa (room temperature instead of cold as it sometimes is elsewhere) and Hakusan, the house sake. There is a full bar, too.

The large servings extend to dessert: banana bread pudding with a richly caramelized outside, huge bowls of intense passion fruit sorbet and unusually creamy red bean ice cream served with bits of mango and orange. The Japanese hot fudge sundae—or should we say profiteroles?—was transcendently good: hot fudge sauce snuggled inside greaseless fried wontons, with vanilla ice cream and a garnish shred of star anise.

Mica Sharon has never lived in Japan, world traveler that she is. But she has created her own, offbeat Japan.

MOUSTACHE PITZA
90 Bedford St.
(212) 229-2220

HOURS: Tuesday–Sunday, noon–midnight.
PRICES: Entrées and appetizers $1.50–$12.
ACCESS: Wheelchair-accessible.
KIDS: No children's menu but pizza is served.
HOW TO FIND IT: Between Grove and Barrow Streets; subway line 1 to Christopher Street/Sheridan Square station or lines A, D, E or F to West 4th Street/ Washington Square station; bus line M8.

Take to heart the words "slow food establishment" on Salam Al'rawi's T-shirt. Salam is the one who makes huge, puffy, ethereal pita breads to order at Moustache, and he can only do it at a certain speed. There is great intelligence and integrity behind all Al'rawi's food, so don't pester him to hurry up.

For months we have looked forward eagerly to the opening of a second Moustache Pitza. (The other one, which Al'rawi sold, is at the corner of Atlantic Avenue and Bond Street in Brooklyn.) Like everything else at Moustache, this happened in its own good time.

Finally, the space once occupied by a cobbler and then vacant for months has become a peaceful, comfortable little eatery in one of the prettiest parts of the West Village. Small tables are covered in bright copper sheeting, and a beautiful fabric mosaic in rich colors decorates one wall. On the other are appealing paintings in a sort of primitive style. Gleaming black and white tiles connect the out-front part of the kitchen where Salam tirelessly rolls out and bakes his pita to the behind-the-scenes part where salads are assembled. The woodwork and door are a soothing shade of green, and the wide plank floors, so typical of old buildings in this part of town, have been freshly sanded. You feel happy here, even before food arrives.

On two visits we ate lahambajin, the soulful mideastern pitza—pizzas baked on pita bread—composed of well-seasoned ground lamb and beef with tomatoes, parsley and onions. It was wonderful both times. We ate zatter bread twice, too; it's an unbelievably delicious, slightly salty blend of the wild thyme from which it takes its name, olive oil and sesame seeds. (In Couscous and Other Good Food From Morocco, Paula Wolfert described zatter, or za'atar, as a sort of hybrid of thyme, oregano and marjoram.) Attention to detail here is so minute that even the thick boards that pitzas are presented on were custom-made by a friend.

Spinach and cheese pie was light and fresh, and falafel, the little chick-pea balls, were crunchy on the outside, subtly spiced and fresh.

We ate merguez, the Moroccan lamb sausage, in a pita bread sandwich with tahini, or sesame seed paste. The sausage was mildly spiced, but then, several things seemed less spicy on opening night than they did a few days later. By then, foul, the delightful stew of fava beans with garlic and tomatoes, was much zippier than it had been on the first try. Baba ganoush, the mashed eggplant salad, was delicate, light on garlic on a first try, but even so, impossible to stop eating. Next time it was slightly more garlicky.

Even a simple "garden salad with feta" was extraordinary here, with divinely fresh, moist cheese, crisp greens, meaty olives, thin slices of cucumber, a few slices of bell pepper and a dressing of lemon and oil that was simplicity itself. To mop up the bit of oil at the bottom of the plate, order an extra pita, $1.

A word on those pitas: I've had other fresh-baked pita, and none compare. Salam's pitas have that taste and texture that come from making something day in, day out, hour in, hour out, with respect. They are the best. To sniff them as they come to your table steaming is to know in the deepest sense what it is to be thankful for daily bread.

Hummus, the chickpea dip, was a perfect blend of garlic, lemon and tahini, although not as smoky tasting as some hummus. Tabbouleh, the zesty mixture of chopped parsley, bulgur and cubes of tomato, was perfect, lively with lemon.

For a hearty main dish, there was luscious, thin-sliced roast leg of lamb tucked into a pita sandwich with tomato, onion and homemade lemon mayonnaise spiked with mint. Where do the folks at Moustache find these truly red tomatoes?

Tall glasses of steaming mint tea (not presweetened—you add sugar) were a traditional and welcome finale, along with small loaves of basboussa, semolina-flour honey cake studded with slivers of almond. So delicious and inexpensive ($1.50) is the honey cake that we often buy an extra one to take home and eat for breakfast. We also recommend fresh, homemade yogurt with a drizzle of honey, pistachio nuts and fruit (mango, apple and others, depending on what looked good in the market). Phyllo dough stuffed with walnuts and raisins was good, but our love affair with the honey cake is so intense that we have eyes for no other dessert. There is no license for wine and beer, but ayran, a yogurt drink, loomi, a citrus beverage, and powerful Turkish coffee are on hand.

It's hard to imagine that we skipped anything on the menu, but we did skip chicken pitza—lemon-marinated fowl with scallions, plenty of garlic and red bell peppers. Oh well, next time. Believe me, there will be a next time—on my own time.

NHU Y
35 Lispenard St.
(212) 431-0986

HOURS: Daily, 11 a.m.–10:30 p.m.
PRICES: Entrées $3.75–$12.75; appetizers $2.45–$4.75. Lunch $3.75–$4.50
RESERVATIONS: Taken only for dinner groups of 10 or more.

ACCESS: Step at entrance but staff will help; restrooms wheelchair-accessible.
HOW TO FIND IT: Between Broadway and Church Street; subway lines A or N to Canal Street station.

PHO TU DO
119 Bowery
(212) 966-2666

HOURS: Sunday–Thursday, 9:30 a.m.–9:30 p.m.; Friday–Saturday, 9:30 a.m.– 10 p.m.
PRICES: Entrées $5–$12.50; appetizers $3–$8; rice noodle soups $3.75– $4.50; rice dishes $3.75–$5.50.
RESERVATIONS: Recommended.
ACCESS: Dining area wheelchair-accessible, restrooms are not.
PARKING: Garage on Chrystie Street or Allen Street.
HOW TO FIND IT: North of Canal Street; subway line D to Grand Street station or lines J or N to Canal Street station; bus lines M1, M101, M102.

It's a pleasure to find more Vietnamese restaurants opening around town. Finding Nhu Y on Lispenard Street in Tribeca and Pho Tu Do over on the northern edge of Chinatown consoles me for the loss of Saigon Café on Broadway and 20th Street.

Both restaurants turn out excellent meals at friendly prices. The people who run them are accommodating, too. Would you, for example, like an all-vegetarian summer roll instead of one with shrimp and pork? Tell the waiters at Pho Tu Do, and you've got it. The smiling waiters at Nhu Y read back your order to make sure they got it all right.

Nhu Y is bright and cheerful, and, as at Pho Tu Do, there's a gold and red shrine to Buddha. (A food and beverage offering at Pho Tu Do even included a cup of Vietnamese coffee, potent black dripped over a layer of condensed milk. Any deity would be well satisfied with such a cup of java, I feel certain.)

At Nhu Y, we started with the famous Vietnamese shrimp paste molded around a stick of sugarcane and grilled. After spring rolls wrapped in rice paper, a must-have at Vietnamese restaurants, we moved on to pork meatballs served over glutinous noodles scattered with peanuts. Along with lettuce, mint and shreds of carrot and daikon, the meatballs are meant to be rolled inside additional rice papers. (A tip: these steamed rice papers cool very rapidly, so be sure to pry them apart and pass them around the table immediately. If you still can't get them apart, take two and ask for another plateful.) We liked a jumbo shrimp dish with peppers and onions, lemon-grass chicken in a zippy sauce, beautifully cut grilled squid tasting faintly of garlic, and thin-sliced beef with bitter melon over rice. "Hollow vegetable with garlic sauce"—actually stir-fried water spinach—was tasty, too. If you don't want the thick, sweet Vietnamese coffee, lemonade (sweet—and I mean sweet—or salty) is an alternative.

Nhu Y is a place I'd like to return to again and again. One of these nights the pigeon and quail promised on the menu will probably be available.

Pho Tu Do features a huge menu book decorated with its trademark Statue of Liberty and featuring truthful color pictures of much of the food. It's a definite help in ordering. This is the only place I have found Hue, a lively Vietnamese beer. (Hue is also the name of a fragrant rice dish made with dried shrimp.) We had vegetarian summer rolls wrapped in steamed rice paper with the green ends of scallions sticking out like handles and fried spring rolls with shrimp.

Com suon bi, a delicious combination of grilled pork chop and shredded pork on rice, made a wonderful lunch for only $4. Steamed snapper was succulent, a better choice than the fried snapper with lemongrass and chile. But our two absolute favorites were banh beo, steamed rice cakes scattered with peanuts, and hot and sour fish soup enriched with pineapple and chile peppers. It was nothing like Chinese hot and sour soup, but I promise you'll like it.

For dessert, there are the ice-and-fruit extravaganzas served in glasses. The version at Pho Tu Do includes lots of squiggles of a jellylike green substance called pan dan, made out of screwpine leaves, and just enough coconut to sweeten the confection lightly.

ONE CITY CAFÉ
240 W. 14th St.
(212) 807-1738

HOURS: Thursday–Sunday, 11 a.m.–11 p.m.
PRICES: Entrées $4.95–$7, family style offered; appetizers $1.50–$3; sandwiches $5. Discounts for food stamp recipients (50 percent); Medicaid recipients (20 percent) and students with valid I.D. cards (20 percent). For cash and credit-card patrons, add 15 percent service charge. AE.
RESERVATIONS: Recommended for Friday evenings.
ACCESS: Steps at entrance; restrooms are wheelchair accessible.
PARKING: Garage two doors from restaurant.
HOW TO FIND IT: Between Seventh and Eighth Avenues; subway lines L, N or 4 to 14th Street/Union Square station; bus lines M1, M2, M7, M14.

We are all one city. Yet sometimes the contrasts are startling.

Some folks pay $75 for dinner, and others are scrounging 75 cents toward a slice of pizza. Some are paying $10 a glass for champagne, but the guy on the street who accepted an offering of my leftover shrimp and catfish one night asked for a dollar, so he and his buddy could buy "something to wash it down with."

These two groups seldom come together in any but the briefest of encounters—when the relatively well-off hand the homeless a quarter or two. One City Café is a brave experiment in changing that.

It is experimental in that it accepts food stamps as an alternative to cash. Don't worry, if cash is all you have, that's fine, too. I've heard stories, unconfirmed, of some people latching onto friends who have food stamps to get in, but One City welcomes cash and American Express. It is an experiment because about half of the staff are participating in a nine-month job-training program for formerly homeless people.

How is all this working? One night I met a pal at the bar before moving on back to the dining room with more friends. The low-ceilinged space, which once housed Quatorze, had an air of orderliness about it, and the bartender seemed competent and poised. Was he, we wondered to ourselves, a supervisor or a

recently homeless person? We found ourselves speculating that he must be train-
ing others with less experience, and then we realized that this was prejudice sur-
facing. Because he did something well, did that mean he couldn't have been
homeless? Absurd. Once, the barkeep (wine and beer, no hard liquor here) did
have to explain to another staff member that he wanted only an ice bucket, not
the stand, too, but that could have happened anywhere.

After we were seated, a 1993 Taft Street chardonnay from California, $16,
which can't be bought with food stamps, was fine, though not remarkable. In
general, the wine list could use a little more work, but so could the wine lists at
dozens of places in town.

We began with a house salad that was a match for many mesclun salads in
tonier places, and tasty salt-cod fritters. Black-eyed pea salad lacked verve; a few
dashes of lemon or an extra sprinkle of salt would have helped. Black-bean soup
was robust and well-seasoned, however. Two hungry friends split a cornmeal-
dusted, fried catfish po' boy with fine sweet potato fries as a before-dinner snack.

Entrées we liked best were a homey codfish stew, which was a special of the
day, and well-seasoned, though not terribly spicy, ropa vieja, the Cuban-style
beef dish that translated literally means "old rags," or "old clothes," because it
is shredded. To my taste, the kale that came with the ropa vieja had not been
sautéed long enough, but some others professed to like it. I think that kale is
one vegetable that benefts from long cooking. But the mashed potatoes that also
accompanied the dish were top-notch.

The West Indian vegetable curry (potatoes, peas, carrots, red onions) seemed
tame compared to ones I'm used to, and roti, the pancake-like bread that such
curries are often folded into, would have been nice instead of rice. Saucy red
beans, a side plate, had a peppery tang.

Banana bread pudding was my favorite dessert, but flourless chocolate cake
and carrot cake were fine, too. Or you could have batidos, lush Caribbean milk
shakes made with papaya, mango and other fresh fruits.

Just around the corner, you can get hearty meals at La Taza de Oro for about
the same money as food-stamp recipients pay at One City. But the atmosphere
is considerably more casual there. And in this city, you do pay for fancy looks.

And by the way, espresso is 50 cents in food stamps, $1 cash. Even at the cash
price, that's a bargain.

OROLOGIO
162 Ave. A
(212) 228-6900

HOURS: Daily, 5 p.m.–midnight.
PRICES: Entrées $7–$12; appetizers $4.50–$7.
ACCESS: Dining area/restrooms wheelchair-accessible.
HOW TO FIND IT: Between 10th and 11th Streets; subway line L to First Avenue/
14th Street station; bus lines M14, M15.

If time is your obsession, Orologio is your kind of place. The word means, in
Italian, watch, clock, timepiece. Here, you are always aware of time. There's a
wonderful display of old clocks of normal size, including what must have been just
about the world's first digital clock, in charming orange Bakelite. Both outside and

inside Orologio there are trompe l'oeil watches and clocks, and then there is the larger-than-life-size mirror with a clock on it, and the wall-sized painted clock, white with black numerals and hands. Some of these clocks work, some don't. The effect is fresh and handsome, a match for the food.

Claudio Gottardo's Mappamondo on Abbingdon Square and his nearby Mappamondo II were the West Village prototypes for Orologio, and their success is history. So it's no surprise to find the East Village cousin filled with happy eaters, spilling out of the small storefront to the sidewalk tables, on summer evenings. It's not impossible to get in after five weeks, just decently busy.

Even before you order, there's a welcoming basket of warm, crisp foccacia, light and thin as pita bread. We practically inhaled it, but the genial waiters brought more whenever we asked.

While you consider the main order, you might share an appetizer pizza on a foundation of that same crisp crust. We liked a special of the day with goat cheese and arugula, and the margherita (tomato, mozzarella and basil) and sausage-and-red-pepper fillings were topnotch, too.

Salads included the house combination of arugula, avocado and hearts of palm, dressed at the table with good olive oil and balsamic vinegar, and a lovely artichoke salad that was dressed in a vinaigrette creamy with shaved Parmesan over it, a sort of two-cheese salad.

Carpaccio, the thin, air-dried beef, was lovely with arugula and more Parmesan. Portobello mushrooms grilled with olive oil and garlic were another pleasing classic. A salad of warm, moist chicken tossed with goat cheese and arugula was more appealing than an uninspired sautéed shrimp with mushrooms and white beans. Warm vegetable patties—zucchini, spinach, asparagus, carrots, potatoes and garlic—served with arugula (most things do seem to come with arugula here, which is fine by me) and goat cheese were another felicitous starter. Homemade mozzarella, served with peppers and tomato, did not seem fresh and milky enough. A couple of these antipasti plates could be a dandy summer supper.

Or choose a few pastas to share, as we did one time. The taste of wild mushrooms had really permeated the pappardelle al funghi, wide noodles luxurious in a swath of garlic and oil. Black and white tagliolini came in a zesty tomato sauce that delivered spice, as promised. Farfalle, or bow ties, were exquisite in a creamy sauce flavored with smoked salmon and bits of asparagus. Ravioloni filled with a delicious mixture of asparagus, mushrooms and zucchini nestled under a blanket of perky tomato sauce.

The gentle prices mean that entrée portions are not large, but they're plenty large enough if you split a pasta beforehand. We favored peppery marinated grilled tuna, red snapper in a sauce of sun-dried tomatoes, black olives and wine, and moist, golden grilled chicken with polenta and mushrooms. A dish of thin-sliced roasted chicken with artichokes was tender and tasty, and so was thin-sliced leg of lamb with white beans and a scattering of mushrooms. Some main dishes were plated with small roasted potatoes; side dishes you may want to consider included spinach or broccoli sautéed in garlic and oil, or sautéed fresh mushrooms.

Sitting at Orologio over excellent espresso and well-made tirami su, ricotta cheesecake or crème brûlée, it's hard to believe this is Avenue A. Maybe it isn't—maybe we are in the midst, as one friend imagined, of the floating clocks in the opening credits of The Time Machine, the movie with Rod Taylor and Yvette Mimeux.

PO

31 Cornelia St.
(212) 645-2189

HOURS: Dinner Tuesday–Thursday, 5:30–11 p.m.; Friday–Saturday, 5:30–11:30 p.m.; Sunday, 5–10 p.m. Lunch Wednesday–Sunday, 11:30 a.m.–3 p.m.
PRICES: Entrées $10–$15. Lunch $7–$8. AE.
RESERVATIONS: Required.
ACCESS: Dining area wheelchair-accessible; ladies' restroom wheelchair-accessible, men's is not.
HOW TO FIND IT: Between Bleecker and West 4th Streets; subway lines A, D, E, or F to West 4th Street/Washington Square station; bus line M8.

A friend glanced around at Po's understated decor. She took in the good looks of the lean eaters who were taking up every available chair. "This is a bit more of a scene than you usually are willing to put up with," she said, "but now I see why."

The why was this: We had just eaten another memorable dinner at Po.

Po opened last year with Mario Batali, a star chef who had gotten raves at Rocco and Café Tabac, at the stove and Steven Crane as his partner. Po got some instant fanfare, and I had wanted to stay away until the crowd that always must do the latest restaurant went elsewhere. But the crowd never left, because it's hard to find food this imaginative, flavorful and satisfying at any price. It is nearly impossible to find such fare on a menu where the entrées top out at $15. So I made a reservation and braved the scene. You should, too, and don't be late. Po has so few seats (34) that it's rude to ask them to hold tables.

Batali's impressive depth and breadth of experience includes Bolognese cuisine in Borgo Capanne, Italy, and seafood in San Giorgio di Piano, between Ferrari and Bologna. His earthy style, right down to his sandy-colored ponytail and the shorts he favors over more traditional garb, is his own, and sure. Batali makes amazing things out of simple ingredients. Everybody around town is doing white beans these days, but Batali does it better; bruschetta with perfectly cooked, creamy white beans on top is one example. One piece each will be brought to the table, and an additional order costs only $1. Everybody does a mesclun salad, and many of those delicate little lettuces are organically raised, but who else is putting a stunning white-bean vinaigrette on the mesclun? I am utterly smitten, too, with white-bean ravioli in a rich sauce of butter and balsamic vinegar, one of Batali's signature dishes.

At lunch, you might start with an antipasto selection for $4 or, for $7, make a larger selection your meal. At dinner, I was enamored of watercress salad with raw artichokes and shavings of cheese. Impossibly thin-shaved fennel combined with watercress in a lively lunchtime salad. A grilled Portobello mushroom came with lovely arugula and thin-shaved Parmigiano.

One evening when spring was a tease in the warm air, both ceiling fans and raw spring mushroom salad, tossed with dried tomatoes and pea sprouts, were welcome. Po's celebratory seasonal menu has such enticing entries as "gnocchi in a spring onion amartriciana," which I haven't yet tried.

I passed it up for the reassuring comfort of meat sauce over tagliatelle, a special. This humble dish was made with great care, the meat and vegetables so finely chopped that the sauce married to the noodles in a manner that suggested the pasta had been partly cooked in the sauce. I was wild about the plump gnocchi with pesto and pecorino cheese. Penne with a tomato and basil sauce that might, to some, seem artless was actually the height of elegance; it has that sure simplicity that comes of making a dish again and again, adding and taking away until it becomes intuition. Once in a while, something is ever so slightly off the mark—a gritty mussel in an otherwise blameless broth, fresh salmon that didn't seem to meld into the lusty caper and olives in a puttanesca sauce over penne.

The knockout dish was monkfish with preserved lemons, a Moroccan touch, and black mustard, and of course, some of the beautiful white beans. Quail were marinated, then "painted" with a reduction of balsamic vinegar and paired with black plums and frisée. Roasted sweet sausage combined with leeks, new potatoes and Cinzano for another glorious dish. We admired the freewheeling doodles of citrus glaze on the edges of a plate of tender baby octopus in a spicy dried-orange-tomato zuppetta (a "little" broth). A special of sea bass in a more delicate broth was merely good.

Service was smooth. One touch that seemed especially sensible is that a few bottles of wine from the list are opened for house wine each day, and refills are poured directly from the opened bottles, at table. Sometimes, I have seen this done in such a hasty way that diners are surprised to find they have to pay for wine refills, but at Po, the servers ask first, pour later.

Of course the bread was superb here, good Tuscan-style loaves that we devoured with fruity olive oil. And, of course the espresso was wonderful. And desserts don't get much better than a seductively smooth rhubarb compote swirled with slightly runny fresh mascarpone. There was a delectable warm apple tart with lush hazelnut gelato, a chocolate and caramel terrine that was rich as fudge, strawberries that became a new taste thrill when teamed with black pepper and Batali's beloved balsamic.

So what if my trendier friend did see the actor Eric Bogosian on our way out one night? (To me, he just looked familiar, somebody I had seen around the neighborhood.) Oh, well, as long as I have those mellow white beans with vinegar and garlic, I can endure a little brush with celebrity once in a while.

RANGOON CAFÉ
81 St. Mark's Place
(212) 228-2199

HOURS: Daily, 4:30–10:30 p.m.
PRICES: Entrées $4.95–$5.50; appetizers $3–$3.50.
RESERVATIONS: Recommended.
ACCESS: Ramp at entrance.
HOW TO FIND IT: Between First and Second Avenues; subway line N to 8th Street station; bus lines M1, M2, M8.

Rangoon Café is small, and the food is served on disposable plates. But the savory tastes are big and expansive, and so is the welcome.

One night, the host quickly rearranged tables to make our party of three comfortable. When we asked a question about Aung San Suu Kyi, the Nobel Peace Prize laureate who is in her sixth year of house arrest in Myanmar, formerly known as Burma, the same fellow took time to tell us with great passion about the political situation back home.

In Burmese, the name Myanma Naing-ngan, of which Myanmar is an English derivative, means "Land of the Swift and Strong." When it comes to food, we might add "Land of the Delicious" to the list.

Although Burmese food does resemble Indian and Thai food in a few ways, it is unique, a knockout cuisine in its own right. There's a certain delicacy combined with fire, a winning combination in life or cooking.

Such a simple, relatively familiar dish as saté with peanut sauce took on new nuances of flavor; the peanut sauce was coarse, with some substance to it, not the thinned-down peanut butter we have come to expect at all too many Thai restaurants. I've had crispy lentil fritters at a few other Burmese restaurants, but never have I had better than the crisp, spicy version served here.

Burmese ginger salad, threads of ginger with peanuts, toasted chickpea flour, and a myriad of other ingredients, the whole moistened with lemon or lime juice, was refreshing, a perfect summer entrée.

Sesame string beans and peanuts wowed us, too, in a version far superior to lots of Chinese-style string beans about town. Rangoon night-market noodles with duck were zesty, the fowl meaty and almost greaseless. Chickpea-potato salad and vibrant watercress salad were top-notch too. And oh, the rice! Butter-raisin rice, dun-paod in Burmese, was fresh and delightful, better than the sum of its parts—buttered rice with raisins, bits of chicken, a touch of bay leaf and cinnamon and a handful of green peas.

With everything, you may have sweet Burmese iced tea and of course, the multi-layered bread called thousand-layer bread here, and in Burma, hundred-layer bread. Who knows why? Never mind; by any name this carefully handmade bread is a delight.

There's just one problem; eating the bread takes up valuable space that I might be filling with lentil fritters, raisin rice or ginger salad.

SEMO & NEMO
120 W. 3rd St.
(212) 979-0433

HOURS: Sunday–Thursday, noon–11 p.m.; Friday–Saturday, noon–midnight.
PRICE RANGE: Entrées $9.95–$11.95; appetizers $3.95–$6.95; soups $6.95–$10.95; noodle and rice dishes $6.95–$9.95. AE.
RESERVATIONS: Recommended.
ACCESS: On 2nd floor; not wheelchair-accessible.
PARKING: Garage next to restaurant.
HOW TO FIND IT: Between 6th Avenue and MacDougal Street; subway lines A, E, D, F to W. 4th Street/Washington Square station; bus line M8.

My friend and I huddled inside our woolens one clear, crisp lunchtime and dipped our spoons into bowls of flavorful broth and noodles, thin and fat ones. We marveled over delicate steamed dumplings, scalloped on the edges so they looked like flowers. We indulged in one of our favorite daydreams, the one where we stay out late listening to jazz at the Blue Note across the street and end the night at Semo & Nemo (open until 2 a.m.) with spicy-hot kimchi fried rice.

Semo & Nemo, which is a near-perfect little noodle house, inspired us to feel hopeful. Maybe we could manage to stay up late some night.

A capacity crowd at Semo & Nemo is about 16 people. There's a tiny kitchen in the back, behind a wall that holds hundreds of tape cassettes. When everybody, including lots of Korean diners, is sipping steaming barley tea out of pottery mugs and eating noodles and kimchi hot pots and smoking and talking, there's no place quite like this one in the Village. It's the Asian equivalent of a Village coffeehouse, where lingering is a way of life.

To start, you might try tender fried squid or zesty, pan-broiled squid or duk bok ki, hearty rice cakes in a spicy, slightly sweet, red sauce with scallions. Along with the tea, kimchi—spicy, pickled sprouts, cabbage, spinach—will appear. You will never go wrong with the aforementioned steamed dumplings, in which meat and scallions are minced extra fine for a delicate treat. There's a chile-spiked oil for dipping the dumplings. Bi bim bab, the homey rice dish with eggs, sprouts and hot chile, was mixed at the table. We are partial to shiitake yaki dong, rice and mushrooms, and to kimchi fried rice, which brings tears to the eye, partly from hotness and partly from happiness. Miso larmen, a robust soy-paste broth with thin and thick noodles, was satisfying on a chilly day. Rice dishes in cast-iron pots were presented sizzling, and they have a homey appeal. Be sure to toss the rice with your chopsticks to mix it; the rice that's next to the pot will definitely stick to it if you don't. The rice pot we tried included shrimp, spinach and thin slices of fish cake. And don't miss that kimchi fried rice.

SHABU-TATSU
216 E. 10th St.
(212) 477-2972

HOURS: Sunday–Monday, 5–11:45 p.m.; Tuesday–Saturday 5 p.m.–2 a.m.
PRICES: Dinner for two $28–$34. AE, DC, MC, V.
ACCESS: Not wheelchair-accessible.
RESERVATIONS: Taken only for groups of 5 or more before 7 p.m.
KIDS: No children's menu but will accommodate.
HOW TO FIND IT: Between First and Second Avenues. Subway line L to Third Avenue station, line N to Eighth Avenue station or line 6 to Astor Place; bus line M101, M102.

Shabu-shabu is the sound that thin-sliced meat makes as it's swished through bubbling hot broth, and it's the name of a dish. You can get it at Shabu-Tatsu.

This kind of at-table cooking has been traditional in Japan for at least 100 years. But in New York, there's no other place quite like Shabu-Tatsu, as far as we know. The menu is on the cutting edge of Japanese fashion. Besides shabu-shabu, it features the Japanese interpretation of Korean barbecue, quite the rage in Japan just now, and even bibim bap (sometimes written bibim bab on other menus), the Korean meal-in-a bowl—a tossing together of rice, cooked beef, vegetables, raw egg and zenmai, a kind of bracken sometimes called "mountain vegetable."

There's usually a wait to get into this small, sleek East Village spot. We were directed past tables where meat and seafood were being grilled, through the kitchen and down the back stairs to an even more snug room where a few tables are covered in paisley cloths. There, you can cool your heels while having a cold sake or beer or the warm sake to which Americans are more accustomed.

We sipped chilled Onigoroshi sake out of a masu, or wooden box, as is customary. The word masu means measure, and at Shabu-Tatsu, the measure was generous; a water tumbler was filled to the brim and beyond. Since the tumbler was presented inside the box, any spillover was caught and did not go to waste.

Eventually, we were directed back upstairs to one of the gleaming highly varnished tables. Other diners are cooking, talking, smoking. Warm, moist face cloths await, and you're glad you waited.

When you order, the waiter is likely to ask if you want bowls of rice right away or later. A friend who has lived in Japan extensively said that many customers have rice last, after much sake and lots of festive shabu-shabu or barbecue. Is this so the sake has a chance to make you feel euphoric and the rice would buffer it too much? Is it because they are waiting to see if they will have any room left for rice? Either way, it seems reasonable to me.

Besides kimchi, the peppery pickled vegetables without which no Korean barbecue is complete, there are delightful sunomono, or vinegared things. In this category, we sampled sprightly mixed seaweed salad, watercress in a sesame dressing, spinach in a light soy mixture sprinkled with dried bonito flakes, and tender octopus on a bed of wakame, a kind of seaweed.

Barbecues may be ordered à la carte or as a full dinner. For a fair-sized group, you might want to order one each of the two assorted barbecues, as we did. The excellent beef assortment for two ($29) included boneless short ribs sliced so thin they seemed delicate; delicious liver; marinated tongue so good it might convert those who are squeamish about that beef body part, plump pieces of chicken and slices of eggplant, zucchini and carrots. (The pieces of beef stomach seemed too chewy for my taste, though I did try to like them.) Another deluxe barbecue for two was the seafood assortment of topnotch shrimp, lovely squid, gorgeous baby octopus complete with heads, scallops, and salmon laid to steam in a foil packet. Several dipping sauces, one a soy-based ponzu floating a slice of lemon, came with the barbecue, and other appropriate sauces appeared with our prime rib-eye shabu-shabu.

After cooking meat and vegetables in the broth, shabu-shabu style, you add plump noodles. Each diner gets a roomy white mug with salt and pepper at the bottom and then ladles out a serving of noodles and broth into the cup. After that, sip a mug of tea, made with roasted tea leaves, and try a small bowl of green-tea ice cream, which had an appealing molasseslike undertone.

One night a passerby clutching a box of instant noodles peeked wistfully through the window at our steaming bowls of noodles, then presumably went on home to "add boiling water." We hope that next time he will be inside, part of the group around a big bowl of shabu-shabu.

TANTI BACI
163 W. 10th St.
(212) 647-9651

HOURS: Sunday–Thursday, 11 a.m.–11 p.m.; Friday–Saturday, 11 a.m.–midnight.
PRICES: Entrées/lunch $10.50–$13; pasta $5.50–$7.50; appetizers $3–$7. Brunch $8.50. No liquor license, bring your own wine. MC, V.

RESERVATIONS: Taken only Sunday–Thursday; in-person wait list Friday–Saturday.
ACCESS: Not wheelchair-accessible.
KIDS: No children's menu but will accommodate.
HOW TO FIND IT: West of Seventh Avenue; subway line 1 to Christopher Street station; bus line M8.

Tanti Baci means many kisses. How apropos. Along with other well-satisfied customers, I am blowing loads of kisses to Tanti Baci, a restaurant that is simple, from its apricot-sponged walls to its pared-down menu.

Oscar Del Nodal, the waiter who wears his hair in a neat French twist, welcomes you. Paola Tottani, the enthusiastic co-owner (with Luna Pariente), welcomes you. The lively smell of sautéeing garlic welcomes you. Then a basket of chewy, flour-dusted rolls welcomes you. Tanti Baci is a welcoming place and, in its own way, a daring one.

It takes a lot of brio to serve only four kinds of salads, four sandwiches and quite a few kinds of dry (asciutta) and fresh pasta with just five choices of sauce. And strictly speaking, you are not even allowed to choose from all of those. "No," the opinionated Tottani told my friend Kitty, "Not the fresh pasta with the vongole," or tiny clams. Kitty must, Tottani declared, have dry pasta—linguine would be perfect. Tottani's daughters, Valentina and Francesca, pushed her to open the restaurant "because I have always so many people at home."

When we said things like, "Well, I'll have the Number 16 with sauce B"— translation, pesto-filled ravioli in lush pesto sauce—Tottani waved her hand dismissively. "I do not know the numbers," she said. So we gave her words, and she gave us lessons in Italian food.

Martin, the young man at our table who recently discovered a passion for gnocchi, obediently ordered one of the two sauces Tottani recommended with it, a simple, fresh tomato sauce pungent with basil and garlic. The other permissible sauce with gnocchi, said Tottani, was the hearty yet subtle bolognese, a savory, rosemary-accented mingling of ground beef, onions, tomato and, of course, garlic.

But we digress, forgetting the appetizers. Characteristically, they are few: White beans—fagioli all'uccelletto—were a creamy coming together of well-cooked legumes, garlic, a bit of tomato and a bit of the rosemary this kitchen loves so well. The name means "beans like birds," because the way they are seasoned is supposed to make them taste like small game. Bruschetta was based on chewy, substantial bread, topped with bright chopped tomatoes, garlic and snippets of basil. It is in the details that so many larger, flashier restaurants neglect that Tottani shows her pride and care. For more slices of the lovely red tomatoes, soon to be gone until next tomato season, order fresh mozzarella with basil, olive oil and black olives. Such food is elemental, and wise, and you feel better for eating it.

There are times, for example, when nothing cures "Broadway Stomach" brought on by too many rich foods, as the author of one curious old book called it, better than al dente linguine with garlic, oil and a generous hand with the red pepper. Pomodoro sauce, too, was just the kind we crave, a coming together of fresh tomatoes, basil, garlic and olive oil. So simple, so simpatico.

Tottani advises against meat sauce over fresca pasta. "What if my brother came," she asked rhetorically, "and I served that? He would throw it out the window. It is not Italian. How would I explain?" If you want a meat sauce and a fresh pasta, the solution is simple; just order a side of lightly seasoned but savory meatballs.

There is as yet no license for wine, but besides a good acqua minerale there's fresh-squeezed orange juice, hot or cold chocolate, fresh fruit shakes and espresso. Desserts are the imported Italian tirami su and torte—pine nuts, chocolate or frutta di bosco, poetically named for the berries of the woods.

I don't really care about dessert, though. I could just listen to Tottani talk. She teaches her familial recipes to chef Edmundo Garcon, Ecuadoran by birth but surely Italian somewhere in his soul, and she praises him generously: "He immediately understands the taste. He is subtle." When asked if the white beans ought to be made with sage, the way Waverley Root has it in *The Food of Italy*, she had the courage to say. "People used what they had in the yard" for seasoning, back home in Italy.

Tanti Baci is an original. Cherish it.

TAQUERIA DE MEXICO
93 Greenwich Ave.
(212) 255-5212

HOURS: Monday–Friday, 11:30 a.m.–11 p.m.; Saturday, noon–11 p.m.; Sunday, noon–10 p.m. Counter service.
PRICES: Tacos and enchiladas $2.50–$6.50.
ACCESS: Wheelchair-accessible.
HOW TO FIND IT: Between Bank and 12th Streets; subway lines A or E to 14th Street/Eighth Avenue station; bus line M14.

I never thought I'd say it: There are so many taquerias in New York that some of them give tacos a bad name. Not so with Taqueria de Mexico.

Along with lots of other New Yorkers, I used to whine about how there was no real Mexican food in New York. Then suddenly, there was a taqueria (or a premium-coffee establishment) around almost every corner. In Manhattan, most of these new places did not actually claim to serve Mexican food but variations on the theme, Cal-Mex or Tex-Mex. (In Brooklyn, there are a few Mexican taquerias.) Call it what you will, this trend was a definite improvement.

In the meantime, a kind of revolution was brewing. No history of recent Mexican food in New York would be complete without a tip of the hat to Jose Hurtado-Prud'homme, who in 1991 with his wife Marzena opened Mi Cocina, a restaurant where extraordinary Mexican fare is served. At Mi Cocina, vegetable tacos might contain such items as bok choy and Swiss chard, bread was served instead of corn chips, and regional Mexican menus were offered. There was a wine list. In short, New Yorkers had never been to a Mexican restaurant quite like Mi Cocina.

Hurtado-Prud'homme, who hails from Queretaro, north of Mexico City, had been executive chef at Cinco de Mayo, but now, in his own place, he soared. The small but appealing Mi Cocina, nestled in the West Village, became a destination restaurant.

I tell you all this to give you just a glimmer of how thrilled I was when I got word that Hurtado-Prud'homme had opened a taqueria, an authentic Mexico City taqueria. It was in my neighborhood, besides. And when I called up Hurtado-Prud'homme and learned that there were five kinds of tamales every day at his new Taqueria de Mexico, my joy knew no bounds. Tamales are labor-intensive—you have to wrap all those little bundles of cornmeal stuffings in corn husks (or sometimes banana leaves)—and in New York they are seldom a regular menu item.

My favorite tamale happens to be a simple vegetarian one—poblano chile in a sauce of roasted tomatoes, with a bit of queso blanco, the Mexican white cheese. The sauce blends pleasingly into the earthy, crumbly cornmeal steamed inside a corn husk. Beautifully moist chicken in a green tomatillo sauce also made a fine tamale, but Veracruzano de camaron, a shrimp-filled tamalé with olives, capers and roasted tomato sauce, did not work out as well. The whole shrimp, just a few per tamale, seemed to soak up all the tomato sauce, leaving too little to keep the tamale from being dry. Pork in guajillo-chile sauce also made for a slightly dry, if tasty, tamale; however, this can easily be remedied by pouring a tiny container of green sauce or one of fresh, chopped-tomato salsa (pico de gallo) over it. There are several other sauces, too, $1.25 per side order: ranchera, which is merely hot, or salsa picosa, which is very hot.

Teleras, small egg-washed buns for making the Mexican sandwiches known as tortas, are baked fresh in small batches throughout the day. Most satisfying among the tortas was spicy chorizo with beans and jalapeño peppers. but roasted loin of pork was good, too, either in a cubana torta with ham, cheese, avocado and chipotle chile, or on its own. But pork in pumpkin-seed molé seemed a bit dry on two small, soft corn tacos.

My vote for best taco goes to a tangy pork taco, al pastor, for which the meat was marinated with cilantro, onion and pineapple. But if you are used to the brittle, crunchy shells that often pass for tacos in these parts, Hurtado-Prud'homme's true Mexican soft tacos may take some getting used to. (By the way, don't expect an actual casserole of food when you order "tacos de las cazuelas"; that's merely how the taco filling was cooked.)

Wild-mushroom quesadillas, with cheese and onions wedged between two lightly grilled flour tortillas, were excellent. And to round out the menu, there was soup—corn and tomato was dandy—and a lovely tossed salad of pristine mesclun, with avocado (perfectly ripe) if you wish, in a classic vinaigrette.

Mild but good guacamole ($1.95) was always sparklingly fresh, but remember to order chips (65 cents) separately. All side orders, including mellow refried beans, are vegetarian, by the way.

When I got a big takeout order and brought it to friends in the office, quiet fell as everyone stopped talking and started eating. Some of the converts to this new taqueria actually went there to eat the very next day. "The best stuff I'd had in the city," said one aficionado. "It was so delicious I couldn't eat supper that night."

For dessert, besides a smooth chocolate pudding and a very lush rice pudding, there's flan de elote, a sort of sweet-corn pudding that may take some getting used to. And there is a traditional pink dessert tamale made with raisins, butter and milk. Thumbs-up for the old-fashioned paper plates; thumbs-down for the Styrofoam soft-drink cups. (Strong, hot espresso came in a real cup.) The look of this small place is bright and friendly, with peach-colored walls that look sort of like adobe, mirrors framed in Mission-style wood and whimsical yellow tiles.

When we talked by phone, Hurtado-Prud'homme was clearly excited about his new venture. He said that well-heeled Mexican-Americans are stopping by late in the day for a snack, just as they might in Mexico City. And one rainy day we saw an elderly anglo come in and study the menu carefully. He ordered a rice pudding and coffee and appeared to be content. Who knows? Maybe next week he'll be back for a tamale.

There can never be too many taquerias as honest, and as good, as this one.

CAFÉ BEULAH
39 E. 19th St.
(212) 777-9700

HOURS: Dinner Monday–Tuesday, 5–11 p.m.; Wednesday–Saturday, 5 p.m.–midnight. Brunch Sunday, noon–5 p.m.
PRICES: Entrées $12–$15; specials $18–$23. Brunch $10–$14. AE, DC, MC, V.
RESERVATIONS: Recommended.
ACCESS: Wheelchair-accessible; restrooms equipped for disabled.
HOW TO FIND IT: Between Broadway and Park Avenue South; subway lines N or R to 23rd Street station or lines L, N or 4 to 14th Street/Union Square station; bus lines M1, M2, M7.

Café Beulah is not cheap, but I don't mind.

I am prepared to pay almost any price for deluxe-quality country ham, divine black-eyed pea cakes, grits and greens, warm biscuits with butter and true southern fried chicken. It's not so easy to find these seemingly simple foods in these parts.

It would be calming to sit in this well-ordered space, lined with old photos, even if all you did was drink iced tea. (Yes, there was a real Beulah, and her picture is going up on the wall soon, maybe near Johnnie Mae Smalls, mother of owner Alexander Smalls. The photos were copied and framed by Lorna Simpson, whose photographs are at the Whitney and the Museum of Modern Art.)

The food is what Smalls, a baritone who has sung at Carnegie Hall and in the role of Jake in "Porgy & Bess" on Broadway, once described as "Southern revival . . . southern food with a French presentation." Homage is paid to traditional favorites, without dissing them. Example: arugula salad (restaurant food) with black-eyed peas (down-home), and it's great. Smalls, who started cooking at five years of age, developed recipes and hired Leslie Parks (who went to the French Culinary Institute and is the daughter of photographer Gordon Parks) to run the kitchen. Service was, for the most part, suave and sure. Glasses of iced tea were freshened, place settings unobtrusively added or removed as called for.

It takes plenty of confidence to charge $6 for mellow macaroni and cheese, served in a terrine with a little dish of Creole sauce to pep it up. The lively condiment—peppers, tomatoes, corn and okra—added a new dimension. Someone dotes on sage, and one of its best uses is as a component of zesty black-eyed pea cakes, crisply fried and served with a swath of satisfying mushroom gravy one time, a peppery Creole mayonnaise the next. The bread basket costs $3. But what a basket! Warm biscuits, both plain and sage, and crumbly, non-sweet (hallelujah) corn bread.

She-crab soup was ambrosial essence of crab, and deviled crab cakes were another winner. Gumbo, the most steeply priced entrée ($23), was dry, despite first-class ingredients; meaty, brittle-skinned duck, jumbo shrimp, fresh crab and okra, ringed around a helping of rice. Plating tenderly sautéed chicken livers in barbecue-mustard sauce with turnip greens made the dish as pretty as it was tasty. For a homey supper, there's a humble bowl of grits, greens and smoked ham, all served together.

Free-range chicken was southern fried, all crisp crackle and juice, as it ought to be. And fried catfish was nicely done but not really suited to the sturdy white bread on which it was served. Tangy potato salad accompanied a sandwich of ham fragrant with cloves and a smidgen of mace, and that worked better. Still, that bread was New York bread; the bread basket is not. Lemon-candied yams were glazed almost black, so intense they needed to be eaten as a separate course. Sautéed collard greens and stewed turnip greens were comforting.

There's a full bar and a wine list with excellent, affordable choices. But iced tea is really the right wine with this food, even in winter. We found the lemon coconut cake unexciting, but had exemplary pecan pie and light, fragile-crusted sweet-potato-custard pie. Sweet-potato ice cream was a smash hit.

A friend reported that she once had pecan pie at Beulah's that might have been frozen. And alas, another friend reported a cold bread basket. But there is an aura of competence and confidence at Beulah, apt, I think to save the day. I want this place to succeed, so I can keep going there to listen to Nina Simone on CD and eat sitting beneath the high ceiling fans. I'll be surrounded by those wonderful faces—grave, brave, saucy and reassuring faces.

CARAVAN
741 Eighth Ave.
(212) 262-2021

HOURS: Daily, noon–11 p.m.
PRICES: Entrées $6.95–$10.25; appetizers $2.95–$3.50; kebobs $8.95– $12.75. AE, DC, MC, V.
ACCESS: Dining area wheelchair-accessible, restrooms are not.
RESERVATIONS: Taken only for parties of 10 or more 6–8 p.m.
HOW TO FIND IT: Between 46th and 47th Streets; subway line 1 to 50th Street/ Broadway station; bus lines M7, M50.

Caravan does not bill itself as a kebob house. This is as it should be, because Caravan takes the food of Afghanistan far beyond the meat-on-a-stick experience.

From the moment you walk through the door you'll be surrounded by hunger-producing smells, by the fine fragrances of basmati rice and scallion dumplings being steamed. You may catch a whiff of grilling lamb or chicken, besides, and you won't go wrong ordering kebobs here. But don't neglect such delectable first courses as dainty pumpkin turnovers to dip in a mint-yogurt potion, smooth and heavenly homemade noodles dressed in yogurt-and-garlic sauce, delicious "palow" (as they spell pilaf or pilau here) made of basmati rice. Don't, whatever you do, miss delicate sautéed rounds of eggplant in more yogurt.

And that's not all the good news at Caravan, which is attractively decorated with gleaming samovars and rich-red wall hangings. Prices were modest in the extreme; a more-than-ample dinner for six (count 'em, six) cost only $126 (before tip), and that included two bottles of wine and five Turkish coffees.

There is no bad news. Well, almost no bad news. On a second visit, they were out of the Australian Shiraz we had liked at $16 a bottle, but that will probably be remedied. Before curtain in the theater district, the restaurant got very busy, and there were slight delays in service. But the waitresses and busboy managed handily.

If you harbor any lingering resistance toward yogurt, this is the place to cure it. Strong men ate yogurt here without complaint. (Strong women liked it just as well.) It's so good the way the chef does it here, mixed with big doses of garlic and blended with mint. It's a dip for all manner of good things: those steamed scallion dumplings, fried scallion turnovers known as boulanee, and boulanee kachaloo, a fried potato turnover. (The aforementioned sautéed eggplant, with or without a zesty meat sauce, is called badenjan boulanee.) A second order of boulanee kadou—fried, spiced-pumpkin turnovers—was hard to resist; we didn't.

A favorite with our table was sautéed spinach called sabzi chalow, seasoned with coriander, cumin, scallions, and a bright splash of lemon, then scattered with plump kidney beans. I'm wild about ash-e-keshideh, those noodles in garlic sauce. Another excellent vegetarian choice was kabuli palow, basmati rice with raisins, carrots and almonds. Saffron, orange peel and pistachios were added to another "palow," one that came with moist pieces of chicken in it.

Boneless chicken was tender, marinated and then grilled. Cornish hen was similarly marinated and grilled. Other dandy grills included beef filet, minced beef, yogurt-marinated lamb and garlicky shishlick, or tenderloin. With them or with lamb curry, pickled cucumbers were just right.

For dessert, light, honey-drenched cookies are safe. But how well you take to other Afghani desserts will depend on your tolerance for rosewater. You'll either like the soothing, cardamom-flavored rice pudding called firni, or you won't. You'll either like the saffron-scented Persian rice pudding, or you won't (I did).

If you don't, content yourself with strong Turkish coffee or a pot of steaming mint tea.

FOOD BAR
149 Eighth Ave.
(212) 243-2020

HOURS: Monday–Friday, noon–midnight; Saturday–Sunday, 11 a.m.–midnight.
PRICES: Entrées/lunch $6.45–$9.95; appetizers $3.75–$6.95. Brunch Saturday–Sunday, $9.95. MC, V.
RESERVATIONS: Taken for groups of five or more.
ACCESS: Dining area wheelchair-accessible; restrooms downstairs.
HOW TO FIND IT: Between 17th and 18th Streets; subway line 1 to 18th Street/Seventh Avenue station, line E to 23rd Street/Eighth Avenue station or lines L, A or E to 14th Street/Eighth Avenue station; bus lines M14, M23.

Despite a name that calls to mind a salad bar or maybe a feeding trough on a farm, Food Bar is a fantasia of whirring ceiling fans, lamp shades made of laminated slide photos—and customers, the best decoration of all. We adored the bald patron who wore a daisy behind one ear.

Summertime, when some of the regulars are away for the season, is the best time to experience some of the simple dishes that make Food Bar special—sliced tomatoes with white bean purée and basil olive oil, sublime with ripe, red beef-steaks, what the menu calls "a nice big salad" (and it really is), and biscuit-dough strawberry shortcake, that most appealing of all summer desserts.

Green beans, too, are in season locally for a fine starter salad of beets, roasted new potatoes and green beans. Cayenne-peppered onion rings, lightly battered calamari and a lovely grilled artichoke with red pepper sauce are other first-course possibilities. And crisp, onion-laced potato pancakes with apple sauce and sour cream are irresistible any time of year.

Chef Joe Fontecchio's appealing main courses included roasted chicken (served with one of those potato pancakes), grilled leg of lamb with green beans and small roasted potatoes, and seared curried salmon served with sautéed Savoy cabbage and lemon vinaigrette. Gnocchi with wild mushrooms, escarole and roasted garlic was tasty, as was its gentle $7.50 price tag. Angel hair was tossed with fresh artichokes, tomatoes and lots of crushed black pepper. Grilled tuna was good, and the fried rice-noodle cake with it was better than that. There's not a single main course that costs more than $10; burgers are $5.25 ($5.75 for cheeseburgers). All this, with margaritas, daiquiris and a sensible wine list, too; nothing costs more than $20, except sparkling wines. (It is possible to run up quite a bill for mineral water, though, with a big bottle priced at $5.50.) Desserts were cozy—lemon pound cake, smooth chocolate pudding and a "tunnel of fudge" cake, runny in the center.

FRANK'S TRATTORIA
371 First Ave.
(212) 677-7140, 677-7141 or 677-2991

HOURS: Daily, dinner 3:30–11 p.m.; lunch 11 a.m.–3:30 p.m.
PRICES: Entrées $12–$14, appetizers $6. Lunch $10–$12. AE, DC, MC, V.
RESERVATIONS: Suggested for Friday–Sunday.
ACCESS: Wheelchair-accessible; restrooms equipped for disabled.
KIDS: No children's menu but will accommodate.
HOW TO FIND IT: Between 21st and 22nd Streets; subway line L to First Avenue/ 14th Street station; bus lines M2, M15, M23.

Frank's is the homey, cozy, old-fashioned, sensibly priced kind of Italian place that you probably thought you could find only in the outer boroughs these days.

The waitresses exude good cheer and always try to save you money. The bus-boy attentively refills the water glasses. Frank Pino, the owner, offers a smashingly good Spanish wine for something like $16 a bottle. You don't often get treated this well in expensive restaurants. And half the time, you don't get food this good, either.

In truth, places like Frank's are hard to find anywhere anymore. So when my friend Joan called to tell me about the incredible dinner she and her husband Archie had eaten at Frank's, $13.95 per (including wine), I met her there at the next available lunch hour.

From the street, Frank's looks like a pizzeria, and in fact, you can get good pizza at Frank's. If you walk past the front counter and pizza ovens, you'll find a dining room—billed on the menu as the "country Italian dining room"—with tables covered in checkered cloths. Here, as Joan quipped, you can always "see what the boys in the back room are having." Some of "the boys," and the women, too, are elderly customers. Some eat alone, some come as couples, but all are made to feel comfortable and all get a kindly word from Hortensia, Frank's wife. Many of these regulars have the daily specials, and you should, too.

At lunchtime, for around $6, you can get a pasta with an exceptionally crisp, varied house salad. That first day, we ate farfalle, the bow-tie shaped pasta, with broccoli, and linguine alla amatriciana, in a hearty tomato sauce fortified with pancetta—that's Italian bacon—and onions. Other days, there were other pastas: pesto on green fettucine, a pasta sauce made with delicious, lean sausage and peppers, and fresh, well-made homemade lasagna. Pasta e fagioli, that simple soup made of pasta and beans, was tame until we added hot pepper.

When we tried a pizza—roasted garlic, smoked mozzarella, fresh oregano and basil on a thin, crisp crust—we realized why Fabre is kept so busy making pies. They're great.

One night a friend had a special of liver with onions and bacon, and the liver was pink as ordered. Alongside dinner specials, besides bread and salad, there are generous plates of vegetables—one night sautéed potatoes and carrots. These little extras keep people coming back to Frank's.

Fried calamari, tentacles and all, was light and delicious, and clams posilipo with a forthright, garlicky sauce, were so fabulous we used bread to mop up every last smidgen.

Linguine was topped with marinara sauce and fresh, plentiful seafood, including nicely cooked lobster, for one daily special. Luscious little lamb chops, simply done with brown pan juices, were superb, and deep-brown osso buco was finished with wine in the sauce and served with gnocchi. Nuggets of flavorful, on-the-bone chicken scarpariello was satisfyingly lemony and garlicky. These are not startling dishes, just very good renditions of comforting classics.

For dessert, an Italian-style Napoleon, layers of pastry and cream and as light as the proverbial air, was wonderful. There's good-quality tartufo, spumoni and tortoni, too. No new coffee bar serves better espresso, and at Frank's, Sambuca gratis is the rule, rather than the exception.

ISLAND SPICE
402 W. 44th St.
(212) 765-1737 or 765-2995

HOURS: Dinner Monday–Thursday, 4–11 p.m.; Friday–Saturday, 4 p.m.–midnight; Sunday, 2 p.m.–10 p.m. Lunch Monday–Saturday, noon–4 p.m.
PRICES: Entrées $8.95–$18.95; appetizers $6.50–$15.95. Lunch $6.50–$9.50. AE, DC, MC, V.

RESERVATIONS: Recommended.
ACCESS: Dining area/restrooms wheelchair-accessible.
HOW TO FIND IT: Near corner of Ninth Avenue; subway lines A, E, 1, 2, 7, S or N to 42nd Street station; bus lines M16, M42.

Marva Layne began winning customers to her Caribbean cuisine with a small takeout shop, Sweetie Pie, on Ninth Avenue. Now, she has ventured west of Ninth to open Island Spice, where the sweet potato pie, when you can get it, is just right and not too sweet.

Crossing the invisible barrier past Ninth Avenue used to freak out some people, but jerk pork, codfish fritters and stewed cabbage à la Layne are winning converts. I'd been watching for Island Spice to open, and the first time I wanted to go there, friends demurred. One thought the food might be too spicy, another didn't like straying that far from the beaten track.

Too spicy is never a problem for me, and judging by the crowds lining up outside the door lately, it's not a problem for lots of other happy eaters, either. But for more timid tasters, there are subtle flavors, too, tastes that won't overwhelm.

If zippy homemade ginger beer (nonalcoholic, but plenty sprightly) or sorrel drink laced with more zingy ginger is not your idea of a good time, just order the many-fruited island punch, or for a cocktail, island punch with champagne. There are also thick shake-like drinks of sea moss (traditionally thought to have aphrodisiacal properties), gentle sour sop, the fruit of a tropical tree, and carrot juice thickened with sweetened milk and enriched with ginger and vanilla. At times, the kitchen can scarcely send out pitchers of these lovely concoctions fast enough to meet the demand. Red Stripe, the Jamaican beer, and Stone's ginger wine are also available.

Often, there are long waits—the wait to be seated, the wait to order. But always, the servers do their best and are unfailingly good-natured in trying circumstances. While you wait, study the blackboard specials and be ready.

One night's meal began with salt fish and ackee, the mellow yellow fruit that looks like scrambled eggs, and "bammy crisp," toasty triangles of bammy, the bread that's made with cassava flour. When it's available, don't pass it up. The same goes for fish tea, which is really a lively fish broth. And callaloo, or spinach when callaloo is not available, was made into a soup that was like essence of greens, sure to cure whatever ails you. Another irresistible starter when it was on the menu was codfish fritters, here in a handsome wide, flat rendition that resembled potato pancakes in looks. Mini beef patties were not the least greasy, refined compared to the version you might get on Flatbush Avenue in Brooklyn, but not quite as spicy as those.

Layne said the menu will undergo changes as she goes along but predicted optimistically that it will only get better. Examples of current entrée offerings have been tender jerk chicken in a sauce enlivened by Scotch bonnet peppers, tidy medallions of jerk pork given the same treatment, ginger-lime chicken fried and tanged with citrus, kingfish in coconut-curry sauce, oxtails cooked falling-apart tender in a brown stew with butter beans. Crisp escovich fish (one of many spellings, but "coveech" on this menu) blanketed with pickled onions and tomatoes was another winner. Curried goat, like the curried chicken stew and jerk pork, may sometimes be had in roti, the flat Indian bread, when available.

With these came red beans and rice, turned out of timbales to make an appealing shape, and such side dishes as fried or boiled bananas, sautéed cabbage or callaloo. Even side salads had little extra touches, such as slices of perfectly ripe avocado.

Vegetarians can fare well here, with such dishes as stunning sautéed cabbage gussied up with tomatoes, onions and a rich coconut-curry sauce. "Ital" stew, as the dish called Italian stew has come to be known, was a savory combination based on big kidney beans, tomatoes and spices. Why this is called Italian stew is a mystery I've never been able to unravel.

Sunday brunch includes a mimosa, punch or wine for $8.95 and features a few items not on the regular menu, including banana pancakes. Hominy or corn-meal porridge and cream seasoned with vanilla and nutmeg is also available.

Everything at Island Spice had that down-home taste that meant it had been made in small, careful portions. The small space is attractive, with sponge-painted walls, green painted ironwork visible through the windows, baskets of fruits and vegetables that diminish during a night of cooking and a tropical-looking tree.

Later, there may be Taste the Tropics ice cream, auntie's plum pudding and mom's bread pudding. For now, we have been happy with excellent carrot cake and positively smitten with individual sweet potato pies—sweetie pie, indeed.

JAIYA
396 Third Ave.
(212) 889-1330

HOURS: Monday–Friday, 11:30 a.m.–midnight; Saturday, noon–midnight; Sunday, 5 p.m.–midnight.
PRICES: Entrées $7.95–$17.95; appetizers $3.75–$9.95. AE, DC, MC, V.
RESERVATIONS: Required after 7 p.m.
ACCESS: Dining area small but wheelchair-accessible, as are restrooms.
HOW TO FIND IT: At corner of 28th Street; subway line 6 to 28th Street station; bus lines M101, M102.

Jaiya is here! At last, the Thai restaurant that's a legend in Queens has opened a Manhattan location. Jaiya began in 1978 in a miniscule storefront on Broadway in Elmhurst. The food was extraordinary.

Spiced with bright, startling flavors of lemongrass, coriander and chile, the cuisine at Jaiya lured explorers out of Manhattan. Even star chefs came to eat and learn and exclaim in joy.

Once again, Jaiya's chefs are demonstrating what good pad Thai, the popular noodle dish, can be like: a happy balance of barely sweetened stir-fried rice noo-dles, vinegar, fish sauce, scallions, roasted peanuts, chile and small dried shrimp, all cooked with egg in a kind of noodle version of fried rice. Alongside the dish came a condiment tray with extra ground peanuts, sauce and roasted, ground chile. Even crunchy mee krob, the deep-fried rice-vermicelli noodles that are prepared with goodly quantities of caramelized sugar, was especially good here, not cloyingly sweet as it so often is elsewhere. Happily for vegans or those who are cutting back on meat, noodles and many other dishes, some featuring bean curd or wheat gluten, are available on a page-long vegetarian menu.

Pork and beef saté were listed on the menu, but it was also possible to order hefty strips of chicken saté. We tried all three versions and liked pork least, because it was slightly too fatty and ought to have been trimmed more carefully. The traditional sweet-hot cucumber sauce that came with saté was especially good here, but the other usual accompaniment, peanut sauce sparked with coriander, chile, ginger and garlic, seemed artificially thickened. These satés were all so luxuriantly meaty, though, that side sauces weren't all that important to their success.

There was also a minced barbecued beef, nur yang-num-tok, spiked with onion, fresh mint, lemon and chile. Don't pass up delectable Chinese-sausage salad, an always-appealing combination of thin-sliced sausage, cucumbers, chile, onions and lime juice. Larb, here made with ground beef instead of pork, had a slightly rough texture from coarsely crumbed chile and was refreshing and lively with the flavors of mint, scallions and lemon.

Our most hearty endorsements among appetizers, however, go to two breath-taking shrimp dishes. For dancing shrimp, raw shrimp were "cooked" with a marinade of lemon, onion, chile and generous amounts of what the printed menu insists is fresh mint, though I could have sworn there was fresh coriander, too. Never mind, for the flavor of any green plant would be almost obliterated by other strong, pungent flavors. The second killer shrimp preparation was barbecued shrimp in a similar marinade.

For shrimp main dishes, try No. 67, made with ground pepper and garlic, or the house special baked version in a rich, complex brown sauce (No. 69). Baked crab, which was hard to coax any meat from, was less successful. Crab-meat dumplings made of a well-seasoned ground crab mixture were the right choice.

Admirably fresh whole red snapper was a treat either with a triple-taste chile sauce or in Jaiya's house version, a smooth coconut-milk curry sauce.

Just as its food is given life by the Thai seasonings, Jaiya's calm gray walls are brightened by pictures painted in rich jewel tones, and the ubiquitous vivid red shrine or temple that all Thai restaurants seem to have was tucked into a corner. New-restaurant plants adorned in red ribbons provided greenery. Waiters wore snazzy white shirts embroidered with the restaurant's logo.

KABUL CAFÉ
265 W. 54th St.
(212) 757-2037, (212) 246-8387

HOURS: Dinner Monday–Thursday, 3–10 p.m.; Friday, 3–11 p.m.; Saturday, noon–11 p.m.; Sunday, noon–10 p.m. Lunch Monday–Friday, noon–3 p.m.
PRICES: Entrées $8.50–$16.95; appetizers $3–$5. Lunch $4.95–$11.95. DC, MC, V.
RESERVATIONS: Recommended.
ACCESS: Dining area wheelchair-accessible, restrooms are not.
ENTERTAINMENT: Saturday evening, belly dancers.
PARKING: Municipal lot across from restaurant.
HOW TO FIND IT: Between Broadway and Eighth Avenue; subway line E to 50th Street/8th Avenue station or line 1 to 50th Street/Broadway station; bus lines M50, M104.

I remember my first Afghani kabob meal and then, a little later, the first one that really knocked my socks off. It is a source of comfort and joy to realize that nowadays, there are more kabob houses around and more better-kabob houses. Kabul Café is one of the best.

Kabob menus run true to a certain pattern, with slight variations. But there are certain subtleties here. The service is polished and concerned, the upstairs dining room quietly handsome, the basmati rice cooked to perfection, the spiced Persian tea uncommonly soothing. Kabul Café is one of those places where you feel better just by virtue of being there, even before you order.

Tea and atmosphere would not be enough, though, without good food. A friend reported that when an eggplant hater and his daughter, who has an aversion to carrots, ate at Kabul Café, they actually gave up their prejudices against those foods. If the eggplant was kashk-e-badenjan, it's small wonder. This thin-sliced eggplant in a bewitching yogurt sauce could likely convert anyone to anything. People who hated yogurt would probably forget their dislike after one bite, and that's not hyperbole. And if that didn't do it, aushak—irresistible, scallion-filled dumplings swathed with yogurt and meat sauce—probably would crumple all resistance.

Other appetizers were equally appealing—grape leaves lightly stuffed with seasoned beef and rice; delicate sambosa, pastries filled with vegetables, chickpeas and ground beef; bulanee, a pastry stuffed with seasoned potato or zingy scallions; hummus, the chickpea dip, swirled with olive oil and lemon; salad Olivieh, a chicken-potato combination with the bright spark of pickles.

Speaking of pickles and food dislikes, anyone who claims to dislike turnips probably can be persuaded otherwise with a sample of the turnip pickles, colored with beet juice, that often are brought to the table before you ask. If this is not the case, do ask for turshi, $2, a relish combination of these and other pickled vegetables, including carrots, cucumbers and cauliflower. Chopped salad built around cucumbers and tomatoes in a lemony vinaigrette makes another welcome tonic.

At lunch, there often are specials, such as the one a friend chose, kadu chalaw, mellow pumpkin stewed in a lush brown sauce and served over a heap of basmati rice. Another pleasing vegetarian possibility is what the menu undersells as "vegetarian dish," eggplant and other baked vegetables, carrots and raisins served over brown and white rice. We also liked sabzi chalaw, spinach sparked with coriander.

Khorest-e-Ghormeh sabzi was a wintry stew founded on kidney beans and tender beef seasoned with pungent dried lemon. And who could pass up khorest-e-ghieimeh, beef, yellow peas and dried lemon topped with fried potato? It lived up to this promising description.

Other satisfying entrées we tried included hearty lamb shank, tikka kabob made of beef and kabob kobideh, highly seasoned ground beef formed into a strip and char-broiled. Marinated Cornish hen with saffron and kabob barg, marinated filet mignon, were other good choices, as was a special kabob of swordfish.

Stews and char-broiled meats seasoned with fragrant, fresh spices are the mainstay of this cuisine, and their apparent simplicity does not detract from their goodness. Anyhow, they aren't really quite as simple as meat and rice; try at home to produce the exact combination of, say, cumin, coriander, nutmeg and dried lemon that makes a dish taste so delicious, and you'll see that it is an art.

Turkish coffee made a bracing end to the meal, and we always enjoy the smooth simplicity of firni, a white pudding topped with pistachios. The best-of-all pistachio treats, though, was rich, smooth Persian ice cream with a calorie count we don't even want to think about. For those who want more than coffee or tea, there is beer, and there's a wine list.

KRUNGTHEP CITY
45 Lexington Ave.
(212) 532-6402

HOURS: Dinner Monday–Friday, 3–11 p.m.; Saturday–Sunday, 4:30–11 p.m. Lunch Monday–Friday 11;30 a.m.–3 p.m.
PRICES: Entrées $3.50–$13.95, appetizers $3.50–$8.95. Lunch $5.95–$8.95. AE.
RESERVATIONS: Suggested for Friday–Sunday and for groups of five or more.
ACCESS: Dining area/restrooms wheelchair-accessible.
HOW TO FIND IT: Between 24th and 25th Streets; subway line N to 23rd Street/ Broadway station.

I used to pass K.C. Place on Lexington Avenue and think about going there, but I never did.

Well, I was wrong. K.C. Place, which became Krungthep City about a year and a half ago, turns out to be Thai, and that's a kind of food I hardly ever pass up. It also turns out that K.C. Place was not quite the same as Krungthep City, which is the old name for Bangkok. In the old days, the commitment to Thai food was not so wholehearted. Chef-owners Anuree and Thavat Thitibordin were cooking at other places back then; Anuree at Seeda Thai, and her husband, Thavat, at such American kitchens as The Four Seasons and Tavern on the Green. Now, with the two of them minding the stove, Krungthep City is all Thai, and it's really cooking.

"What kind of beer do you have?" we asked shortly after sitting down in the cheerful little dining room.

"We have Thai beer! The best Thai beer!" cried Dum Huntakul, our manager-waiter, with irresistible enthusiasm. Naturally, we asked for some. It was Singha, a beer with which we are quite familiar, but somehow, it did taste better than usual. Partly, the beer might have tasted so good because Dum's mood was contagious, but it was also partly because it was chilled to the absolutely perfect degree of coldness.

We started by trying a few favorite dishes from the menu and a selection or two from the specials board. Tom yum, chicken soup pungent with lemongrass, chile peppers and lime juice, was gratifyingly sinus-clearing. We hardly ever miss a chance to have the Thai salad made of thin-sliced Chinese sausage, lime juice, peanuts and red onions, and the one at Krungthep City was sprightly. Chicken saté, which we tried another day, came with a substantial peanut sauce, thick and delicious.

Squid quickly seared with a scattering of chile, shrimp with a red coconut-milk curry, scallops beautifully and lightly cooked with Penang curry sauce, and red snapper in a garlic and chile sauce were all topnotch. Tell Dum you like it hot, and the kitchen will oblige. Perhaps we neglected to do that when we had a special of snapper steamed with ginger and wrapped inside banana leaf; it was a bit tame compared to some of the other taste thrills.

Other dishes we can recommend include kai yang, the Thai barbecued chicken, and duck several ways—on the specials list one day with a tamarind sauce, and also with a red curry with pineapple (shades of that imagined Hawaiian eatery), tomato and onion. We also liked Krungthep's version of the noodle classic pad Thai, with shrimp, chicken, peanuts and bean sprouts.

At meal's end, Dom insisted we try the house brandy, in which raisins had been soaking for several months. Both brandy, served in big snifters, and raisins were delicious. After one or two disastrous versions of fried ice cream, I was dubious about trying it. But after our second meal at Krungthep City, persuaded by Dum's tantalizing description, we ordered Krungthep's fried ice cream. Like everything else at Krungthep, it was a delight.

LIPSTICK CAFÉ
885 Third Ave.
(212) 486-8664

HOURS: Monday–Friday, 7 a.m.–3 p.m.
PRICES: Breakfast $1.25–$1.75. Lunch $5–$13. AE, DC, MC, V.
ACCESS: Dining area wheelchair-accessible, restrooms are not.
PARKING: Commercial lot next to restaurant.
HOW TO FIND IT: Between 53rd and 54th Streets; subway lines E or F to Lexington Avenue/Third Avenue station; bus lines M101, M102.

In New York, believe it or not, a fresh fruit cobbler must seem as exotic to some as puff pastry once did, back when Julia Child introduced us to French food.

"What is the cobbler of the day?" we asked our waitress at the new Lipstick Café, named for the open space it occupies in part of the lobby of what is known as the Lipstick Building. We didn't mean "What is a cobbler?" but she told us anyway.

"It is peaches and blackberries, sort of like a compote," she explained in accented English, "with a little bit of pastry. Not too sweet."

The word pastry sounded an alarm. Was this fancier than the normal, country kind of cobbler? Not to worry. This cobbler was runny and juicy, as blackberry cobbler always ought to be, with a bit of typical biscuit-dough pastry. It was less sweet than most versions, always fine with us, and it came with a slathering of crème fraîche instead of a pitcher of the heavy, clotted, unhomogenized cream you might expect to find on a midwestern farm. There's no harm in that slight twist.

Go early to the Lipstick Café, because by slightly past noon, a line forms for food much like what Jean-Georges Vongerichten serves at his stylish Jo Jo on East 64th Street. (Lunch begins at 11:30 a.m., so stake out a table then.) Many of these people are standing in line to taste what they might not be able to afford at Jo Jo.

Breakfast, by the way, is a particular bargain, with gentle prices on a par with those at the streetside coffee wagons. Tasty ham-and-cheese biscuits, for example, were 80 cents. We doted on toasted almond brioche and a lemon-raspberry muffin, but apple turnover was saturated with cooking fat the one time we tried it. There's also a big, tiered display of tempting fruit, including hard-to-find yellow plums. Prices were pleasing indeed; a plain croissant will set you back a modest 90 cents; coffee is 65 cents (80 cents for large), cappuccino $1.75 and $2.25, milk (the kind that's poured from glass bottles) 65 cents.

Besides iced tea (80 cents), there were lovely summer drinks: a refreshing "icy infusion" of mint and thyme, a zesty nonalcoholic cocktail of ginger, pineapple and lemongrass and a blackberry spritzer (each $2.50). The spritzer was heavy on fresh blackberry juice, and we would ask for more soda water next time, but that was a fault of generosity.

At one lunchtime this week, the soup ($4.50) was a perfectly balanced purée of potatoes, leeks and Swiss chard. And very rare, pepper-coated fresh tuna served over the varied baby greens known as mesclun, with a few haricots verts, all dressed with a strong, lemon-confit vinaigrette, was a fine variation on salade Niçoise. Another winner was a chicken club sandwich with black-pepper mayonnaise and spicy, marinated corn salad. The robust roast chicken was sturdy enough to stand up to these strong flavors, but the fresh, near-white corn kernels were almost overwhelmed.

If there is a fault to this well-regarded chef's lusty, flavorful cuisine, it is that occasionally, flavors out-shout each other. Sometimes the salad dressings could do with a tad more oil and less lemon or vinegar. And fresh coriander, lime and hot pepper elbowed out the nutty taste of wheat berries in a seven-grain salad topped with shrimp marinated in a super-spicy mixture that must have included lemongrass. Don't get me wrong; I love these flavors. But with eyes closed, the only grain that held its own was wild rice.

With desserts, however, there is little fault to find. The strong, true flavors of the ultra-bitter chocolate tart, the aforementioned cobbler and a walnut-caramel tart with vanilla ice cream all were sublime. And for those who want to have their cheese and ice cream too, there is Vongerichten's revivifying fromage blanc sorbet.

LITTLE SAIGON
374 W. 46th St.
(212) 956-0639

HOURS: Dinner Monday–Saturday, 3–9 p.m. Lunch 11 a.m–3 p.m.
PRICES: Entrées $4.25–$12.95; appetizers $5.25–$6.45; soups $1.95–$5.45; noodles and rice $4.45–$6.45. Lunch specials $3.95–$6.15 (served between noon–3 p.m.).
RESERVATIONS: Recommended.
ACCESS: Dining area tight but wheelchair-accessible; restrooms accessible.
PARKING: Garages on West 44th and West 46th Streets.
HOW TO FIND IT: Between 8th and 9th Avenues; subway lines A or E to 42nd Street staion; bus lines M16, M104.

L ittle Saigon is surely the smallest restaurant on Restaurant Row. It's hard to think of another restaurant quite so little as this one; only Chez Brigitte, the venerable French lunch counter on Greenwich Avenue, comes to mind.

Merry, round-faced Kim Duyen does not speak French, only Vietnamese and a very few words of English. Yet in a space that might grandiosely be described as a galley kitchen, more accurately a cubbyhole, she turns out fresh, made-to-order Vietnamese food by cooking the numbers customers circle on paper menus. Some of her 12 children (beaming, she shows photographs and tells you the English words for their successful careers)—must help her with menu printing and other paperwork.

After spending a bit of time with Duyen, who runs the whole show, you will find yourself pitching in and helping; I help myself to extra napkins and get my own chopsticks.

Try No. 1, Vietnamese spring rolls, with pork and shrimp rolled in delicate rice paper and fried; No. 2, summer rolls, not fried, wrapped in ultra-thin rice paper; No. 4, which can either be shrimp salad or shredded chicken salad, slightly spicy and very good; No. 8, thinly sliced beef tangy with lemon. After the first page of the menu, you begin to run into a bit of trouble, because there is a No. 1 under the rice noodle section (try it—it's grilled beef with sesame), under the beef section, and so on. Chicken, shrimp and rice have their own sets of numbers.

As for beverages, focus on No. 3, "French black condensed milk coffee," or No. 4, an iced version of the same, unless you crave "orange juice in box." This Vietnamese coffee is what the French would call café filtre, dripped slowly through individual filters into the glass, which already holds a layer of condensed milk. Since the hot version is never quite hot enough by the time the coffee drips, ask for the iced coffee unless you don't mind your brew lukewarm.

From noon to 3 p.m. there are lunch specials (No. 1, No. 2, No. 3, and so on, once more) for $1 (vegetable soup) to $5.95 (stir-fried shrimp).

LOFTI'S MOROCCAN CUISINE
358 W. 46th St.
(212) 582-5850

HOURS: Dinner Tuesday–Saturday, 5–11:30 p.m.; Sunday, 4–9 p.m. Lunch Tuesday–Saturday, noon–2 p.m.
PRICES: Entrées $12.95–$14.95; appetizers $2.75–$3.75. Lunch $10.95–$12.95. AE, DS, MC, V.
RESERVATIONS: Recommended, especially during peak hours, 6-8 p.m.
ACCESS: Wheelchair-accessible; restrooms equipped for disabled.
KIDS: No children's menu but will accommodate.
PARKING: Two commercial lots on 46th Street.
HOW TO FIND IT: Between Eighth and Ninth Avenues; subway line E to 50th Street station or lines A or E to 42nd Street station; bus lines M16, M42, M104.

More Moroccan is my mantra—more good Moroccan food in New York, that is. There is never enough to satisfy me.

So it was a red-letter day when Lotfi's reappeared. In previous incarnations of the restaurant, I had sampled Lotfi's considerable delights—fragrant stews known as tajines, intriguingly spiced eggplant salads, couscous with fiery ground-chile paste called harissa. There used to be a Lotfi's in Brooklyn, then there was one in the Village, and also an upstairs one on 45th Street. All had disappeared, and the absence lasted nine months.

But Abdellatis (Abdel for short) Rebbag and his wife Susan were apparently just biding their time, waiting to open the best Lotfi's yet, on Restaurant Row. "We needed a break," said Susan, who is from Australia but passionately loves the food of Abdel's homeland.

After their rest, the proprietors of Lotfi's seem happy to see their old customers, and the feeling is mutual. Perhaps it is that absence does make the heart grow fonder, or maybe Abdel is cooking better than ever after his sabbatical.

The long, low room glows with rich-colored hangings. Here and there, you'll notice handsome, cone-shaped eathenware vessels known, like the stews that are cooked in them, as tajines. Through an open door, you'll see the tall, amiable Abdel capably jockeying his pots and pans, working his magic. Susan "helps," she says modestly, working the front of the house. Everything is homemade, even the preserved lemons that are an important staple of this cuisine, except for the Turkish delight (a delight, nonetheless) and the ice cream.

And everything is good. The odors of steaming semolina grain and pungent spices—cumin, saffron, turmeric, cayenne, anise and more—make you hungry when you walk in from the street. Start, perhaps, with a salad sampler platter, a pleasing smorgasbord of tastes—spicy puréed eggplant, garlicky mashed chickpeas, tangy marinated olives, and delicate carrot salad lightly flavored with orange water, a lovely counterpoint to the sharper tastes. Smear these on warm pita bread.

Another exceptional starter was the braewats, or "cigars": small, irresistible crisp pastries filled with savory seafood, chicken, chicken livers, ground beef, vegetables, cheese or merguez, the Moroccan sausage. Moroccan sausage was terrific on its own, too.

If nobody in your party is inclined to order bisteeya (Paula Wolfert's spelling in Couscous and Other Good Food from Morocco, also transliterated as bistilla or b'stilla), you might consider ordering this fragile, many-layered pastry as an extra, to share. It was filled with chicken or seafood, eggs, toasted almonds, cinnamon, lemon, ginger and other good things, then dusted with powdered sugar. The powdered sugar part may sound odd, but it works.

Tajines, the Moroccan stews, were impressive here, and if anything, have gotten better than they were at the old midtown location. Lamb tajine made with prunes, sesame and almonds was tender and tasty, and chicken with zesty preserved lemons was flavorful, if just a mite dry. But Berber chicken with saffron, chickpeas and onions, stewed to a glorious golden color, was perhaps most satisfying of all. The cone-shaped tagine pot traps the steam as the food cooks and pushes it back down into the dish, so that flavors become more intense.

Couscous, or steamed semolina grain, was served in several different versions, with more well-cooked, falling-apart lamb, or with chicken, and piles of hearty root vegetables. With the couscous, ask for harissa, a hot, hot chile condiment that you should add cautiously at first, until you find yourself developing a taste for it.

Gazelle's horns, pastries stuffed with almond paste, are a favorite with some of Lotfi's happy eaters, but I can never pass up ghoriba, simple cookies made of butter and semolina flour. It is hard to improve on a plate of these, but they are perfect "dipping" cookies and to gild the lily, add a scoop of ice cream. (Most desserts may be ordered with ice cream.)

End with a cup of incomparable mint tea, which perfumes the air as it is being poured from a height, or maybe some lusty Arabic coffee. I like to linger over the coffee, because meals at a favorite restaurant are always over a little too soon. Nowhere is this more true than at Lotfi.

MAVALLI PALACE
46 E. 29th St.
(212) 679-5535/2606

HOURS: Dinner Tuesday–Sunday, 5–10 p.m. Lunch Tuesday–Sunday, noon–3 p.m.
PRICES: Entrées $9.75–$13.95. Lunch $7.95–$9.95. AE, DC, MC, V.
RESERVATIONS: Recommended.
ACCESS: Dining area wheelchair-accessible; restrooms downstairs.
HOW TO FIND IT: Between Park and Madison Avenues; subway line N to 23rd Street/Broadway station; bus line M23.

Mavalli's vegetarian fare is so well made that I promise you'll like it even if you aren't a vegetarian. It also happens to be the best Indian food I know of in New York right now.

First, the caveat: Service can at times be maddeningly slow, both in the restaurant and away from it. Because we were so enamored of Mavalli, we decided to order food from there for a small office party. Two hours later, when we were ready to faint with hunger, the food arrived.

And it was wonderful. We felt faint with pleasure instead of impatience.

Rest assured that chef Narayan S. Swami is cooking your food to order as quickly as humanly possible. Food this good should not be rushed. So sip a drink from the bar or a mango lassi made with yogurt, and let your hunger take on an edge. Subtly spicy cashew nuts (or almonds or peanuts) were the perfect crunchy accompaniment for a cocktail, by the way.

If you have not made the acquaintance of iddly, don't wait another minute. Iddly are small, steamed cakes of ground rice, and while the plainish lentil and rice cake with sambhar—a soupy mixture of split lentils, coriander, cumin and other spices—was tasty, you simply haven't lived until you have tasted kancheepuram iddly, a sort of deluxe rice cake flavored with bits of cashews, ginger and coriander.

There are many other delightful first courses. Mavalli's bonda, or potato dumplings, and the vegetable fritters known as pakoras were crisp and virtually greaseless. Aluchat, cool and zesty curried potatoes, were a hit, too.

There's no better place, too, for trying masala dosai, the huge Indian crêpes filled with a savory potato and onion mixture. Carried away, we ordered seconds. The house dosai filled with uncommonly fine hot chutney was a winner, too.

What makes Mavalli so special is that each food tastes separate and like itself, a quality to prize when it comes to Indian restaurants. Frankly, at too many other restaurants, dishes are smothered in sauce and have an alarming tendency to taste the same, all of them sort of sludgy. Here, cubes of potato (sukka alu) dry-cooked with green curry leaves were clearly potato; chanamasala, chickpeas with pomegranate, were clearly chickpeas. Other top-notch curries included mutter paneer, green peas and cottage cheese with tomatoes, and palak paneer, the spinach version. Baked eggplant and peas, in a dish called baingan bharta, and dhingri gobhi, mushrooms with cauliflower, broccoli and coconut, were other excellent choices. Korma, a subtle vegetable-yogurt curry and avial, a coconut curry with lots of root vegetables, were mild but far from uninteresting. In the latter, we happily located wedges of peels-on potatoes.

Other things that set Mavalli apart from the competition are the well-made chutney of sun-dried mango, the yogurt-based raita with roasted cumin, and the other condiments. The lentil sambhar is so good that after we had used it as a dip for fritters and turnovers some of us, not so surreptitiously, ate the rest of it with spoons. (If you crave more, spend 75 cents on an extra side order and eat it all yourself.)

And then there is the rice. What rice! The lemon rice, with its hint of saffron and tart wallop of fresh lemon, is so satisfying that it would be easy to eat a whole order, instead of sharing, and call it a meal. Then we tasted bagala bhath, an amazing yogurt rice with mustard seeds and lentils, and perhaps a pod of hot pepper, and realized that nothing in the world could be better than that. Now we order both rices each time we go to Mavalli. With everything, we like Flying Horse, a full-flavored Indian brew from oversized bottles meant for sharing.

As a finale, our set is wild about the mango ice cream; it's commercial, but fresh mango cooked in syrup is sometimes folded into it for a voluptuous treat. We also liked rice pudding flavored with rosewater, and kulfi, molded ice cream made with cooked-down milk, saffron, cardamom and pistachio.

MENCHANKO-TEI
39 W. 55th St.
(212) 247-1585

HOURS: Lunch/dinner Monday–Saturday, 11:30 a.m.–12:30 a.m; Sunday, 11:30 a.m.–11:30 p.m.; dinner starts 5 p.m. Breakfast Tuesday–Sunday, 7 a.m.–9:30 a.m.
PRICES: Entrées $7.25–$13; appetizers $3.75–$7.75. Breakfast $6.75–$11.75. AE, DC, MC, V.
ACCESS: Not wheelchair-accessible.
HOW TO FIND IT: Between Fifth and Sixth Avenues; subway line E to Fifth Avenue/ 53rd Street station or lines D or F to Rockefeller Center/47th–50th Streets station; bus lines M1, M2.

It may sound unsophisticated, but you may as well know it now. I confess.

I've never been totally wild about sushi. I can eat raw fish pretty much without fear or squeamishness, so that's not the problem. I admire the beauty of an artfully arranged selection of sushi, and that, actually, is part of the problem.

Sushi always seems almost too glitteringly attractive to eat, too remote, somehow. Food can, of course, be art, and vice versa, but should we eat art? (I never feel bad about destroying the symmetry of the rigatoni in a plate of Bolognese sauce, and I have no qualms about disturbing the perfection of a mound of mashed potatoes.)

Whatever the reason for this failing, I have no such misgivings about Japanese noodles. They are not too beautiful to eat. They are user-friendly, served up in generous bowls, adrift in clouds of steam. I even find myself craving them late at night when a chill is in the air.

So do lots of other New Yorkers, apparently, for most any day or night you will find a line of people waiting for seats at Menchanko-Tei, one of Midtown's premier noodle houses.

Men means noodles, and chanko-nabe is a mixed hot pot—the dish that sumo wrestlers eat with scads of rice to make themselves strong. In Japan, dedicated eaters go from spot to spot comparing ramen noodles (made with wheat flour and egg), just as we might debate the merits of one pizza versus another.

Edamame, boiled green soybeans, are an easily acquired taste, and an almost addictive first course. At Menchanko-Tei you may also start with oden, the nibbles that in Japan would often be found on pushcarts. These little goodies are cooked in a savory broth flavored with bonito, the dried fish flakes, and probably a bit of soy sauce and mirin; the exact broth is, of course, a house secret.

Five pieces, your choice, cost $6.25, or $1.35 each. We wanted to have kinchaku ("pouch of gold"), bean curd filled with seaweed or glutinous rice cake, but none was available that evening. We liked atsuage (on this menu, spelled atuage), the deep-fried tofu, a fish cake called satsuma-age and konnyaku (konjak frour on the menu), a gelatinous yam that, spongelike, absorbs lots of flavor from the broth and also is supposed to be a great diet aid. Daikon and hardcooked eggs rounded out our selection.

Kikuzo ramen, named after a famous Japanese comedian, was perhaps our favorite. Fresh noodles were cooked in a rich broth flavored with soy sauce, along with excellent roast pork, a thin slice of white-and-pink fish cake, lightly pickled bamboo shoots, scallions and a sheet of nori, or seaweed. Menchanko, the house bowl of noodles with shrimp, rice cake, Chinese cabbage and other vegetables, was milder, with thicker noodles. And nothing could have been more satisfying on a drizzly day than kimchi zosui, a hearty dish with lots of rice and chile-fired pickled cabbage.

There's a chalkboard of specials, written in Japanese, and, on blue paper, a list of side dishes and additional oden. As a side dish we liked a small, utterly delicious soy-braised snapper served with cold spinach and scattered with bits of fresh ginger. Kimpira gobo, or shredded burdock root with colorful bits of carrot, was refreshing sautéed with a bit of mirin and soy sauce. Don't miss niku jyaga—literally, beef, potatoes and carrots—a warming and homey stew. There were also wonderful, lightly salted cucumbers with bonito to eat with rice, Japanese-style. During the meal drink chilled sake. At meal's end sip sencha, the tart roasted green tea.

No dessert here—lingering over noodles is not the Japanese custom, though patrons may linger over Scotch, gin, Bourbon or beer. In fact, the rakugo performer Hayashiya Kikuzo, who has his own brand of ramen, tells a story poking fun at diners who linger over ramen in Spain, where they don't know from ramen, so others cannot sit down to eat. And if you are in a rush, sit at the bar that looks like a sushi bar. Here, it's a noodle bar.

PARADIS BARCELONA
145 E. 50th St.
(212) 754-3333

HOURS: Daily, dinner 4–11 p.m. Lunch noon–4 p.m.
PRICES: Entrées $15–$24. Lunch $13–$19. AE, DC, DS, MC, V.
RESERVATIONS: Recommended, especially for weekends.
ACCESS: Dining area/restrooms wheelchair-accessible.
KIDS: No children's menu but will accommodate.
ENTERTAINMENT: Flamenco dancers Sunday–Thursday, 8 p.m.; Friday–Saturday, 7:30 p.m. and 9:30 p.m.
HOW TO FIND IT: Between Lexington and Third Avenues; subway lines E or F to 53rd Street/Lexington Avenue station; bus lines M101, M102.

"**M**eet me at the tapas bar," I told my friends.

"Topless bar?" they said incredulously.

I hate puns, and I tell you this only because it happens nearly every time I mention "tapas bar." I try to enunciate clearly, but still they misunderstand.

So I have a better idea. Just tell your friends to meet you at "the bar," no tapas, at Paradis Barcelona. Then make them happy; have the tapas lunch, a steal at $9.95.

I've eaten once for full price at the handsome, swanky Paradis Barcelona, for a friend's birthday, and it was a treat. But the $9.95 lunch—two tapas selections and a beautiful bowl of soup—is a treat in its own right for both the taste buds and the wallet.

All the soups I have tried were first-rate—a curried mussel soup rich with saffron, a tangy and refreshing gazpacho, a deeply satisfying purée of white beans, leeks and tomatoes. While you savor a bowlful, take stock of the huge array of tapas. (They change a bit from day to day, but some favorites are offered all the time.) They're so tempting that it is hard to choose just two, so sometimes I get carried away and pay a bit more to have extras.

If I have the potato-and-onion omelet or the savory "farmer" omelet made with turnips, ham, roasted peppers and peas, and then I order a helping of spicy grilled chorizo with creamy white beans, that means I'd have to pass up the wonderful, ultra-lemony marinated fresh sardines escabeche. And I can never do that. So it goes, and lunch is likely to cost $20 instead of $10, including a glass of crisp white Portuguese house wine or aged Emilio Lustau sherry and perhaps a small taza of heavenly espresso, dark and strong. Still, I consider it money well spent.

The choice is hard because Paradis Barcelona has such a big selection, the best I know of in New York. Chef Frank Rhodes seems to be having a wonderful time here. Huge garlic prawns with garlic mayonnaise were heaped on one tapas tray. Tender octopus vinaigrette came with roasted onion, and small new potatoes were stuffed with fearless garlic mayonnaise, a tidbit of smoked salmon and a garnish of curly frisée. Scallops empanada was a huge wedge of flaky, two-crusted pie filled with scallops and red pepper. Is it any wonder I can't decide?

There are so many attractive tapas: rustic bread rubbed with tomatoes and olive oil and served with sheep's milk cheese or other accompaniments, thin-sliced serrano ham with escalivada, a chopped mixture of grilled eggplant, peppers, onion and tomato; light, crisp-fried calamari; grilled Portobello mushrooms with paella rice; smoked tuna with a zesty salsa of chopped tomato, olives and capers; delicious brandada, mashed potatoes and salt cod, stuffed into peppers; roasted spiced almonds; small green olives in a lemony marinade.

Paradis Barcelona's magnificent tapas are the same ones lunch patrons are eating at tables. If you reserve a table and the roasted half chicken in a broth of white beans, fennel, tomatoes and olives is on the menu, do try this happy melding of flavors. Or order a casserole of saffron rice with clams, saffron-pasta squares called panuelos, or duck braised in Rioja wine and seasonal dark greens. It's a thrill to encounter a kitchen where somebody has a liberal hand with saffron, one of the most expensive of ingredients.

The tapas bar is such a convivial place to be—well-heeled businessmen, many of them Spanish-speaking, come in to read the paper, eat the tapas lunch or sip espresso and exchange a few words with Jose Lado, the genial, bow-tied bartender in a many-colored vest. The setting, too, is serendipitous—Mexican tiles, a gleaming swath of bar, a curtain of hanging beads to hide the entrances to the restrooms.

The incredibly smooth, lush crème brûlée Catalan makes a fine dessert if you are so inclined. Ice cream, sherbets and fresh berries are also top quality.

It is the tapas, though, that keep me coming back for more.

SILK BAR & GRILL
378 Third Ave.
(212) 532-4500

HOURS: Dinner daily, 5–10:30 p.m. Lunch Monday–Friday, noon–3 p.m.
PRICES: Entrées $14–$25; appetizers $5–$14. Lunch $11.50–$18.50; appetizers $5–$8. AE, CB, DC, MC, V.
RESERVATIONS: Recommended, especially for weekends.
ACCESS: Wheelchair-accessible; restrooms are tight.
PARKING: Garages nearby.
HOW TO FIND IT: At corner of East 27th Street; subway line 6 to Park Avenue South/28th Street station; bus lines M101, M102.

Silk looks posh enough to justify its name. The subtly striped upholstery on the banquettes, the unusual scones that make the lighting soft and the near-flawless service—all these are too luxe for a cheap lunch.

It's not a cheap lunch, but it is affordable. Go ahead, treat yourself. It would cost a lot more to get food this good, and this prettily plated, Uptown.

Besides, the attitude is endearingly down to earth. One day, our waiter asked if we would like more of something, and we said we couldn't have more, as we hadn't had any yet. (This was a minor error, and about the only one I can recall.) The waiter actually smiled, and he speedily set matters right.

Pacific-Rim cuisine is a coming-together of flavors from that increasingly important region. It's not just Chinese, or Malaysian, or Thai or Japanese, but a little bit of all those—and more. It's the culinary buzzword of the '90s. At Silk, these pan-Asian influences are blended with what owner Henry Tao calls nouvelle French. The results are never boring, and they are often delightful.

You might start with a deeply satisfying curried carrot soup ($3.50) when that's the du jour, and you won't go wrong any day with the succulent baby greens that make up the mixed salad ($4.25) in a soy-ginger vinaigrette that's just tangy enough; there are baby-greens salads all around town, but nobody does it better. Both crabmeat fritters and wonderful sizzling calamari salad were served with wasabi tartar sauce, a perfect example of an Asian flourish. On the dinner menu—you may also order from it at lunch—don't miss a lush sake-cured salmon in "lemonade" sauce; don't worry, it's not sweet, just lemony. Grilled tofu on ratatouille over a Sichuan peppercorn pesto was a coming-together that didn't quite work, though the pesto was stellar and would be good on most anything.

Caesar salad ($4.50 at lunch, $6.50 at dinner), another entrée salad that might be shared as a starter, was a perfect execution of a classic, with a nontraditional fillip of house-smoked salmon jerky instead of anchovies. This did work, admirably. Beef satay ($7.50 at dinner as an appetizer, $8.50 as a lunch entrée) was tender and tasty with tangy peanut-miso sauce. Even Silk's burger was special, served with gingery coleslaw and thin shoestring fries.

I'd have grilled tuna steak ($17.50 at dinner) again, just so I could eat the horseradish mashed potatoes and bitter greens that came with it; but I'd eat it for its own sake, too, because it was moist and was swathed in a balsamic-teriyaki sauce that was delicious instead of merely weird. Tuna steak was also a hit at lunch, as a club sandwich.

Flawlessly pan-seared scallops were a case of overkill, though, what with apricot curry sauce (too much like jam) and risotto made with beets. Don't spend $16.50 on this one, which is on the dinner list; there are too many other good things to consider.

At lunch, salmon cakes with vegetable couscous will set you back only $8.75, and you won't regret it. Grilled chicken teriyaki with brown rice was satisfying, but my favorites were pastas. Pan-fried angel hair with slivers of bright vegetables, small, tender shrimp and yakisoba sauce was savory, and fresh tomato linguine was happily paired with wild mushrooms for another memorable pasta. There's a full bar, and there are some interesting wines, by the glass or by the bottle, but iced tea was good at Silk and glasses were refilled with alacrity. Consider tea to keep the calories low, whether or not you need to keep your wits about you in the afternoon, because it would be unthinkable to miss dessert.

Mango sorbet and cinnamon ice cream were highlights, and a slab of macadamia chocolate cake with orange marmalade was pronounced divine by chocoholics in our party. But the day I had deeply green, green-tea ice cream with a huge almond cookie—nothing like those you see in Chinatown, more like shortbread—I was smitten. The almond cookie was a special, so it may not be available every day, but Silk is the kind of place you'll eat at again and again, and not just in case it's the day for almond cookies.

SILVER SWAN
41 E. 20th St.
(212) 254-3611

HOURS: Dinner Monday–Friday, 3 p.m.–midnight; Saturday–Sunday, 4 p.m.–midnight. Lunch Monday–Friday, noon–3 p.m.
PRICES: Entrées $15–$24. Lunch $12–$13. AE, MC, V.
RESERVATIONS: Recommended.
ACCESS: Dining area wheelchair-accessible, restrooms are not.
HOW TO FIND IT: Between Park Avenue and Broadway; subway line N to 23rd Street station; bus lines M1, M2, M7.

The name Silver Swan has the ring of a posh night club. Instead, this new German restaurant has an air of sweet innocence reminiscent of a visit to grandmother's house.

Everywhere, there are pretty embroidered tablecloths and runners, many of them made by the loving hands of Renate Koplin, chef and owner. Potted hyacinths, primroses and other posies adorn tables. Rustic-looking wreaths hang on walls, and there are knick-knacks galore.

Before you go home, ask for a gumdrop from the glass jar on the bar. That is, if you can spare room for a single morsel more by then; true to its reputation, the German fare here is hearty and filling.

Plump, cold herring three different ways (wine sauce, cream sauce, or in a salad with slivers of pickled beet) leads the menu. All were excellent, if you like herring. If you don't, you might ask, as a friend did, to have a plate of sprightly salads: potato, cucumber, beet and cabbage on a bed of frilly lettuces. Or begin with excellent and crisp potato pancakes, $3.95 for two or three huge ones.

Sauerbraten was a succulent, tender marvel, accompanied by red cabbage and a large dumpling. I'm afraid even the best of this sort of dumpling seems a little leaden to me, but here it was only a little, not a lot, heavy. Spaetzle, the small potato-flour dumplings, were more to my taste, and they came with a tasty, homey beef goulash and with jaeger schnitzel, one of five schnitzel preparations here. The schnitzel was flavorful, though not the most tender cut of veal, beneath mushroom gravy.

"Meat loaf is my favorite thing in the world," sighed a friend happily, eating the "French" version of an exceptionally good one. It differed from the German meat loaf only in that it came with onion gravy, which could have been a little more generous, instead of mushroom gravy. Either way, it was served with splendid, real mashed potatoes.

Other dishes that were accompanied by those fabulous mashed potatoes and sauerkraut accented with juniper berries were handsome weisswurst, the white veal sausage, and satisfying bratwurst. With sausages, a three-mustard assortment was presented, but none were quite tangy-sharp enough for us. Kassler ripchen, a lightly smoked, thick pork chop, came with the same accompaniments. Wild boar, from the current game menu, didn't taste very wild and would have seemed a lot like pot roast if not for the bone. But maybe that's good, for those who are timid about trying game. There's venison and a selection of game sausage, too, this winter. Baked spinach casserole was an intense green color but tasted fine; with an order of potato pancakes, it would have made a good vegetarian meal.

Delectable dark-grain raisin buns, onion rolls and other breads from the estimable La Boulangère nearby on 21st Street filled the breadbasket. There is a full bar, and the beer list featured Poulaner Weiss poured into tall glasses and served with a lemon wedge.

For dessert, there's a light Black Forest cake, less gooey than most, feathery yellow cake layered with cream and berries and decorated with kiwi and berries for strawberry shortcake, and apple strudel. The strudel was best when slightly warmed before serving.

TAPROBANE
234 W. 56th St.
(212) 333-4203

HOURS: Daily, 11:30 a.m.–10:30 p.m.
PRICES: Entrées $11.90–$14.90; appetizers $5–$6 (for up to two people). Lunch $4.50–$7.50. AE, CB, DC, DS, MC, V.

RESERVATIONS: Recommended.
ACCESS: Not wheelchair-accessible.
ENTERTAINMENT: Occasional live music.
HOW TO FIND IT: Between Broadway and Eighth Avenue; subway line N to 57th Street station or lines A or D to Columbus Circle/59th Street station; bus line M7.

"First Sri Lankan restaurant in New York City," promised a flier announcing Taprobane. So far as I know, this really is the first one, and it's an exciting introduction.

In Sinhala, the language of most Sri Lankans, the name of the country means "Resplendent Island," according to Roloff Beny's book "*Island: Ceylon.*" Beny added: "I myself prefer the name given to it by the first travellers from China, which in translation is, 'The Land Without Sorrow.'"

Sorrows would surely be few if you always could look forward to food of this variety, quality and spiciness. One good starter was the assorted appetizers—small, crisp-fried fish croquettes, beef turnovers and mildly spicy sausage rolls. Mulligatawny soup made with a chicken-broth base was creamier and milder in Taprobane's version than in the usual Indian-restaurant rendition, but no less pleasing.

Vegetarian red-lentil soup with a faint hint of tomato was delicious, too. The chile-pepper bang was not the least bit faint, however, in deep-fried lentil patties. Well-seasoned minced beef and vegetables filled deep-fried crêpes to make something vaguely resembling a giant eggroll, but better yet was the savory beef mixture stuffed into mild frying peppers and deep fried. Warm shrimp salad came in a light cream sauce spiked with cilantro and enough chile for pep but not fire.

To our group's disappointment, there were no iddi appe, which translates as stringhoppers, or fine strings of rice noodles formed into pancakes. This dish is available only on Saturday and Sunday, because making them is very time-consuming. We did get to try a pilaf in which stringhoppers were shredded and cooked with fine threads of carrots. (I wouldn't be surprised to learn that pilaf is a good way to use up broken string hoppers, or leftover ones. Having read glowing descriptions of stringhoppers, however, I suspect there are seldom any leftovers.) Carrots were also made into crunchy, spicy pickles, and when we asked whether carrots were especially prized in Sri Lanka, owner Nalin Fernando told us that root vegetables are used a lot and carrots are readily available here.

Among the "accompaniments," at least two are worth mentioning as possible appetizers: deviled hot potatoes, slightly al dente and more than slightly peppery, and fried eggplant, which is devilishly spicy, too.

In the incendiary category, count on braised lamb in a deep "black" curry with roasted coconut and pork mustard, which could have come from Sri Lanka via North Carolina: "sliced loin of pork onions and capsicums in a mustard vinegar sauce," promises the menu, and Marie Fernando, co-owner and chef, delivers on the promise. Red-curried pork was nearly as good.

Sautéed lamb with cilantro, tomato and onion was tasty, and curried meatballs were wonderful. We favored kingfish marinated in tangy tamarind instead of a rather plain baked flounder. Squid stuffed with mung lentils was slightly chewy.

And beef "smore" is not, as you might expect, marshmallows between graham crackers but a delightfully spicy pot roast cooked in coconut milk, vinegar, cinnamon and other spices, but it had not been cooked long enough to fall apart the way pot roast should. Another favorite was a vegetarian curry of potatoes and skinny green beans. Mallun, a chopped kale and coconut side dish, and rice pilaf accompanied most main dishes.

Desserts are seldom served in Sri Lanka, except on festive occasions, when beautiful ripe fruits such as pawpaws and mangoes appear. There, too, avocados are served with sugar and cream. Alas, that dish was not available at Taprobane. But ice cream with mango syrup, yogurt with treacle ginger-poached pear and unremarkable tapioca pudding were on hand. I liked the ice cream best, and mango lassi, a sort of shake made with yogurt and fruit, was delicious, too. Cold strawberry soup made with sour cream, listed as a starter, might also make a happy ending.

TURKISH KITCHEN
386 Third Ave.
(212) 679-1810

HOURS: Sunday–Tuesday and Thursday, 5:30–11 p.m.; Wednesday and Friday–Saturday, 5:30–11:30 p.m.
PRICES: Entrées $12.50–$15.50; appetizers $5.50–$7.50. AE, DC, DS, MC, V.
RESERVATIONS: Recommended, especially for Friday–Saturday.
ACCESS: Not wheelchair-accessible.
ENTERTAINMENT: Monday evening, jazz; Wednesday evening, Turkish music.
PARKING: Garage on 29th Street.
HOW TO FIND IT: Between 27th and 28th Streets; subway line N to 28th Street/Broadway station; bus lines M101, M102.

Turkish Kitchen is a duplex of twin dining rooms, a handsome, tall-ceilinged space outfitted with rich wall hangings and gleaming samovars highlighting red matte walls. One night there was an accordion player for an even more exotic atmosphere. Good smells of wood-grilled lamb and fragrant rice waft a welcome, and service is attentive.

Sigara boregi was a big favorite with our crowd, tangy feta cheese stuffed into fragile phyllo dough and pan-fried to delicate crispness. Turkish potato pancakes, patates koftesi, were croquette-shaped. Ciger tava, stir-fried nuggets of calves' liver, turned out to be the McLiver of the Turkish menu, a dish sure to convert those who never touch liver. Small squares were lightly breaded, fried and served with a raw onion salad that included parsley and sumac, the paprika-colored seasoning that is a mainstay of this cuisine. Calves' liver was as far as our group was willing to venture into the exotic, and nobody volunteered to try poached calves' brains. (Not that brains are so very offbeat; in my midwestern college town we frequented Dale's Café, where the trademark was brains and scrambled eggs. But I digress.)

Dry-cured sausage was served with browned potatoes for another winning first course. And don't miss barbunya pilaki, small Turkish red beans tossed with lemon, garlic, olive oil and a bit of carrot. Another night, a similar marinade mixture with carrots and peas in it swathed a delicious fresh artichoke heart. A kindred treatment was given to plump New Zealand mussels in a marinade with carrots and potatoes. And moist grilled quail was served over rice that contained pine nuts and currants. Tarama, or carp roe, was made into a spread to eat with the small loaves of warmed bread, which disappeared at a rapid clip.

Two salads on the menu were wonderful: a lemony mix of chopped tomatoes, mint, parsley, cucumbers, onions and green peppers, and a toss of perfectly fresh arugula in a lemon vinaigrette.

Turkish Kitchen may be the perfect choice for a group that includes both fish eaters and those who prefer meat. There usually are several fresh fish specials, besides the wood-grilled swordfish kabob, and we sampled fresh, although slightly dry, whole porgy and fresh, although plainish, mackerel. The only disappointment was that the fish dishes were not highly seasoned, but you can make up for that by ordering a sprightly salad on the side.

Friends who have been to Turkey were thrilled to order Adana kebab, long strips of spicy lamb on a bed of pita bread, served with a charred hot pepper. (Chef-owner Orhan Yegen, who is from Adana, does not, by the way, like to serve pita bread on the side, only as a foundation for this dish, and he gets cross if you ask him, one server said.) Kasarli kofte, small patties of ground lamb mixed with tangy kassari cheese and generously spiced was served with excellent rice pilaf.

Beef dumplings in a mint-garlic sauce were comfort food to eat with a spoon. A gigantic, tender lamb shank with lightly pickled tomato alongside was the best possible dish for a snowy night. We also liked cabbage leaves lightly stuffed with ground meat and rice, in a zesty yogurt sauce, but on another visit, the cabbage was paired with a stuffed tomato in a vegetable assortment and seemed a bit lackluster.

Some of the more timidly seasoned dishes may be attempts to make Turkish cooking more mainstream in a neighborhood where there are not as many savvy eaters as there are in Weehawken. One attempt that has been overlooked is decaf coffee, which is perhaps too much to ask of a culture that dotes on strong, sweet Turkish coffee, muddy at the demitasse cup's bottom. Amber Turkish tea, in small, gold-rimmed glass cups, is an alternative. Uludag Gazozu, imported Turkish Sprite, with its perfumy fragrance, is a curiosity, but fresh-squeezed lemonade was a delight.

One dessert, a sort of pistachio cake, was dubbed "pistachio kugel" by a fellow-diner. I kept eating first a spoonful of delicate almond pudding sprinkled with almonds and pistachios, then a spoonful of creamy rice pudding, cozy under its browned surface. Which did I like best? It was a toss-up, so forget about skimping; order both.

VERONICA RISTORANTE ITALIANO
240 W. 38th St.
(212) 764-4770

HOURS: Monday–Friday, 7 a.m.–5 p.m.
PRICES: $4.50–$13.50.
ACCESS: Dining area wheelchair-accessible; restrooms downstairs.

HOW TO FIND IT: Between Seventh and Eighth Avenues; subway lines A or E to 42nd Street/Eighth Avenue station or lines 1 or 2 to 42nd Street/Broadway station; bus lines M16, M27, M42, M104.

For something like a quarter of a century, Veronica has been a favorite spot with denizens of the Garment District. Partly, this is because of Veronica's delicious food, served cafeteria style. Partly, it's because the prices are fair. But mostly, Veronica is a treasure because of the cozy, cheerful atmosphere; owner Andrew Frisari treats you like family.

Andy, as most everyone calls him, is the kind of guy who remembers what you had yesterday, and maybe even last week. He offers tastes of new specials he thinks you might enjoy. And he has a twinkly-eyed smile for everybody.

The only time I saw him come close to frowning was when a customer mentioned Hasta La Pasta, the name of an eatery downtown. "I've been saying that for years, haven't I?" Andy asked rhetorically. "I always said I would name a place that."

In truth, new eateries pose no challenge to Andy's hold on loyal customers. Just as fashions change—if you want to see the latest style in winter hats, check out what the customers are wearing here—Andy has added new wrinkles over the years. This is probably the only cafeteria in town where you can get creamy fresh mozzarella made on the premises and smartly arranged with a generous portion of sun-dried tomatoes and wedges of fresh tomato. Arugula? Radicchio? Endive? In a cafeteria? You bet.

Salads are first as you enter the line, and at strategic points all along the line you will find help-yourself pepper grinders. After salads come a huge array of entrées and a choice of good, chewy breads.

Appetizer selections, besides salads, usually include wonderful rice balls served with a helping of red sauce, and stuffed mushrooms, which we probably should have asked to have warmed. Speaking of asking, at Veronica, if you ask and if your request is within the realm of reason, you shall receive.

If pasta with pesto and potatoes, Genovese-style, is on the menu, don't miss it. Another pasta winner was penne Portobello, a no-cholesterol, no-fat wonder of lusty tomato-wine sauce embellished with meaty mushrooms. Penne also was swathed in a similar sauce, this one enriched with excellent chicken sausage made in the house. Homemade ravioli filled with spinach, broccoli and mushrooms came in a creamy tomato sauce. Gnocchi in a robust meat sauce with bits of prosciutto was irresistible, too. And don't forget an order of delicate spinach cannelloni.

True to form, Andy became concerned that we were missing other specialties in favor of pasta and encouraged us to taste a lemony, juicy chicken-breast special, also first-rate. We were less fond of a vinegared fish dish, but maybe that was just because the pasta was so satisfying. (How did we miss the spaghetti all'Grattugio with basil, parsley, garlic, pine nuts and toasted bread crumbs?) Even the chicken soup is made with defatted broth.

Today, as we write, we are missing penne alla Rosalina made with homemade sausage, beans, potatoes, mushrooms, peas and, no doubt, other alluring ingredients. We know this is so, because we just had Veronica's menu faxed over. We also are, to our profound regret, missing risotto di Parma, made with fresh spinach and prosciutto.

Wine, beer and mineral water are available for washing down all these good things. Hot chocolate? No problem. There is even sparkling wine on hand for celebratory occasions. On an ordinary day, help yourself to a glass of plain water from the cooler at the back of the room. For dessert, there is excellent tirami su and rich fudge cake, though we can never resist a side order of fresh, homemade truffles with our dark, strong espresso. Andy practically divines what we want. When I thoughtlessly started to order an espresso for a friend who has given up coffee, he said to her solicitously, "What would you like, darling? Some herbal tea?" Yes, that was just what her heart desired, almond, please. "My favorite," he said, beaming. All this and some of the best people-watching in town, too.

Next week I will be back for breakfast—Andy's own, from-scratch brioche and croissant, or a bagel from H&H, one of the few items he doesn't make.

MANHATTAN ABOVE 57TH STREET

CICCIO & TONY'S
320 Amsterdam Ave.
(212) 595-0500

HOURS: Monday–Friday, 6–11 p.m.; Saturday, 5:30 p.m.–midnight; Sunday 5–10:30 p.m.
PRICES: Entrées $9–$12; appetizers $5–$7. AE, MC, V.
RESERVATIONS: Recommended for groups of 4 or more.
ACCESS: Dining area wheelchair-accessible, restrooms are not.
KIDS: Children's menu, $6.
HOW TO FIND IT: At corner of 75th Street; subway line 1 or 2 to 72nd Street/Broadway station.

How do they do it? That's the question New Yorkers always ask in a skeptical tone when they find a good restaurant with fair prices. There's got to be a catch somewhere, right?

In this case, there's only an explanation. The Lanza and Bertone families own a lot of restaurants besides Ciccio & Tony's: Josephina, Coastal, Coastal Café, 107 West and Memphis. By buying in bulk for all the eateries, they have a lot of bargaining power, and they pass the savings along.

Co-chefs Anthony Lanza and Dino Parton have come up with an appealing menu that includes old favorites and some new twists. In the latter category, you'll find frittelle, risotto flattened into thin pancakes and fried crisp, then served under a variety of sauces. We tried calamaretti, or baby calamari, in tomato sauce, and cannellini beans in a similar tomato-based sauce with roasted garlic. We wish these flat, crisp rice cakes were available unadorned, for a change of pace; the tasty sauces are so robust that they overwhelm the frittelle.

A frittelle and a big salad would make a pleasing summer supper, perhaps best eaten at a whimsically painted sidewalk table. My favorite, insalata de Antonio, was a refreshing combination of shaved celery, crunchy romaine and hearts of iceburg, tossed in a zippy vinaigrette. So simple, so summery. Or choose arugula and sun-dried tomatoes in a black-olive dressing, topped with shaved Parmesan. Smoked mozzarella grilled with radicchio was arranged on bright Fiestaware and drizzled with garlic-infused olive oil.

Other appetizers worth checking out included crusty polenta, the Italian version of cornmeal mush, with superb, zesty homemade sausages and shiitake mushrooms, and grilled eggplant rolled up with soft goat cheese and fresh basil. White bean soup with a hint of tomato and Parmesan-dusted croutons was a winner, too. And for a steamy night, try the cold antipasti, an attractive platter of pepperoncini, salami, pecorino cheese and red tomatoes, all dressed with lemon-herb olive oil. The polpo salad, too, was a terrific hot-weather choice—fresh, tender octopus tossed with capers, small black olives, chunks of potato, tomatoes and that good lemony olive oil.

We eyed pizzettes (small, thin-crusted pizzas) as they went to other tables but could not in good conscience order more than we already had. There's welcome news for those on dairy-free diets: a dairy-free pizza made with tomato and fresh herbs—thyme, oregano and sage. If the pizzettes are as good as the focaccia in the bread basket, which was served with dipping olive oil, they are well worth ordering. Oh, well, next time.

From the specials menu, we ordered a comforting dish of spaghettini with light, well-made meatballs and liked it a lot. Another favorite with our table was a calamari steak, pounded flat, pan-fried and served in a lush, lemony sauce. Wide, al dente pappardelle noodles were felicitously paired with veal braised in Barolo wine. Also from the specials menu, chicken breast with mushrooms and Madeira was flavorful, and tuna, the fish of the day, was rare enough to be admirably moist.

Pollo arrosto, chicken breast with sliced eggplant and mozzarella in Cabernet sauce, came with risotto, but osso buco, which was pan-roasted with shiitake mushrooms, was plated with polenta instead of risotto. Orecchiette, the small ear-shaped pasta, soaked up a delicious sauce of pancetta, thin-sliced cabbage, garlic and fava beans. (We wished for more fava beans.)

The all-Italian wine list, written on a wine bottle that doubles as a vase, is available by the glass. Best bottle buy: a 1991 La Collegiatta Montepulciano D'Abruzzo for only $12.

Hazelnut gelato and the usual tirami su were better than usual here, but for something different try creamy risotto pudding with dried figs and honey. There's also a fine vanilla custard with toppings of caramel and chocolate. The coffee list is long; for a fusion of Italy and the New World, try a Tuscan mocha milk shake.

COLUMBUS BAKERY
474 Columbus Ave.
(212) 724-6880

HOURS: Monday–Friday, 8 a.m.–10 p.m.; Saturday–Sunday, 9 a.m.–10 p.m. Lunch from 10:30 a.m.
PRICES: Soups $3.50; sandwiches $5.95; scones, brioche and pastries $1.15–1.50. AE, DC, DS, MC, V.
ACCESS: Wheelchair-accessible; no restrooms.
HOW TO FIND IT: Between 82nd and 83rd Streets; subway line 1 to 79th Street station.

"This is the way a Danish used to taste," sighed my friend as he bit into a small, buttery one, made with fresh raspberries, not the thick, too-sweet jam used in so many pastries about town.

It tasted real.

This is one of the best things about Columbus Bakery. Everything tastes real.

The other best thing is that maybe, just maybe, Columbus Bakery, overseen by star chef Jonathan Waxman, will be in the forefront of a revolution in favor of small.

Baked goods are usually too big. You know those meal-sized muffins that often taste of too much baking powder and leave you feeling unsatisfied. Full maybe, but not happy. Sometimes, I take one bite and throw the whole thing away. Not at Columbus Bakery.

At Columbus Bakery, a homey-tasting banana muffin was small, the size you bake at home in your own muffin tins. It tasted of banana and maybe a whiff of cinnamon, no baking powder aftertaste, nothing that didn't belong.

Think small muffins. Think small, period. The buttery croissants are small and fragrant with yeast, in a town where most croissants, too, have become over-risen and triple their normal size. One customer pointed to the croissant he fancied and said, "I'll have that little guy there." There's something about small that makes it seem as though this roll was baked just for you—not in a mass-produced way. (Odd, because that is just what is happening—these items are baked for eateries as elegant as An American Place, as average as America.) The chocolate brioche, too, is a small, restrained affair. OK, you know what small is.

What is real, when it comes to baked goods? It's a taste you remember nostalgically, I think. Butter has a lot to do with that taste, and so does a certain hands-on approach. (And this, too, is ironic, because in reality we watched a worker, wearing a brace to protect his back, heft a sack of flour into a giant dough-mixing machine. So I can't tell you exactly how all these good breads end up tasting so homemade. Partly it's small, partly it's magic.)

There are some comfortable caned chairs and some marble-top tables for sitting, but table service is more a sometimes amenity for large groups than it is a given. Usually, you assemble your own food and drink from counters on either side of the cash register and then converge in the middle to pay; it helps to take a friend along. Or you can just pick out supper to take home. (When you're eating at the bakery, the commodious plates are sometimes too big for the small tables, if you order a lot.) You can have luscious, fresh-squeezed blood orange juice, mineral water, beer, wine (Les Jamelles Merlot or Chardonnay, $15.95 the bottle or $3.75 the glass), and, of course, espresso with a proper head of crema. More, too: tea, aperitifs such as Pastis or Lustau sherry, cocktails, cordials and brandy.

The food is simple and wonderful: Parmesan toasts that go well with wine or aperitifs; focaccia made with fontina and prosciutto or fresh tomato and several cheeses; moist smoked turkey with cranberries on a crusty roll; a robust roasted-beet salad, tossed with arugula and shavings of aged Monterey Jack cheese; a toss of wild rice, bulgur, barley, dried fruits and walnuts. Heartier specials included a salad of shredded duck (miraculously nongreasy) with roasted potatoes and artichokes. (Less successful was a small roasted hen, but the green salad with it was fresh, varied and perfectly dressed.)

Save plenty of space for dessert. The cookie-crusted tart of blood oranges is refreshing and positively addictive, and a triple-layered, mousse-filled chocolate cake was amazingly moist, covered with a slab of top-notch dark chocolate. Besides those little brioche chocolate buns I'm so fond of, there are yummy little sticky buns, and there are irresistible plates of cookies—oatmeal with dried apples and dates, buttery chocolate chip.

FALAFEL 'N' STUFF
1586 First Ave.
(212) 879-7023

HOURS: Daily, noon–midnight.
PRICES: Entrées $10–$15; appetizers $3–$4. Lunch $6.50–$10; appetizers $2.75–$3.50. MC, V.

RESERVATIONS: Recommended.
ACCESS: Dining area and restrooms wheelchair-accessible.
HOW TO FIND IT: Between 82nd and 83rd Streets; subway line 4 to 86th Street station; bus line M15.

You don't have to date back to the days of green eyeshades to realize that not all publicists can be trusted all the time, or even much of it. After all, they are being paid to say nice things about the restaurants they promote.

But how reliable are recommendations from others? Can you believe a friend of the restaurant owner? A relative? Or, to get down to cases, a wife? If the wife is Kay Ragab, the answer is yes.

Kay Ragab handwrote a letter to tell me about Falafel 'n' Stuff, a restaurant run by her husband, Moustafa. "It's a small place with all homemade foods," she said modestly. She added that actors Michael J. Fox and Meryl Streep and singer Roberta Flack had all eaten there, and later, on the phone, she mentioned more actors, Jill Clayburgh and Anthony Quinn. But, said Kay Ragab, "he [Moustafa] has no idea who anybody is," not having been raised in this country. There was something sweet, even romantic, about this letter. I fell, and it was swell.

The reality lived up to the advance buildup in almost every way (no celebs I recognized, though). The walls of what might have been a nondescript store-front were hung with lush, bright Egyptian silk pieces. We considered the menu over tall glasses of wonderful, frothy homemade lemonade that had rind in it.

You might start with delightfully lemony tabbouleh, the salad of parsley and bulgur, or smoothly addictive sesame tahini, or garlicky hummus, the chickpea dip, with little balls of fresh, crisp chick-pea falafel. Pale, elegant baba ganoush, the eggplant dip, came with piles of warmed pita, as did most everything throughout the meal. Grape leaves stuffed with rice put others about town to shame with their pristine freshness.

That's the way with Moustafa Ragab's food; everything is always done by hand, always a cut or two above the competition. The extra touch that's a trademark is toasty brown rice that's always being served in a pyramid. (What could be more Egyptian?)

This care and attention made me feel entirely forgiving when a sprinkle of salt was needed on foul (pronounced fool) mudammas, brown fava beans stewed with spices to a melting tenderness, then swirled with fruity olive oil. There's something elemental about this dish, an elusive flavor that makes you feel that surely it has been eaten since the beginning of time. Nothing else tastes quite the same when it's foul mudammas I crave. Here, there's a second, little-seen version, foul eskandarani, which was the same creamy fava beans with tomato and arugula added.

Was there ever a time when humankind did not eat garlic? If so, I'm glad it was before my time. Here, there were breathtaking amounts of it in the Cairo salad, a heady combination of chopped greens, heavy on olives, hot peppers, lemon juice and olive oil. Cleopatra salad was a pleasant enough second choice, a heap of hand-chopped watercress, scallions, cucumber and parsley, tossed with chips of toasted pita bread, lemon juice and olive oil. By contrast, though, it was tame.

Both chicken kebab and Pharaoh chicken, Egypt's (or perhaps Ragab's own secret) version of marinated barbecued chicken, were moist and tender. (Once, undercooked chicken was swiftly corrected.) There's couscous, Egyptian-style moussaka, made with eggplant and lamb with artichokes or okra, and kibbeh, chopped lamb combined with bulgur and pine nuts and baked.

But the main dish we simply couldn't get enough of was melokhia, a dish of greens that makes a nice spring tonic. Melokhia is a kind of green herb made into a soupy broth seasoned with garlic and coriander; as a meat dish, it may contain chicken or lamb, and we liked it both ways. Since melokhia, which flourishes in Egypt, does not grow here, it must be purchased frozen, but luckily, like spinach, it seems to hold up well.

Desserts are the usual sweetly honeyed items, all of them better than usual—baklava, ladyfingers, bird's nest with walnuts and pistachio, a devastatingly good custard whose humble name is "custard from our kitchen." When we went for lunch, thick, dark Turkish coffee seemed in order. Later in the day, a glass of gentle mint tea soothed.

How did Kay Hickman Ragab, who hails from Middle Village, Queens, ever find herself writing a letter about her Egyptian husband's restaurant? Well, the way the couple tells it, he was working in a Middle Eastern grocery store, and she was buying cheese. It was love, not across a crowded room, but across a slab of feta. "Not that minute," said Kay Ragab, careful not to exaggerate, "but within hours."

To this day, Kay Ragab can't stand melokhia. But she's crazy about her husband, and she would like us to be, too.

THE FISH
2799 Broadway
(212) 864-5000

HOURS: Dinner Monday–Thursday, 4–11 p.m.; Friday–Saturday, 4 p.m.–midnight; Sunday, 4–11 p.m. Lunch Monday–Friday, noon–4 p.m. Brunch Saturday– Sunday 10:30 a.m.–4 p.m.
PRICES: Entrées $9.95–$14.95, specials $11–$18; appetizers $3.95–$6. Lunch $6.95–$7.95. Brunch $3–$12. AE, MC, V.
RESERVATIONS: Recommended.
ACCESS: Dining area wheelchair-accessible.
HOW TO FIND IT: Between 107th and 108th Streets; subway line 1 to 110th Street/ Cathedral Parkway station.

The Fish. It takes chutzpah to bestow such a name upon a restaurant. The Fish is a name that takes some living up to, and I don't mean the colorful fish that decorate the walls.

In this case, the proprietors have no cause for worry. This is indeed the quintessential place for fresh, well-prepared fish at fair prices. This formula—good fish, low prices, a free hand with garlic—is irresistible to folks in the neighborhood and beyond.

At The Fish, even when you are told to cool your heels, it is good news. "How much are a dozen oysters?" I asked. "Thirteen dollars," said the waiter, "but it will take a while, because we open them when you order them." I said I didn't mind.

Mind? Such care is so seldom taken that it seemed a minor miracle to this oyster fancier.

While our dozen pristine bluepoints were being opened we ate a few other things, the very best of which was a lobster and smoked Gruyere quesadilla with a biting side salsa of habañero peppers (high on the heat scale) and roasted tomatoes. The tortillas were thin and crisp, the cheese divine. (A few days later, we had the quesadilla again and there wasn't much lobster that time, but it still tasted wonderful.)

Even such a dubious-sounding combination as grilled shrimp with hearts of palm and vanilla bean sauce was good, the vanilla adding an elusive bite when not sweetened. Fried calamari looked too pale but was crisp and practically greaseless, good with mayonnaise made zesty with anchovies and roasted garlic. Fried zucchini with red sauce was delicious, too. (Another night, the zucchini-calamari combo—an alternative to ordering each separately if you cannot decide on which—was not as skillfully cooked, the breadings heavier and more oily.) Lightly deep-fried oysters were rolled in cracker crumbs (the ideal coating, as far as this Midwesterner is concerned) and served with ginger-wasabi mayonnaise. Caesar salad actually contained anchovies, a plus. Sautéed escarole and white beans was admirably garlicky, but the beans were underdone.

A ravioli of the day, stuffed with shrimp and scallops and swathed in a fresh pomodoro sauce, was one of the best entrées. Talapia, which we tried twice when it was a special, was best the night it was quickly seared so it was still moist inside and served in a mild jalapeño-tomatillo sauce. Another night, talapia in tomato-basil sauce was less exciting; the sauce and fish didn't really go together. Pompano was equally lush in a sauce of lime butter. Best side dish: scalloped potatoes.

The sterling quality of grilled sea scallops needed no gilding, so a light citrus vinaigrette seemed just right. Excellent prawns came in a luxurious, mildly peppery Creole cream sauce, and whole catfish in a light cornmeal breading would have been dandy even without the orange-tahini sauce. A thick slab of grilled tuna with shaved fennel and roasted-garlic consommé was smashing. And the one nonfish entrée we sampled was sensational: a juicy hanger steak, the choicest of cuts, with mushrooms and deep-brown cognac demiglace.

Desserts seem to vary, so without telling you which ones we found less appealing (they seem to change all the time anyway), we'll just say that the so-called cobbler (more like a crisp) contained caramelized apples and is a clear winner, especially with vanilla Haagen Dazs. One night, to our great dismay, they ran out of ice cream. (They also ran out of the decent Sebastiani chardonnay, $11 a bottle.)

But when oysters on ice are so good, I can do without ice cream. I subscribe to the wisdom of A.J. Leibling, who wrote about Proust's remembrance of the madeleine, the little cakelike cookie: "In the light of what Proust wrote with so mild a stimulus, it is the world's loss that he did not have a heartier appetite. On a dozen Gardiner's Island oysters, a bowl of clam chowder, a peck of steamers, some bay scallops, three sautéed soft-shelled crabs, a few ears of fresh-picked corn, a thin swordfish steak of generous area, a pair of lobsters and a Long Island duck, he might have written a masterpiece."

IDEAL RESTAURANT & BAR
322 E. 86th St.
(212) 737-0795

HOURS: Daily, dinner 5–10 p.m.; lunch 11 a.m.–5 p.m.
PRICES: Entrées $8.50–$11.95; appetizers from $2.95. Lunch $7.50–$10.95.
ACCESS: Dining area wheelchair-accessible; restrooms downstairs.
KIDS: No children's menu but will accommodate.

HOW TO FIND IT: Between First and Second Avenues; subway line 4 to 86th Street station.

One of the last bastions of German food, Ideal on 86th Street, was destroyed by fire about 15 months ago, and devotees mourned. Now, Ideal is back, "famous for outstanding German food since 1932," as the menu declares.

"Sometimes I was worried, too" said Bill Smith, who bought Ideal about two years before the fire. "Were we going to be lucky enough to find a place near home?" That meant Yorkville, preferably 86th Street.

Smith found what used to be Café du Soir, and in the new location the potato pancakes are as good as ever. This is, to its many neighborhood fans—and quite a few from beyond the neighborhood—cause for rejoicing.

Right off, one Ideal fan asked me in a wistful tone if the restaurant still served the food on divided plates, in school-cafeteria style. I swear that at lunch I once got my roulade, tender stuffed beef (one of Tuesday's specials) with well-browned, oniony home fries and sauerkraut, on such a plate. (But at a later dinner, we got normal plates, and Smith told me over the phone that they have no divided plates now. Oh, well.)

The new place is roomier and a bit spiffier, with a highly polished wood floor. The kitchen, twice as big, is hidden from view—no more watching the cooks flip sizzling eggs and potato pancakes on the grill. Many of the faces, both customers and staff, are reassuringly familiar. Everybody's glad to be back.

Me, too. The potato pancakes were fresh, crisp, wonderful. The applesauce was on the side, of course, as my German dining companion noted with approval.

At one downtown German eatery, wiener and other schnitzel is at least $4 more than here, where a fine piece of breaded veal cutlet with all the trimmings will run you $10.95 at lunch, $11.50 at dinner. (There's also pork schnitzel, if you prefer.) Koenigsberger klopse, well-seasoned meatballs with a caper gravy, were delicious, too. Bratwurst, nicely browned in a pan, was tasty, and so was veal goulash, another Tuesday special. Our only disappointment about the goulash was that there was no spaetzle to substitute for noodles. But our plates contained such comforting food—smoothly mashed turnips, creamed spinach, red cabbage, long-cooked string beans, perfect mashed potatoes.

There's such a lot I haven't even gotten to try yet—pot roast, roast fresh ham, oxtail ragout and smoked pork tenderloin (Wednesday specials), lamb stew (that's Friday). Servings are generous, and besides a cup of soup (chicken noodle was ho-hum, but I haven't tried all of them) and the vegetables, you get a big stack of bread thrown in for the price of the meal.

Desserts include apple strudel and a commendable rice pudding with sweet strawberry sauce. German pancake with strawberries (baked into the crepe-like pancake) or other fruit is listed under pancakes instead of dessert, but I have it last anyway.

There's a counter, the way there was at the old Ideal, though nobody is cooking behind it at the new place. And the gravy is as homey as ever.

What has changed a bit is the staff. At lunch, our well-cushioned waitress looked as though she had enjoyed a few platters of potato pancakes in her time. I'm sure I remember her from the old place. But at dinner, there was a different waitress, a little too svelte for us to believe that she had enjoyed enough of Ideal's food in the past. But like her, you can make up for lost time by eating at Ideal now.

LE SELECT

507 Columbus Ave.
(212) 875-1993

HOURS: Dinner Tuesday–Saturday, 5:30 p.m.–midnight; Sunday–Monday, 5:30–11 p.m. Lunch Monday–Friday, noon–3:30 p.m. Brunch Saturday–Sunday, 11:30 a.m.–3:30 p.m.
PRICES: Entrées $10.25–$18.75; appetizers $4.50–$6.75. Lunch $7.50– $14.50; appetizers $3.50–$5.50. Brunch $12.50. AE, DC, MC, V.
RESERVATIONS: Recommended.
ACCESS: Wheelchair-accessible; restrooms equipped for disabled.
KIDS: No children's menu but will accommodate.
PARKING: Commercial lot on 83rd Street.
HOW TO FIND IT: Between 84th and 85th Streets; subway line 1 to 86th Street station; bus line M7.

You can probably count the French restaurants on the Upper West Side on the fingers of one hand—La Mirabelle, La Boîte en Bois, Poiret . . . and now, there's Le Select.

Eric Demarchelier, owner of the oh-so-French restaurants Demarchelier and Jean Lafitte on the East Side opened Le Select and the crowd includes neighborhood types with babies in carriages, well-dressed older people, customers from across town who are there to say bonne chance, and folks who fall somewhere in between young and middle-aged, wearing an assortment of T-shirts (Mickey Mouse, for one) and baseball caps. All of them like the food, and the surroundings. I do, too.

The space that had been Honeysuckle has been transformed into a comfortable dining room where tables are reasonably spread out. The huge, fanciful sconces may have been in a Busby Berkeley musical, but they're practical, too, providing just the right amount of light, neither glaring nor so dim you can't identify the food on your plate. Ceiling fans whir on high. The shadows cast by backlit window shutters in the raised dining area at the back of the restaurant make it seem as though it's still daylight outside. Banquettes were comfy, too. The wine list is practically a miracle, with a French merlot as the house red and such bottles as a 1989 Medoc from Chateau La Cardonne for $24. (The list tops out at $35, save for Champagne.)

Even in such an attractive place, you could feel out of sorts if the food were not up to snuff. Happily, it is mostly wonderful and so is the service.

You won't find a more traditional and delicious onion soup, cozy under its blanket of melted cheese, than the one at Le Select. A flavorful mussel-saffron soup, the du jour, was perfection. There were a few grains of sand in leeks that came on a plate prettily painted with several shades of vinaigrette, but not enough to ruin the dish. No fault could be found with artichokes vinaigrette, creamy brie tart (like a tomato pizza made with brie) and sprightly tomato salad made with curved slices of tomato from the outside of the fruit. (In this presentation the tomatoes can be both firm—not mushy the way they sometimes are in the center—and ripe at the same time. *Bonne idée.*) I liked the coarse, rustic character of a pâté served with traditional cornichons, those perky French pickles. A companion objected to the amount of fat in it, but fat makes for flavor, I say.

Escargots, at $6.50 the most expensive appetizer, came in pools of potent garlic-parsley butter, fine for mopping with the sturdy bread. Fresh baby lettuces were dressed in classic vinaigrette.

Simple, bistro standards were comforting—mellow coq au vin, roasted half chicken (juicy) and mashed potatoes (stiff but tasty) and hamburger (no bun) served with good, thin french fries and a small tumble of salad. Lamb shoulder braised to a rich brown tenderness was a delight, as was duck confit with mellow, long-cooked green cabbage.

It's not easy to get a bad dish at Le Select. Oh, all right, grilled salmon Provençale style might have been slightly boring, but it was fresh and fine. A special of sautéed red snapper served with ginger-lemon beurre blanc was dandy, and on the regular menu red snapper is available in a leek and celery broth.

Juicy grilled pork chops scattered with chopped tomato and served on spinach were bliss. Steak au poivre (it came with ultra-thick bearnaise sauce on the side, for good measure) delivered. This handsome hunk of meat was well worth its $16.50 price tag, steepest on the menu. Use those fries to mop up any remaining bits of lush brown pepper sauce. Steak is a better choice than shepherd's pie, a burning-hot layer of savory ground meat covered with equally hot mashed potatoes.

A pasta special of penne tossed with creamy, melting goat cheese and a few shreds of roasted pepper sounded simple. It was, but it was also utterly satisfying.

In general, vegetables are treated with care instead of being an afterthought, as too often is the case. Meats are cooked exactly to the desired degree of doneness. And even the least experienced waiters on the mostly French, mostly trained, staff try so hard and are so charming that a longish wait for dessert when the room is crowded is easily overlooked.

A "black chocolate" mousse cake pleased a chocaholic, and blueberry mousse cake with a chocolate layer was pleasant, but my pick was a huge portion of crème caramel, big enough to share and richly burnished with burnt-sugar syrup. Decent apple tart was not warm as promised on the menu. But when the floating island promised on the menu materializes, I'll be back for some. Espresso reminds you, in these days of burned, "over-roasted" coffee beans, of just how good espresso can be.

I live in the Village, where restaurants are a way of life, and I have a job that allows me to eat many well-priced and distinctive ethnic meals in other boroughs. So I confess to being a bit of a snob about Upper West Side restaurants, too many of which seem just like each other.

Le Select isn't like anything else in nearby blocks. It would be good in any part of town. It's wonderful, and welcome.

LEMONGRASS GRILL
2534 Broadway
(212) 666-0896

HOURS: Monday–Thursday, noon–11:30 p.m.; Friday–Saturday, noon–12:30 a.m.; Sunday, 1–11:30 p.m.
PRICES: Entrées $5.95–$13.95; appetizers $2–$5.95; noodles and rice $5–$6.50. MC, V.

RESERVATIONS: Taken only for five or more.
ACCESS: Portable ramp used to access dining area, call ahead; ladies restroom wheelchair-accessible, men's restroom is not.
PARKING: Garage on 95th Street beetween Broadway and Amsterdam.
HOW TO FIND IT: Between 94th and 95th Streets; subway lines 1 or 2 to 96th Street station; bus line M96.

In another part of town, Lemongrass Grill might not be causing such a stir as it is on the Upper West Side. In some other parts of town, Thai restaurants have become almost commonplace in recent years. Not so here.

From practically the moment Lemongrass Grill opened there were waits for tables and for takeout.

Lemongrass lives up to its name with a long, open grill area where all the cooking is done in plain sight. The kitchen workers all wear sanitary headgear, in almost striking contrast to the lush-looking surroundings—whirring ceiling fans, dark-stained ceiling beams, herbs and banana leaves hanging from the kitchen rafters, a shining Buddha ensconsed on a shelf, a slatted pie safe painted in deep green and mahogany tones. A matching slatted window opens onto what is really a mirror, but it creates the impression of another room. The restaurant is more spacious than the original Lemongrass Grill in Park Slope, Brooklyn—but it's still not enough space for Thai-hungry diners.

You might start your meal with tom yum gung, a zesty hot and sour lemongrass broth containing tree-ear mushrooms and a few plump shrimp (fresh, not the more authentic dried shrimp). Vegetable dumplings came in a steamer on a bed of greens, with a garlicky, basil-accented dipping sauce, and they were among the best things we sampled here. Next time, I plan on getting two orders and skipping the lackluster fried eggrolls. Chicken saté with peanut sauce was only adequate, and barbecued chicken wings were juicy but did not taste strongly enough of garlic, turmeric and lemongrass— all promised in the menu description. Calamari salad, however, was fine in a dressing of lime juice, lemongrass, chile and fish sauce, tossed with fresh mint leaves.

When available, water spinach flash-flamed with garlic, chile and black bean sauce is a seasonal treat that's not to be missed. Stars mark the spicier dishes on the menu, and one of my favorites in that category was gai pat prik king, chicken stir-fried with fresh string beans, basil, soy and chile paste. (It's not really all that hot, just well-seasoned.) We also liked Siam chicken, the fowl marinated with lemongrass and served with braised onions and black bean sauce. Shrimp were grilled with garlic, peppers and scallions in such a fashion that they tasted almost sweet, good counterpoint for chile-fired dishes. Lemongrass pork chops were well-flavored with a marinade of galanga, a pinkish root that resembles ginger, garlic, lemongrass and lime juice. Two noodle dishes, lar nard, broad rice noodles with broccoli in a brown oyster gravy, and khao soi, egg noodles with yellow curry and chicken, were tasty.

Thai sticky rice, served as it is at the Brooklyn location in cunning little covered baskets, was too gummy and it clumped together. It wasn't worth the $1.75 per order when plain jasmine rice can be had for only $1.

But the sweet sticky rice that was served with fresh mango for dessert was much better, no doubt freshly made, and a tiny, delicate coconut pudding sprinkled with sesame seeds was a delight.

LUZIA
429 Amsterdam Ave.
595-2000

HOURS: Daily, dinner 5–10 p.m. Lunch Monday–Friday, 11 a.m.–5 p.m. Brunch Saturday–Sunday, 9 a.m.–3:30 p.m. Breakfast Monday–Friday, 9:30 a.m.–11:30 p.m.
PRICES: Entrées $9.95–$13.95; appetizers $2.50–$5.95. Lunch/brunch $5.95–$8.95. Breakfast $2.95–$7.95. AE, DC, MC, V.
RESERVATIONS: Recommended.
ACCESS: Wheelchair-accessible; restrooms equipped for disabled.
KIDS: No children's menu but will accommodate.
HOW TO FIND IT: Between 80th and 81st Streets; subway line 1 to 79th Street station; bus lines M7, M79 and M104.

With this write-up, I depart from tradition. Luzia, named for its chef and owner Luzia Pinhao, is mostly a takeout shop. There are only eight or nine chairs and a few small tables tiled in blue and white.

So why write about a place where only eight people can sit down to eat? Because Pinhao is an extraordinary cook, a culinary wizard, an answer to prayer.

My friend who has eaten in Portugal said that Luzia's wonderful caldo verde was better than any he'd eaten in that country, because in restaurants there the soup is often based on a Knorr's product instead of real potatoes. No need now, said he, to go to New Jersey for Portuguese food, not while there's Luzia on this side of the Hudson.

Luzia and partner Murray Wasserman—they're the sort of folks you get to be on a first-name basis with after a meal or two—are all enthusiastic smiles as they tell you this comely little place was the fruition of a dream. Luzia worked for other people and has cooked at the Portuguese Embassy, but now she shines on her own, doing things her way. Even what you suspect will be ordinary, such as roast turkey, often is a surprise, the fowl amazingly moist and tender.

As you eat dense, chewy Portuguese cornbread made with wheat flour and nibble at the rich brown olives in little pottery bowls that Murray brings to the table, consider the source of some of Luzia's wizardry; all around the counters and windows are terra-cotta pots and small wooden boxes filled with rosemary, parsley, basil, marjoram and chives. A big wooden box holds a beautiful array of fresh apples and oranges. Just growing herbs and displaying apples, would not, of course, a restaurant make. Luzia's cooking does that.

Be warned that not everything is available every day, and there is no printed menu. Vegetables we have taken much pleasure in eating include carrots and fennel lightly steamed together, small-chopped fresh string beans with bits of tomato and a delicate dressing, crisped potatoes that Luzia seemed to intuit that we wanted (we didn't even know they were available) and then, wonder of wonders, seconds of spuds without our having to ask. Then there was the savory salad of chick-peas and the unusual and felicitous couscous tapioca, a special Portuguese kind, subtly perfumed with the fresh basil that had been cooked with it.

By special order, Luzia will make a trip to Newark for the ingredients for her superb fish stew, a heaping platter of whiting, squid, flounder and other fish, cooked with plenty of onion and some bright red peppers. Or perhaps she can be persuaded to make that light, superb caldo verde, an ethereal potato broth floating with bits of fine-chopped kale. There's her sturdy, spicy chicken Milanese (no special order necessary—but you may find that it is a special on the day you visit).

A few things were less delightful than others—a simple vegetable soup was chock-full of good things but tasted flat, compared to the caldo verde. And zucchini boats stuffed with vegetables and cheese were fresh but lacked pizzazz. Never mind, just have another helping of the sparkling green beans.

Portuguese sodas and the Spa brand of cassis soft drink are good accompaniments, but there is no license for wine or beer.

For dessert, there is sometimes a sliver of dense, deep-chocolate loaf cake or some other sweet, and often there are tasty, plump peanut butter cookies, along with Murray's blend of coffee—American, but strong enough to be good.

MISS ELLE'S HOMESICK BAR & GRILL
226 W. 79th St.
(212) 595-4350

HOURS: Dinner daily, 4 p.m.–midnight. Lunch Monday–Friday, 11:30 a.m.–4 p.m. Brunch Saturday–Sunday, 11:30 a.m.–4 p.m.
PRICES: Entrées $8.95–$14.95, appetizers $3–$5. Lunch $4.95–$7.95. Brunch $8.95–$9.95. AE, CB, DC, DS, MC, V.
RESERVATIONS: Taken only for groups of six or more.
ACCESS: Two steps down at entrance; restrooms not wheelchair-accessible.
KIDS: No children's menu, but children's items are offered.
HOW TO FIND IT: Between Broadway and Amsterdam Avenue; subway line 1 to West 79th Street/Broadway station; bus lines M7, M104.

Miss Elle's menu has things on it that are never found in restaurants. When was the last time you saw onion dip and potato chips on a restaurant menu? Never, I'll bet. I never had until the other night, when we ordered three rounds of them.

Yes, the dip ($1.50) is the one made from the recipe on the back of the Lipton Soup mix box. And on the back of Miss Elle's menu, there's a whole category of "make-believe" food, the kind that spoils your appetite for the rest of the meal: milk and cookies (Oreos), a grilled-cheese sandwich, "leftover sandwich" du jour, peanut butter and banana sandwich and, at the low end of the scale, a pretzel, 10 cents.

Miss Elle's, named for owner Ellena Parrino, a former Playboy bunny (and bunny mother—kind of like a sorority house mother), also will order take-out food for guests who find nothing quite to their taste on the down-home menu. Even more amazing, she will allow guests to bring over a favorite recipe, and she and head chef Jimmy Lam will cook it for them. (Could I, I asked, just clip a recipe out of the Sunday paper, one I didn't particularly feel like making, and bring it in? Well, the waitress said, that might constitute an abuse of goodwill.)

That's not all: Every day, Miss Elle offers a 400-calorie dinner, usually something based on a chicken breast, salad and sugarless Jell-O.

The bread basket contained slabs of warm, delicious whole-grain and pumpernickel, the kind of bread that makes butter irresistible. And when I asked for iced tea, which wasn't on the menu, the waitress graciously made a tall, fresh glass.

This place is so accommodating that when a friend who needed comfort ordered five kinds of potatoes, the waitress did not bat an eyelash—"Would you like gravy on the mashed?" was her only comment.

No, said my friend, she thought that might sort of detract from the potatoes.

"I know what you mean," said the waitress sympathetically. "That might be too many colors."

Here's what my friend got: wonderful, crisp fries and sweet-potato fries, a dandy baked potato (no foil wrap), satisfying mashed potatoes (with a lump or two so you knew they weren't instant) and Italian potato salad, the only one we felt lukewarm about. Four potato dishes, my pal admitted, might have been enough.

The rest of us feasted on mom's escarole soup, the kind with tiny meatballs in it; char-broiled filet mignon; prime-rib roast; a special of shoulder lamb chops, slightly fatty but tasty; another special, nicely broiled salmon with a touch of Dijon; pot roast with a good gravy and more mashed potatoes, charcoal-broiled pork chops with the obligatory applesauce alongside. There were side dishes galore: fresh, lightly creamed spinach; mushrooms sautéed with much garlic, and creamy macaroni and cheese. (We weren't wild about cooked carrots with cinnamon, but pass more of that spinach.) Even wines are user-friendly; our favorites from the short list were a crisp Stone Creek chardonnay, $13.50, and a Geyser Peak cabernet sauvignon, $20.

We neglected the Italian side of the menu in favor of the meat-and-potatoes part, but there are also such standards as rigatoni with meat sauce, lasagna, and spaghetti and meatballs.

Miss Elle learned to make this kind of food for her two children. "I had a very appreciative audience," she said of her youngsters and husband, "so, ergo, I loved cooking. I used to create these little dinners and then step up and accept the applause when it was over." (Along the way, the husband faded from the picture, but the children have grown up and produced five grandsons.)

"We went for the stuff we grew up with," said Miss Elle, a third-generation New Yorker, "nothing fancy." It's refreshing to find a restaurant owner who doesn't take herself all that seriously.

Miss Elle cooks at lunchtime and does the baking, including a "harvest pie" of dried apricots, pears, apples and walnuts, best eaten with ice cream. And she has taught Jimmy Lam to make all her mother's sauces. "He makes a tomato sauce that smells like Sunday mornin' at home," said Miss Elle.

The friend who ate the many-potato meal sighed contentedly and looked around at the sweet lace curtains, the old family pictures on the walls, the faux-lace plastic tablecloths, the small, pink-shaded lamps. "This would make a nice apartment," she said. "Can't we just move in?" Miss Elle's, with a coziness appropriate to its setting in an 1894 landmark building, is like that, a whole lot like home. Anyone for more chips and dip?

MO' BETTER

570 Amsterdam Ave.
(212) 580-7755

HOURS: Dinner Monday–Thursday, 5:30–10 p.m.; Friday–Saturday, 5 p.m.–midnight; Sunday, 4–10 p.m. Late menu offered in lounge.
PRICES: Entreés $10–$17; appetizers $4–$7. AE, CB, DC, DS, MC, V.
RESERVATIONS: Recommended for weekends.

ACCESS: Wheelchair-accessible; restrooms equipped for disabled.
ENTERTAINMENT: Live bands, predominantly jazz, Wednesday–Saturday, 10 p.m.
HOW TO FIND IT: Between 87th and 88th Streets; subway line 1 to 86th Street/Broadway station; bus line M86.

Once in a while, a dinner is perfect. Everyone has animated conversations, an updated version of the kind you might find in a play by Noel Coward. Baskets of light, warm cornbread disappear as though inhaled. People exclaim happily over their food. People who have never met before like each other instantly.

That's the kind of dinner we had recently at Mo' Better, a new emporium of slightly updated southern cooking on the Upper West Side. Following in the trail blazed by such young, hip restaurants as Shark Bar and Honeysuckle, where savvy young African-Americans own part of the action, Mo' Better was an almost instant success when it opened just short of two weeks ago. On a Friday, the room was packed, and, as someone from the restaurant said later, "we pushed everybody out onto the floor" to wait tables while Muralidhar, a silky-talking new-wave jazz presence, entertained. (There's a $15 minimum when there's entertainment.)

We surmised that our waiter had been rather suddenly promoted from bus-boy, by his timorous manner and lack of knowledge. "What temperature do you want the steak?" he asked. I couldn't resist pointing out that well done is the only possible "temperature" for smothered steak. At the next visit, our large group was served by a pro, a young woman who actually called the manager at home when we complained about the bitter coffee—one of our very few complaints about the meal. This kind of thing hardly ever happens in a big, cold city. The manager returned; they made more coffee.

There's a high-energy feel about Mo' Better, and a hefty portion of the crowd—and the people who run the place, too—look as though they could be movie stars. The room, in walls of sponged yellow, red and green, is simply decorated with Matisse-like drawings on the wood floor and sconces that mimic old gaslights. With the cast of gorgeous people that Mo' Better attracts, you don't even need decor.

Chef Rodrigo leads off the menu with fried chicken wings so spicy they almost send out sparks. Between bites, the slightly sweet cornbread cuts the heat. (I like less-sweet cornbread, but for those who don't, this is some of the best in town.) On two tries, there were no corn fritters with chutney, although the menu promised them. But pecan-bread chicken fingers with honey-peach sauce were a tame but good choice. Fresh green beans were stir-fried with heady quantities of garlic for a winning vegetable appetizer.

Or start with a smooth, suave, smoked-salmon bisque or a deep, long-simmered black-bean soup garnished with sour cream and bits of onion.

A section of the menu called "on the light side" will appeal to those who are trying to get through the year without extra pounds. Blackened salmon strips were amazingly delicious, a reminder of how good blackened things can be, done right. The tangy grilled shrimp also are available over lightly grilled zucchini and yams and a toss of spiffy mixed greens. Shrimp show up again in a peppered grilled version, and all shrimp variations were fresh and peppy.

Lightly pan-fried catfish and crisp, southern-fried chicken were good advertisements for southern cooking. For homey dishes just right for winter nights, try moist smothered chicken or bronzed pork chops, or that falling-apart-tender smothered steak and onions in a rich, brown gravy. On a busy Friday, ribs we ordered as an entrée were too tough, but another time, appetizer rib orders were much better. Grilled chicken was folded inside a pancake, in a variation of the chicken-and-waffles theme, but it seemed odd that a companion was allowed to order coleslaw on the same plate with pancakes.

Side orders are, however, a joy. The mashed potatoes are real, the collard greens delectable, macaroni and cheese creamier one time than another but always "flavorable," to borrow a menu description. Black-eyed peas were cooked just right, until they formed their own gravy. Rice pilaf and yams were the least exciting choices, and at one dinner, green beans were lackluster. Skip undistinguished sautéed tomatoes and corn, heavy on the corn.

Iced tea is really the right wine with this food, but so far only a handful of the wines on the list are available. We are partial to Amaretto-sautéed bananas with vanilla ice cream over pound cake (more fluffy than dense) and to a delightful, rich, chocolate-pecan pie.

Mo' Better is a winner, a gift to jaded palates. Pass that cornbread, please.

NIKO'S

2161 Broadway
(212) 873-7000

HOURS: Dinner Monday–Thursday and Sunday, 5 p.m.–midnight; Friday–Saturday, 5 p.m.–1 a.m. Lunch Monday–Friday, 11 a.m.–5 p.m. Brunch Saturday–Sunday, 11 a.m.–5 p.m.
PRICES: Entrées $10.95–$15.95; mezedes $3.95–$7.95; appetizers $4.95–$6; salads $3.95–$9.95. Lunch $4.95–$7.95; salads $3.95–$8.95; pasta $6.95–$10.95. AE, DC, MC, V.
RESERVATIONS: Taken only for groups of 8 or more at lunch.
ACCESS: Dining area wheelchair-accessible; restrooms downstairs.
HOW TO FIND IT: At 76th Street; subway line 1 to 79th Street station or lines 1 or 2 to 72nd Street station; bus line M7.

All over the menu at Niko's Mediterranean, there are pleas that say "Souvenir menu available soon. Please do not borrow our house menu."

So, folks, it was a challenge to get this one. But I did it for you. And I can tell you it runs 10 pages. A lot of the food is labeled with leaves and hearts, for vegetarian dishes or those relatively low in fat, salt and cholesterol.

Niko's ceiling is festooned with tiny twinkly lights and fake grapevines, and after only a few weeks in business, the tables are filled with happy customers. Perhaps they are drawn to Niko Imirziades' manifesto of eating, a Xeroxed sheet that declares: "When I was a child in Athens, an expensive ingredient like meat was stretched as far as it would go—and never eaten every day." This was the original Mediterranean diet. "My mother Artemis would fix a large plate of string beans braised in tomato as a main dish," so good it equaled filet mignon, said Niko. His mother received a yearly share of olives and olive oil from her own property, an ancient grove on the island of Samos, he writes.

This kind of writing sets up a lot of romantic expectations. The best of Niko's food rises to the challenge.

I could have been perfectly happy eating just appetizers, mezedes: codfish croquettes with an unusual and perfectly delicious form of skordalia made with mashed potatoes, garlic and roasted beets; stuffed grape leaves in the lemon sauce called avgolemeno; lemony artichoke hearts tossed with carrots and potato. And you won't want to miss imam bayaldi—literally, "the sultan swooned"—which is eggplant stuffed with a zesty mixture of onion, pepper and tomato and served with long-simmered broad beans.

Because I like Niko's so much, it grieves me to say that the only first course we didn't care for much was fasolakia, the fresh string beans braised in tomato and onion, with roasted potato besides. Did the tomato come in contact with a cooking surface that was not nonreactive? Was there an undercurrent of dried mint that had passed its prime? Alas, the roasted potatoes, usually another favorite of mine, were tired, too many times reheated. But I think these problems stem from the fact that the enthusiastic Niko is trying to do too many things at once. He'll get on track.

From the rotisserie, we had a delicious slow-roasted baby chicken, juicy and golden-skilled, and even better slow-roasted pork. These entrées were served with more of the unfortunate string beans. Horta, a side dish of escarole or, depending on season, other greens, was the old-fashioned overcooked kind but satisfying.

There are a number of pasta dishes on the menu, a tribute to Niko's other favorite Mediterranean country, Italy. We tried an excellent one: bow ties tossed with rotisserie chicken, Kalamata olives, spinach, pignoli nuts and sage, topped with a fat little pillow of goat cheese to swirl into the pasta at will. For unreconstructed meat lovers, too, there were plenty of choices. We liked rib-eye steak, treated to a tasty marinade and cooked on a skewer with the usual pepper, onion and tomatoes. A reasonably priced wine list and some appealing desserts round out the menu. Vanilla ice cream with wild-cherry sauce was simple and wonderful. We also liked cheesecake with fresh strawberries and a creamy flan.

THE SAVANNAH CLUB
2420 Broadway
(212) 496-1066

HOURS: Daily, dinner 4 p.m.–1 a.m. Lunch noon–4 p.m. Brunch Saturday–Sunday, noon–4 p.m.
PRICES: Entrées $9.95–$14.95; appetizers $3.95–$7.95. Lunch entrées $4.95–$8.95. Fixed-price brunch price $6.95. AE, DC, DS, MC, V.
ACCESS: One small step at entrance; restrooms wheelchair-accessible.
PARKING: Commercial lots on Amsterdam Avenue.
HOW TO FIND IT: At 89th Street; subway line 1 to 86th Street station; bus lines M7, M86, M104.

Food writing adjectives fail me.

New, unsullied adjectives fail me, too.

Eating the cooking of Sara and Teena Bonner at The Savannah Club made me feel so purely grateful that I almost said grace.

I can't think when a meal in New York has made me that happy. Maybe one never has, up to now.

I wasn't expecting very much. There was no hype, to speak of. A simple, straightforward fax informed me of the opening of The Savannah Club, with a mother-daughter chef team from Alabama. I had eaten at Birdland, owned by the same folks, and thought the jazz fine, the food merely passable.

This food is something else. It is a gift to New York. In the graceful, high-ceilinged room, fans whirring overhead, we started with a basket of good corn-bread (not very sweet, glory be) and biscuits accompanied by onion jam (was that a hint of ginger, a mere whiff of clove?) and sweet-potato butter. In minutes, we reduced that to crumbs and asked for more.

Not least of the miracles at The Savannah Club is that the bread basket was cheerfully, swiftly replenished, and the entrées arrived within mere moments of each other. Good service should not be out of the ordinary, but sadly, it has become so in many moderately priced restaurants, and even in high-priced ones. Clear, delicious, amber-colored iced tea, strong enough to stand up to ice cubes, should not be all that hard to find in this city, but it is scarcer than hen's teeth. Here, you'll have a glass of iced tea that conjures up a creaking porch swing and a summer evening lit by fireflies.

Too many cooks try to sweeten up yams, which are already plenty sweet. At Savannah, the crispy yam fries tasted of themselves, with a sprinkle of salt, just right. The fries come on a plate lined with a paper doily, an old-fashioned kind of frill. Thin-sliced homemade garlic sausage, Sara's own, was wonderful with simple, warm buttered potatoes.

I couldn't get enough of the fried oysters with scallion tartar sauce, prettily served in the shells from which they recently came. You won't find better. Griddle cakes made with lump crab and scallion griddle cakes were a joyful interpretation of the southern hankering for hot breads at every meal.

Catfish fritters were lightly battered bits of heaven, served with subtle pickled okra. Speaking of pickling, the tangy pickled collard greens were just fine, too, though they might be even better with some boiled potatoes to soak up more vinegar. Louisiana shrimp boil did come with small potatoes that had been cooked in the boiling broth. Deep-fried okra was served with an amazing corn-and-pepper relish. Where could this tender corn come from? There is no such corn anywhere near New York City, surely. It tastes so akin to summer corn that I imagine squadrons of planes flying it in from some sultry clime . . .

But back to reality, which at Savannah is good enough for me. I have never eaten such dainty dumplings, such firm yet tender stewed chicken as Sara Bonner's chicken and dumplings—not at home, and certainly not in a restaurant. This is the best fried catfish I have eaten in New York. It tasted like catfish I remember—that whiskered fish is part of some of my very fondest childhood recollections—and the clingy, fragile batter is better than most I recall. With the fish came tasty "dirty" rice (made with small-chopped chicken gizzards and livers) and succotash that contained more of that stellar corn. Catfish isn't on the menu, due to a printing error, but don't worry, it's in the kitchen.

Fish and shrimp went into a judiciously spicy fish stew, smelling and tasting of garlic and tomatoes, but never overwhelmed by them. Meat loaf with enough filler to make it almost delicate was blanketed by onion gravy, served with perfect mashed potatoes and succotash. The succotash also was tossed with from-scratch noodles and butter for a homey dish that cannot be called pasta because they're American, and it's noodles, by golly. Moist smothered pork chops came with baked, cut-up sweet potatoes. Seasonings were perfection, so I never even thought of asking for a bottle of Tabasco as I usually do at southern eateries. (A huge, fresh bottle of that vibrant hot sauce arrived with a sizable appetizer of crisp-fried chicken wings, however.)

"Mama's" fried chicken, peppery and crisp, juicy within, would make you proud if your mama made it. Alas, our portion did not have the promised cream gravy on it. With gigantic, meaty ribs there was oniony potato salad fit to take on a church picnic. High-quality ham steak was fried on the griddle and swathed with gingery gravy. Ham hocks with white beans and collards might be too heavy for most New Yorkers, and even I would not have minded a few more beans and a few less hocks. Only bluefish, stuffed with a too-sugary oyster and cornbread stuffing, missed the mark. One other slight criticism: cloth napkins would be a thoughtful addition. Paper ones shred under the kind of hard use they are likely to get with a plate of fried chicken.

Brownie pie with double-chocolate ice cream was inspired, a treat even for someone who usually prefers vanilla. Sweet-potato pie, wisely low on sugar, was encased in a thin crust, a crust that seemed to contain pecans. Apple cobbler and apple turnover (with a winning accompaniment of cinnamon ice cream) were made with feathery pastry, bananas Foster cooked not a minute too long in a bit of butter and brown sugar. (On the bananas, vanilla ice cream goes better than chocolate, so ask for it.) Bits of candied lemon peel were scattered over the ice cream (vanilla) atop the bananas Foster one night.

Many New Yorkers, like the Bonners, came from some place else. I did, too. After a while, New York knocks us around, and we all start to get hard around the eyes. The same sort of thing could happen to this good food. I hope it won't.

TACOMADRE

2345 Broadway
(212) 873-0600

HOURS: Daily, 9 a.m.–11 p.m.
PRICES: Lunch/dinner items $2.44–$9.95. Breakfast 75 cents–$1.75.
ACCESS: Ramp at entrance; restrooms equipped for disabled.
KIDS: No children's menu but will accommodate.
HOW TO FIND IT: At corner of 85th Street; subway line 1 to 86th Street/Broadway station; bus line M86, M104.

The burritos keep coming. For a few months, denizens of the Upper West Side waited, none too patiently, for TacoMadre to open. Months ago, one of my best scouts, Victor, called to mention that something was happening on Broadway just above 85th Street.

"Great news!" wrote another food friend, Molly, who's the bubbly type. She said TacoMadre was set to open Monday. "The menu looks bodacious!" she went on. She mentioned the sincronizadas, the latest thing since tortas hit town. (Tortas are big puffy rolls stuffed with Mexican sandwich fillings.) Sincronizadas have the same fillings—chile-soaked pork to name just one example—sandwiched between thin flour tortillas and grilled.

Monday, on schedule, TacoMadre opened. Barely half an hour later, Ari, another pal who lives nearby, called to report he had eaten a bean-and-cheese breakfast burrito for only 75 cents.

Maybe it was because of the chalkboard outside TacoMadre hawking the 75-

cent special—you can't buy much else for less than a dollar these days. Maybe it was the fact that neighborhood people were pining for salsa and things to eat with it. Maybe it was because TacoMadre looked inviting, with its cool white walls and blue tiles, stainless-steel counters, earthenware pottery and ceiling fans. Whatever the reasons, TacoMadre was popular from practically the moment it opened, with the blue-washed wooden stools at the counters occupied almost all the time.

In the morning, before lines formed for lunch, we wrapped our mouths around the bargain burrito, a flour tortilla with pinto beans and melted cheese tucked inside. We sampled a slightly tough but tasty corn tortilla with scrambled eggs and green chile peppers. These and other breakfast burritos, served 7 to 11 a.m., are not quite as luxuriantly overstuffed as those I remember from South Texas. They are more like snacks. But, hey, I'm just happy to be able to get breakfast burritos in New York. (Based on a chorizo and egg torta I ate one day for lunch at TacoMadre, I am eager to try the chorizo, egg, onion, tomato and potato version of the breakfast burrito.)

In the morning, we like to hang out and watch the grill full of tomatoes being roasted for salsa, the bubbling pots of beans, the wide pan of mushrooms sautéeing for vegetarian sincronizadas.

At lunch, you can't beat a cardboard container of sopa de lima, $1.75, a peppy chicken-tortilla soup zesty with the bright tang of lime. Chicken salad Mexican style, with perfectly ripe avocado and a chipotle-pepper apple vinaigrette, was milder but fresh and fine. Red-chile marinated pork, called al pastor, was terrific inside a soft tortilla with grilled onion and a squeeze of lime juice. (All dishes come with flour tortillas, unless you ask for corn, and are served on red plastic plates.) Chile Colorado was tender beef simmered in red chile and wrapped into a burrito with cheese and beans—a choice of refried, our pick, or charros (pinto beans) or black beans. We tried and liked a savory mushroom sincronizada, too.

Most items come with a choice of sauces: green sauce made from tomatillos, fresh tomato-based salsa, super-spicy salsa Costena, molcajete made of roasted tomatoes and chiles, and ranchero, a less spicy version made with roasted tomatoes.

We were mildly disappointed in the tortas, puffy rolls spread with beans, avocado and a thin slice of onion. Chicken cutlet and egg-and-chorizo fillings were tasty but overwhelmed by the surrounding bread. And the vegetarian torta of avocado, tomato, black beans and sprouts just didn't have enough flavor to take on so much white bread. Scooping out the innards of the roll so there would be more filling in proportion to bread would improve the sandwich.

There's Pepsi, alas, instead of Coca-Cola. But nothing could spoil our impromptu picnic at a nearby bench on a sunny, windy day. We improvised by borrowing milk crates for extra seating, but if you find the setting, TacoMadre will pack you a Mexican picnic ($27.50 for five, up to $80 for 15). If you bring an ice pack, you could even add some scoops of intense mango or coconut sorbet (our picks over the usual lemon and raspberry) to your picnic, though they are not included in the price.

Chef Conrado Ramos heads up a cookline of fast, efficient workers wearing blue TacoMadre caps. Taquerias, wrote Ramos on the menu, "come in every size; some are no more than pushcarts with kerosene stoves. Some are sleek and modern. They have in common their delicious food, fresh and fast." TacoMadre lives up to this description—sleek and modern, fresh and fast. Every neighborhood could use one.

TIBET SHAMBALA
488 Amsterdam Ave.
(212) 721-1270

HOURS: Dinner Monday–Friday, 6–11 p.m.; Saturday–Sunday, noon–11 p.m.
Lunch Monday–Friday, noon–4 p.m.
PRICES: Entrées $6.25–$8.95; appetizers $3.95–$6.25; same menu for lunch but
with specials starting at $5.50. No liquor license; bring own bottle. MC, V.
RESERVATIONS: Recommended for weekends.
ACCESS: Dining area wheelchair-accessible.
HOW TO FIND IT: Between 83rd and 84th Streets; subway line 1 to 86th Street
station; bus lines M7, M86.

At Tibet Shambala, owner Norbu Tsering greets you serenely. The mood is
catching. There's a picture of the exiled Dalai Lama, whom Tibetans call
"His Holiness," on the saffron-yellow wall, and soothing flute music plays in the
background. Once Norbu gets to know you, he may even welcome you with a
little homily.

A friend who is a regular there said that Norbu once said something like this
to her: "We all have a lotus seed inside of us, and when we perform acts of
kindness, it blooms into a beautiful lotus blossom." He then opened his
hands, she said, like the petals of a flower unfolding. Tsering's wife, Tashi, and
daughter Phuntso cook, and Norbu Tsering, assisted by his nephew Tensing,
waits tables.

It was not only the Tserings and the atmosphere that we found appealing,
though. We were wild about spicy chasha tsoila, a sort of shredded chicken
Tibetan style, and equally good was ngo-tse avo, nicely seasoned chick peas and
potatoes with onion for tang and avocado for counterpoint. It's kind of south-
western, actually. Sautéed black-eyed peas were blended with tofu, potatoes, garlic and ginger in a cold dish known as thaba nenzom.

But Tibet is, in some parts, a land where vegetables don't have a long growing season and meat is the main thing. (Vegetables do grow in Eastern Tibet,
next to China; that's the source of the avocados in Tibetan cuisine.) Delicious
possibilities include sha momo, hearty steamed dumplings (a bit like pierogi)
stuffed with beef and scallions, and sha gyathuk ngopa, pan-fried noodles with
vegetables and beef. In the chicken category, you won't want to miss chasa
shamdey, a kind of chicken curry made with yogurt, and chasa khatsa, chicken
braised with chile peppers and onions. Order a bit of dey, the Tibetan version of
pita bread, to mop up any extra juices.

Tibetan desserts are not exactly what you're used to. Even deysee, rice pudding made with yogurt and served warm, is not a typical American rice pudding.
The homemade yogurt is delicious on its own, and if you ask for sho shindok,
you may have it with fresh fruit.

Tibet Sambala is uncommonly peaceful, and it is an uncommon place in other
ways, too. You don't get spices sent from the owner's sister in Katmandu at most
neighborhood restaurants. You don't get philosophy on every street corner,
either. One night, Norbu Tsering said, talking of the teachings of the Dalai
Lama, "I hope more people can learn about Tibet philsophy and way of life. You
do not have to adopt all of it, but maybe there are one or two things that could
be useful to you in this life—or in a future life." I think so.

BROOKLYN

BEST CAFÉ PEARL
303 Brighton Beach Ave.
Brighton Beach
(718) 891-4544

HOURS: Tuesday–Sunday, noon–11 p.m.
PRICES: Entrées $7–$17.50; one menu. AE, DC, DS, MC, V.
ACCESS: One step at entrance; dining area/restrooms wheelchair-accessible.
RESERVATIONS: Recommended for weekends.
ENTERTAINMENT: Varied live music, including Russian, Friday–Sunday evenings.
HOW TO FIND IT: Near Brighton 3rd Street; subway line D to Brighton Beach
Avenue station; bus lines B68, B1.

The Best Café Pearl really is the best.

It's the best for potatoes and pork chops and pickles and pig's knuckles. And
Pearl is the best because it's the one place I know of where it is possible to order
thin, slightly smoky, grilled eggplant wrapped around a subtle walnut filling and
drizzled with deep purple-red pomegranate juice. This dish is unearthly, and all
by itself it would be reason enough to hang out at Café Pearl.

But let's start at the beginning. Anya Von Bremzyn, my friend who wrote the
wonderful cookbook called Please to the Table, discovered Café Pearl. Anya
knew the Café was there, but no listing could be found in directory assistance.
Further investigation unearthed the fact that it was listed as the Best Café Pearl.

Once you're there, please give your coat over to the man who checks coats;
it's the right way to do things here. (In Russia, coats are always checked.)

The dining room has a dance floor with bright lights underfoot, and on weekends there is live music. Then, reservations are a must and there's a minimum of
$10 a person. On a weekday night, though, you are likely to find only a few
other patrons listening to CDs of Natalie Cole.

The ideal thing, of course, would be to take my friend Anya with you for the
ordering. She speaks the native tongue and can, practically without a glance at
the menu, order a parade of delicacies to be delivered to the table family-style.

This is a good thing, since the translation sometimes defies comprehension:
"broiled vegetables on tender hooks" is still a puzzlement to us, and we are not
positive that we had trout "Gordon." Since you may not be lucky enough to have
a translator along, I am going to tell you some of the highlights in plain English,
and if you describe them to the waiter, you should be able to get them. Here goes:

No. 23, herring with onions, is a deceptively simple dish. Order the plump
pickled herring, almost hidden by the generous stack of raw onion rings on top,
as Anya would—with potatoes. The fish is sublime when eaten with chunks of
fresh-roasted potatoes, perfectly browned and showered with fresh parsley. (This
is unusual; in other neighboring cuisines, the potatoes would be boiled.)

Eggplant with walnuts. Is this No. 4, or No. 5? Don't worry about it, just order and be happy. This is utterly unlike any other eggplant dish I've had anywhere else. The zesty walnut filling is magically good inside the paper-thin eggplant, and the drizzle of bittersweet pomegranate is genius.

Dumplings. Tell the waiter you want the lush lamb dumplings, hinkali, that look like little hats. At the top of each beautiful steamed dumpling, there is a small knob, or handle. When the dumpling cools enough, pick it up and suck juice and filling out of the bottom of the dumpling. That's the right way. If you break it with a fork, you will lose lots of the precious juice.

Eggs in Georgian style. This is a typically Georgian dish, hard-cooked eggs in a delicate sauce of fresh coriander and yogurt. (Homemade Georgian yogurt is thin, almost thin enough to drink.)

Pickles. The crunchy, garlicky red-cabbage pickles are my favorite here, but I'm partial, too, to the watermelon pickles (sour and garlicky, not sweet) and pickled lettuce.

Pig's knuckles. These are soaked in a peppery paprika marinade and cooked till tender. Their somewhat gelatinous quality make them just the thing for absorbing shots of vodka—or should I say that vodka is just the thing with pig's knuckles?

Kebobs. Go wild, order them all: marinated pork chops, supremely meaty and tender. Small rib lamb chops, hefty spareribs. (Chicken was too rare near the bone, alas.) The kebobs come piled high on a platter with freshly made wedges of french fries, almost-charred tomatoes and roasted peppers.

Trout kolkhida (or colchis, in English). Steamed inside grape leaves with lots of lemon, the trout we got actually might have been salmon trout, or Coho. Whatever it was, it was delicious, with lots of citrus seeping into the crispy-soft, edible leaves.

Chicken tabaka. This beautifully fried chicken was generous on garlic and good juice, and of course, oh joy, it came with more potatoes. (They make potatoes in all different shapes and sizes at Pearl, and garlic and parsley are never spared.) This dish, perhaps the best-known Georgian dish, is named for a heavy iron pot used to cover the chicken and at the same time press it down to flatten it. On the side in a little pitcher, there's a tangy, garlicky tomato sauce.

Dessert? Turkish coffee or desultory American coffee; have tea instead. And start thinking about the next time you'll come to Pearl. Maybe you'll call a day ahead and bring a big group for a suckling pig roast. I'll see you there.

CAMBODIAN CUISINE
87 S. Elliot Pl.
(718) 858-3262

HOURS: Daily, 11 a.m.–10 p.m.
PRICES: Entrées $3–$6.50; appetizers $2–$3.95. Lunch $3–$3.50.
ACCESS: Dining area/restrooms wheelchair-accessible.
RESERVATIONS: Recommended.
KIDS: No children's menu but will accommodate.
HOW TO FIND IT: Between Lafayette Avenue and Fulton Street, one block from LIRR Flatbush Avenue station; subway line G to Fulton Street station or line 4 to Atlantic Avenue station; bus lines B26, B38, B52.

Just let the folks at Cambodian Cuisine feed you. Even if you think you are familiar with Cambodian or Vietnamese food as cooked in New York City, there are apt to be some unfamiliar, but delicious, things on this menu. The sense of discovery, too rare these days, abounds here.

This food is something like Thai and Vietnamese food—in fact, it used to be called South East Asia Cuisine—but there are French, Indonesian, Chinese and Indian influences. "Less fat—better than Chinese food," says the menu. But no comparison is needed; Cambodian food is its own self—unique.

Chris Ley, the service part of the husband-and-wife team, remembers what you have liked in past visits and suggests dishes you might like to try this time. (Once when I walked in, Chris, who is Khmer, cried, "Oh, we just sold the last B18, the one you liked so much!" Remember that number, for a rich, out-of-this-world curried soup with potatoes.) Chris' husband, Jerry Ley, who is Cambodian-Chinese, cooks food to order, one or two things at a time. They're an unbeatable duo.

You'll find a modest little coffee shop that has minimal decoration, unless you count the little Buddha shrine that blesses the venture. Prices are minimal, too. It is difficult to spend more than $10 per person, even for a feast. Friends I took to the old S.E.A. were so taken with the good food and low cost that they started begging Chris and Jerry to move to their neighborhood, Park Slope.

Maybe some far-distant day, said Chris. The rents are too high there. In the meantime, you'll have to go to where they are, and it's well worth the trip.

You might start with A3, cold Cambodian spring rolls, or naem chao, two wafer-thin rice pancakes rolled around a fresh, crunchy filling of shrimp, bean threads and other shredded vegetables. To some tastes, A7, the "hot & spicy ground meat appetizer," much like the larb found at Thai restaurants, may seem offbeat. To me, it just seemed tasty; you scoop up bits of the greaseless, crisp-fried beef and eat it on top of slices of carrots and cucumbers that come arranged around the meat on the plate. Either of these starts is an amazing $2.

Kuey Teo koke, or "soupless noodles," was a bowl of sesame-sauced cellophane noodles—"Mix it well," Chris cautioned—that put many pallid versions of Chinese sesame noodles to shame. Three dollars! Enough to share! (OK, that was just to get your attention. I'm going to stop telling you every single price. They're all incredible, trust me.)

Similarly, mee bampong, fried noodles similar to the more familiar Vietnamese mee krob, were a mixture of crisp-tangy-slightly sweet taste thrills. For a milder but incredibly flavorful dish, you might try sarmchoke rice broth, similar to China's soothing congee, with lots of squid and other seafood in it.

We imagined we might be getting close to full when "homestyle" bean curd with bok choy, mushroom and cabbage arrived at our table, but our appetites revived as if by magic, testament to the goodness of the dish.

Talapia in a spicy lemongrass sauce was so outstanding that it left me lusting for the Mekong fish chop, which, the menu explained, would be "fried in chili sauce." In the meantime, I was more than content with samlor mchoo srae, a hot, spicy shrimp soup.

It's hard to think of a single thing we didn't like—probably because Chris didn't allow us to order anything she thought we might not enjoy. (At some restaurants, you might chafe at this restraint; here, you simply feel that you are in good hands.) Perhaps the most unusual dish of all, though, was a steamed, shredded chicken dish known as chicken ahmok. The moist bits of fowl were pressed into a kind of cake that included coconut juice, lemon leaf, lemongrass and coriander, and the luscious result was prettily trimmed with slivers of red pepper.

To go with everything else, you may have white or brown rice, Ovaltine, coconut soda, the sweet "French" iced tea or iced coffee Cambodian style, dripped over sweet condensed milk.

Dessert? Don't be silly. I'd rather have another bowl of noodles.

EL MAGUEY Y LA TUNA RESTAURANTE
533 Grand St.
Greenpoint
(718) 963-3333

HOURS: Thursday–Tuesday, 11 a.m.–11 p.m. Closed Wednesdays.
PRICES: Entrées $1.95–$7.95.
ACCESS: Dining area on one level.
HOW TO FIND IT: Between Union Avenue and Lorimer Street; subway line G to Grand Street/Metropolitan Avenue station; bus lines Q59, B48.

Not long ago, Robert Sietsema called to tell me about El Maguey Y La Tuna, a restaurant named for two kinds of cactus, both pictured on the front of the eatery's business card. When Sietsema talks, I listen.

That's because he writes and edits "Down the Hatch," which, as you might suspect from the title, is about things to eat. So we hopped on the L train and headed for Brooklyn.

El Maguey is one spacious room, decorated with some of the usual serapes and sombreros. But there the resemblance to most other Mexican restaurants ends. This is real down-home food, the kind working-class people in Mexico must eat happily day in, day out. You can tell that it's not combination plates and pseudo-Mex the moment you look at the menu and see legnua, or tongue, tacos listed.

The red sauce is that red-velvet sort made of ancho chile peppers. The green sauce is perky but tamer. Even the chips have a satisfying earthy taste. Clearly, they are made in a home kitchen, not mass-produced. The tortillas are mostly—or maybe always—corn here, not flour, which to me is the real way, the Mexican way. The chile peppers are fresh, the cerveza (Bohemia and other Mexican brands) cold.

We tried delicious tacos de carnitas (made with pork), al pastor (with well-seasoned lamb), and de carne, (with crumbled chorizo, or sausage). They were all delicious, but one of the best things about them was that they only cost $1.50 each. We ate steamed tortillas, true daily bread, out of a basket, slathering them with long-simmered pinto beans, and shrimp in garlic sauce (priced, amazingly, at $3.25). And whatever you do, don't miss chile rellenos, fresh peppers stuffed with cheese.

This is one of the three places where you can get molé three ways, all good: there's poblano, a sweetish version with sesame seeds; ranchero, bitey and deeper brown; and verde, chunks of chicken tossed in a green tomatillo sauce.

Good as all these were—and they were excellent—perhaps my favorite was taquitos al guacamole, crisp tacos stuffed with potato and ground meat the night we had them, then topped with guacamole, sour cream and a sprinkle of cilantro. These were so fabulous that we even ordered seconds. Robert thinks they are made different ways on different days, though they are always topped with guacamole. Once, he said, they were made out of chicken instead.

Get the chuletas (pork chops), get the soup—everything is sure to be good here, I think. I don't have time to tell you more right now. I have to rush out to look at the patisserie Robert just told me about, the one with honest-to-goodness baguettes.

HARPO GOURMET RESTAURANT
181 West End Ave.
Manhattan Beach
(718) 743-6900

HOURS: Sunday–Thursday, 4:30–10 p.m.; Friday–Saturday, 4:30–11 p.m.
PRICES: Entrées $8.50–$16.95; appetizers $3.95–$6.95. AE, MC, V.
ACCESS: Two tables near door wheelchair-accessible; otherwise restaurant/restrooms are tight.
RESERVATIONS: Recommended for Saturday.
KIDS: No menu but offers half-portions.
HOW TO FIND IT: Near Hampton Avenue, just over a block from the head of Sheepshead Bay. Subway line D to Brighton Beach station, then take B1 bus line. Also bus line B49 (on West End avenue).

In one of the old Marx Brothers movies, Harpo tests Groucho's food to see if it is poisoned. Harpo keeps shoveling it in and gesturing to Groucho that it is no good—until he has eaten it all, because it's so good.

If Harpo had tasted the food at his namesake restaurant, he would have eaten all of it, too, we feel certain. It's that good.

Manhattan Beach is a quiet Brooklyn neighborhood near the shore, tucked between Brighton Beach and Sheepshead Bay. It's mostly residential, and if pressed to guess on some trivia quiz, most people would probably tell you there are no restaurants in Manhattan Beach. So Harpo is something of a hidden treasure.

The owner's nickname is Harpo, but his real name is Wing Chan. He and his wife Jenny Kuan run the restaurant together when they're not engaged in one of several other lines of work. Chan, who got his nickname because he was quiet, used to hate being called Harpo but found that it was a bonus in his work as a hairstylist. When not styling hair at Salon 3757 in Manhattan, Chan is busy finding the best Chinatown produce, developing vegetable stock for vegetarian patrons and, as a sideline, running yet another company that sells gold-leaf and silver-leaf picture frames.

The attractions of the restaurant, the only one of their businesses with which we are personally familiar, are many. To start, you might try mozzarella cut into cubes and fried, clearly a superior homemade version of the popular prebreaded sticks of cheese one sees in so many restaurants. The creamy mozzarella is also available in another classic combination, with fresh roasted peppers. Fresh mushroom ravioli is always on the menu, though the sauce changes from day to day. And there's a seafood-stuffed ravioli sauced with something so rich and creamy it makes me glad it has been deemed safe (or safer than margarine, anyway) to eat butter again.

For an extravagant seafood starter, you'll want to try amazingly light puff pastry stuffed with shrimp, crab and scallops. If your tastes are plainer, crusty bread topped simply with chopped tomatoes and basil makes a fine bruschetta. Standard appetizers such as thin-sliced smoked salmon, shrimp cocktail and prosciutto with melon are all carefully selected and of excellent quality.

Canadian quail rubbed with thyme and grilled were succulent, and grilled shell steak with an unexpected dill treatment was flavorful. Moist chicken breast with tarragon is a tried and true pairing, but slightly offbeat possibilities—large shrimp with chardonnay and fresh sage—seem to work here, instead of seeming contrived just for the sake of being different. Partly, this is because Harpo's hand with seasonings is restrained. Meat and fish entrées came with lightly sautéed fresh vegetables—lately, zucchini, broccoli or pencil-thin asparagus. The special baked potato is mashed with onions and butter, put back in the shell and rebaked; either the spud or rice also came with entrées.

Penne with shrimp and radicchio in a delicate cream sauce was another slightly unusual combo. For a heartier pasta entrée, consider three-colored fettuccine sauced with an old-fashioned tomato-based veal sauce to which chicken and mushrooms were added. Tagliatelle in fine, fresh pesto sauce and bow ties in a champagne sauce with fresh salmon were other highlights on the pasta section of the menu. If you prefer your salmon without pasta, choose handsomely grilled salmon with capers and lemon instead.

None of these menu items are startlingly different, but they are just different enough to make you notice. Dessert, too, is reassuringly familiar for the most part, just elevated by uncompromisingly high quality. Chocolate paradise (billed as "the ultimate chocolate cake"), a rustic apple torte, good tiramisu, dense carrot cake and suave white-chocolate mousse were all just dandy. But the dessert we were wild about was called ice cream with "starburst sauce." On two different trips to Harpo's, we had seductively soft, lush, homemade vanilla ice cream on a bed of sauce that seemed like essence of fruit, once apricot, the other time raspberry. Espresso, stern and black, seemed an antidote to such sweet pleasure. Lately, alas, Harpo has not been able to find the fruit sauces, which are imported from Paris, but he swears he will keep looking.

JOE'S OF AVENUE U
287 Avenue U
Gravesend
(718) 449-9285

HOURS: Tuesday–Thursday and Saturday, 11 a.m–6:45 p.m.; Friday, 11 a.m.–8 p.m.
PRICES: Entrées $6–$7.50; appetizers $2–$3.50. Lunch $3.75–$4.25.
ACCESS: Dining area wheelchair-accessible, restrooms are not.
KIDS: No menu, but will accommodate.
HOW TO FIND IT: Between McDonald Avenue and Lake Street; subway line F to Avenue U/McDonald Avenue station; bus line B3.

Joe's of Avenue U is one of the last bastions of old-fashioned Italian food. The ingredients are prime: Colavita olive oil, San Marzano tomatoes, top-notch dried pasta, fresh fish that puts most other "fresh" fish to shame. The prices are absurdly low, considering the high quality.

Every Friday, there is pasta con sarde, the humble yet glorious dish of sardines, wild fennel, pine nuts and, on the side, sautéed bread crumbs. Once, perhaps, the bread crumbs were a substitute for more expensive grated cheese; nowadays, they are an authentic detail of Italian soul food—food made from simple ingredients, seasoned with ingenuity born of necessity.

Waverly Root, in his book, The Food of Italy, writes that Palermo is the home of pasta con sarde, and Joseph Ciaramitaro, who founded Joe's in 1955, came from Palermo. In other parts of Sicily, those he questioned seemed not to know of it. "Perhaps," writes Root, "other localities have renounced trying to reproduce this dish, knowing that they would be incapable of holding a candle to Palermo, which makes almost a cult of it." That's easy to understand when you eat pasta con sarde at Joe's.

At Joe's of Avenue U you will find vastedda, a thin piece of calf's spleen folded into a sandwich with both soft and hard cheese, all inside a piece of focaccia. If this sounds odd to you, don't knock it until you've tried it. It is an utterly delicious coming together of flavors. Panelle, thin sheets of fried chick-pea dough, may also be had the same way, tucked inside a wedge of focaccia and smothered in cheese. Or you may order the crisp panelle separately, three nifty little pancakes for the bargain price of $1.25. And the big, homey rice ball, $2, is best under a cozy blanket of cheese and good red sauce.

Tony and Camille Gagliano, the pals for whom Joe's of Avenue U is a tradition, confided that Enzo Ciaramitaro, who with his brother, Paul, does most of the cooking, had told them the source of the well-priced San Marzano tomatoes that go into the sauce. It's generous and neighborly of him to share his source. Enzo's sauce is memorable for what it is not; it is not too gussied up with oregano and other spices, and it is not overcooked. It is tasty enough that you may want to just eat it with a spoon. I did.

One of the finest ways of eating this admirable sauce is with lean, lightly spiced sausage and chunks of falling-apart potato. The potato soaks up the flavor of the tomato sauce to great advantage. Or eat tomato sauce as part of a homey tripe stew with peas and poatoes simmered with the tender tripe.

On your way into Joe's dining room, you'll pass most of the dishes of the day, waiting on warming trays. They never wait for long, evidently, because everything tasted fresh.

Don't miss a sprightly polpo, or octopus, salad; succulent and lemony baked clams and lightly breaded, crisp-fried calamari. On Friday, baccala alla Siciliana, moist codfish cooked with green and black olives, was a special and it was perfection. Cod with escarole, another Friday special, was wonderful, too. And be sure to put in your order for one or two plates of broccoli rabe, steamed with garlic and oil; sometimes Joe's runs out.

The substantial, simple food is so satisfying that you won't really need dessert. Lucky, because none is offered. There is demitasse, however.

Just finish off your second carafe of rustic red vino—$7, and the only choice is the house wine—and be happy. (There's also a house white by the same California vintner, Opici.) As Tony and Camille pointed out, another restaurant they know of is charging $12 for that very same house red.

The food may be Italian, but Joe's is true to that old American slogan: For a square deal, eat (and drink) at Joe's.

This next review is by Suzanne Curley, a Newsday *reporter, but when you fined Senegalese food in Fort Greene, you don't quibble about authorship.*

KEUR N'DYE
737 Fulton St.
Fort Greene
(718) 875-4937

HOURS: Tuesday–Sunday, noon–10 p.m.
PRICES: All entrées under $10.
ACCESS: Steps into restaurant; restrooms not wheelchair-accessible.
HOW TO FIND IT: Between South Elliott Place and South Portland Avenue; subway line G to Fulton Street station; bus lines B25, B26, B38, B52.

Opened by immigrants from Senegal, Keur N'Dye (meaning "The House of Dye"—Dye being one of the proprietors) is a small, inviting eatery with clean lines and a comfortable feel. White and wood-trimmed, with African art on the walls and lighting fixtures carved from hollowed-out gourds, it holds obvious appeal for the many neighborhood residents who flock here for inexpensive, authentic dishes from West Africa. When weather permits, the French doors along the whole front of the restaurant open onto the street, giving the place the air of an urban European café.

Deciding what to eat here is easy because there are fewer than a half-dozen main courses (beef, chicken or fish, with one vegetarian selection) chalked in on the small blackboard hung by the kitchen door. And the affable young man who waits tables enjoys helping newcomers choose.

Appetizers ($2.50) are two: either sautéed slices of perfectly ripe plantain, or pastels, a kind of fried ravioli stuffed with a delicately spiced ground-beef mixture. Entrées, each of which costs less than $7, include chicken with mildly spicy tomato-peanut sauce—other versions of which abound all over Africa. And Keur N'Dye offers a delicious interpretation of yassa, a typical Senegalese dish of marinated chicken or fish cooked in a silky, transparent lemon sauce with onions and green olives; its flavor is much like that of those wonderful Moroccan stews called tagines, which are made with preserved lemons.

Vegetarian couscous is, like the other entrées, served attractively, on a small, curved wooden platter: a mound of couscous with steamed zucchini, carrots, yucca and okra alongside. Although the shiny red sauce looked pretty, it didn't add all that much in terms of flavor. And while our waiter had urged us to try the fish-and-vegetables platter because it is a version of tiebou dienne, Senegal's national dish, the boniness of the fish made it only a qualified success. (All main dishes here come with either plain white rice or seasoned red rice, and with some of the entrées there is a choice of either beef or chicken.)

Among the beverages are a very sweet and spicy (i.e. sharp) home-brewed-style ginger beer and sorrel, a soft drink made from a "weed" that, according to our waiter, is highly regarded in folk medicine as a blood-purifying tonic.

There's no liquor license here (the proprietors are Muslim), so bring your own beer or wine if you like. However, Keur N'Dye itself is so comforting and relaxing and convivial, you may find you don't even feel the need to imbibe.

LA BOUILLABAISSE
145 Atlantic Ave.
Brooklyn Heights
(718) 522-8275

HOURS: Monday–Saturday, 5–11 p.m.; Sunday, 5–10 p.m. Lunch Monday– Friday, noon–2:45 p.m.
PRICES: Entrées $8.95–$18.95; appetizers $4.50–$6. Lunch $6.95–$14.95.
ACCESS: Small dining room, but will help accommodate wheelchairs; restrooms not accessible.
RESERVATIONS: Taken only for groups of six or more.
KIDS: No children's menu but will accommodate.
ENTERTAINMENT: Occasional (call).
HOW TO FIND IT: Between Clinton and Henry Streets, 2 blocks from Brooklyn-Queens Expressway, 2; subway lines 2 or 4 to Borough Hall station; bus lines B25, B38, B45, B52, B65, B63.

La Bouillabaisse is in Brooklyn.

So what, you may say. But the people in this neighborhood don't say that. They say, "C'est magnifique!"

There were plenty of Mideastern places hereabouts, the occasional Mexican restaurant, and even Cajun victuals, across the street. Tucked away in a residential part of Brooklyn Heights, there was even a moderately priced French restaurant. France, however, was hardly one of the ethnic groups you expected to find represented along Atlantic Avenue.

Never before had there been good French food at truly low prices in part of the borough, and La Bouillabaisse is cause for celebration.

This slip of a restaurant is filled nightly with eager patrons, and more are usually waiting by the door. Owner Amanda Green deftly juggles tables. (You may wait while you're sitting at the table, too, but nobody seems to care.) The people become the decoration, and they are people you might want to know. That's a good thing, because the space is so small that joining into conversations at neighboring tables becomes almost irresistible.

"When I saw Janet Reno on Bill Moyers, I just wanted to go there and say, 'Let me work for you,'" said a woman scrunched into a table behind me. How could I refrain from telling her that I am the self-styled president of the Janet Reno Fan Club? "Sign me up," she said.

A few chalkboards are propped here and there to list the dishes of the moment: Meaty Jersey tomatoes plated with fresh mozzarella; skinny, beautiful sautéed asparagus, a crab cake that's nearly all crab, goat cheese with a poached pear as a first course instead of dessert, robust, well-seasoned chicken soup so good you only wish your mother had made it, mussels in a lush, winey sauce perfect for dipping. (The slices of white baguette in the basket will do for dunking, but the multi-grain bread has too much taste of its own and, at most, ought to be dipped in the little bowl of herb-suffused olive oil.) Whether or not you order an appetizer, dinners came with a lovely salad, for which chopped tomatoes are marinated in the vinaigrette and become part of it.

Chef-partner Neil Ganic pays homage to his stint at Elmer's, a Manhattan steak house, with a small, perfect steak mignonette in a pepper-sparked sauce with slightly crunchy carrots and tiny new potatoes carved into fat buttons, a bit of skin left on them. Would that it could be on the menu every night. The hot seafood platter that's often on the menu had a bit of a peppery bite and was generous with lobster and crab as well as the less expensive mussels and clams, but a nutcracker would have helped in extracting the meat from the claws; perhaps you should bring your own. The house trademark bouillabaisse was made of good fresh seafood, too, but one night the tomato-saffron broth seemed was tamely seasoned; more saffron, expensive though it is, would help. The next week, the bouillabaisse had more pep.

The pasta you must not miss is tomato linguine in a fresh tomato sauce; most tomato pasta does not really taste like tomato, but this does, possibly because it was cooked with the pasta briefly. It's a wonderful idea. Less mind-expanding but still tasty were green ravioli in a pink sauce, agnolotti in a creamy sauce. Grilled chicken Dijonnaise was served with gorgeous grilled eggplant and zucchini. Soft-shell crab was lightly breaded and fine. Lamb casserole—a stew, actually—was a homey melange of potatoes, carrots and, sad to say, slightly undercooked meat. But we felt forgiving, because we liked this place so much; "I'll take it home and cook it some more," said a friend. And she did.

Best endings were a delectable, not-too-sweet rice pudding, a dark-chocolate mousse and, another night, one of those super-rich chocolate cakes. Cappuccino mousse had a pleasing flavor but was too runny. Regular decaf coffee was strong and fresh.

LA LOCANDA
432 Graham Ave.
Williamsburg
(718) 349-7800

HOURS: Monday–Saturday, 8 a.m.–9:30 p.m. Closed Sunday.
PRICES: Entrées, $6–$14; appetizers $2–$6; pizza $1.25–$3.50, pies $9– $14, special pie $20.
RESERVATIONS: Accepted on weekends but there are only eight tables, plus outdoor seating in warm weather.
ACCESS: One step up into restaurant; restrooms wheelchair-accessible.
KIDS: No children's menu but will accommodate.
HOW TO FIND IT: Between Withers and Frost Streets; subway line L to Graham Avenue station; bus lines B18, B24, B62.

Grandpa Michael DiGruccio makes the fresh semolina bread, and it comes to the table still warm.

Energetic Maria Colombo, DeGruccio's daughter, makes deliveries in the neighborhood, double-parking and dashing inside with the food. "Come after one-thirty," in the afternoon, she tells regulars, "so I can give you more attention."

Her husband, Cono Colombo, stays behind the counter making pastas as fast as he can. Sometimes, the couple's 10-year-old daughter, Rachele Colombo, even helps her mom, charming customers in Italian or equally fluent English and scrubbing down tables with zeal. (Rachele can write "pasta e fagioli" on a dinner order quicker than you can say it.) Isuf Krasniqi is the pizza maker.

La Locanda is most definitely a family business. It may look like a humble pizza parlor, but don't let that fool you. This is some of the tastiest Italian food in the borough. (Actually, the place looks spiffier in the evenings, when the deep-green lace curtains are drawn for a cozy look.) The Italian men you see sitting in here schmoozing know this, and they probably have been eating Italian food much longer than you have. Trust them.

I ate things at La Locanda that I've never had before, and that's saying a lot. I had never eaten pie filled with escarole and white beans, the airy crust brushed with egg yolk. As soon as I did eat this exemplary, elemental meal of bread and vegetables, I began to think about when I might be able to have it again. There were light little spinach rolls made with the same crust, and eggplant rolls, too, and a two-crusted potato-pepperoni pie, and more traditional open pies. All were absolutely fresh and first-rate.

Instead of just ordering from the menu, go over to the counter behind which pizzas are being slapped into shape and look at the prepared dishes. You are apt to find delicacies you simply can't resist. One such find was pepperonata made of eggplant, peppers, potatoes, zucchini and the like, served warm. Another was chicken with vinegared peppers and potatoes, the good flavors of the peppers soaking into the chicken and the potatoes. The chicken, reheated, was slightly tough compared to the tender, made-to-order chicken scaloppine with lots of lemon and fresh broccoli. Another delicious chicken dish was made with peppers and peas.

Prices for huge platters of wonderful pasta were absurdly low. You won't find better bucatini alla amatriciana, made with tomatoes and pancetta, in any fancy restaurant in Manhattan, and here a generous serving was only $5.50. Ziti alla puttanesca, pungent with anchovies, capers and olives, may be had for that same price, and it was nearly as good. Robust tortellini alla Bolognese—with meat sauce, that is—cost only a dollar more, $6.50.

Hearty soups, a meal in themselves with some of that fragrant semolina bread, cost even less, $4.50. The homemade cavatelli, which is also available with sauce for $6, can't be beaten when it is the soup of the day, flavored with a lightly tomatoey broth. Pasta e fagioli was done the way my Italian friend, Beatrice, does it, the way it always tastes better, with varied lengths and kinds of pasta and creamy beans. (I did need a dash of hot pepper to give the pasta e fagioli oomph.)

When my pal, Gus, was hungry for fish, he persuaded the cook to send him a dish of garlicky scampi, $7, even though it wasn't Friday, usually the only day fish is on the menu. I haven't been there on Friday, but if you go then, you can get shrimp several ways, linguine with red or white clam sauce, fried calamari or a seafood platter, at $10 the most expensive dish on the menu. I usually can't pass up pasta for a chicken or veal dish, but a friend had pounded, grilled chicken with balsamic vinegar and salad, $6.50, and it was unusually juicy.

When a friend begged for dessert, sturdy little Rachele was secretive. "They don't have dessert," I explained. Just espresso with thick crema, and well-made cappuccino. Or how about a Manhattan Special, the beloved coffee soda that is made near here? Just as I was mollifying my friends by saying that we could always go to Fortunato's, a pastry shop and coffee house of excellent repute, four slices of light cheesecake pie appeared. No dessert is listed, or visible, but this sort of thoughtfulness seems to be the norm at La Locanda.

LEMONGRASS GRILL

61A Seventh Ave.
Park Slope
(718) 399-7100

HOURS: Monday–Thursday, noon–10:30 p.m.; Friday–Saturday, noon–11:30 p.m.;
Sunday, 1–10:30 p.m. Closing may be extended one hour in summer months.
PRICES: Entrées $5.95–$8.95; seafood $13.95–$16.95; appetizers $3–$5.95.
ACCESS: Dining area wheelchair-accessible (one step into garden); women's
restroom accessible, men's restroom narrow.
RESERVATIONS: Accepted for groups of six or more.
KIDS: No children's menu but will accommodate.
HOW TO FIND IT: Between Lincoln Place and Berkeley Place; subway line 2 to
Grand Army Plaza/Prospect Park station; bus lines B41, B67, B69.

Hann Low and his family hail from Malaysia, but it seems there is no kind of cuisine they can't tackle successfully.

The Low family owns four Fujisan restaurants, three in Brooklyn and, most recently opened, one in Manhattan's Chinatown. They own Rex, a Manhattan club and restaurant. They also own Christopher's, an Italian restaurant on Seventh Avenue in Brooklyn. Now, the Lows have opened another sure-fire crowd-pleaser, Lemongrass Grill, across the street from Christopher's.

Lemongrass Grill was such an instant hit that a line is the rule rather than the exception.

The gentle serving staff handles this crush of customers in unflappable fashion, and the kitchen staff just keeps cooking at top speed. Chile peppers practically explode over the flames, causing the open cooking area to grow somewhat smoky, which it often does. Somehow, I don't mind the haze; it makes me feel as if we're all in this together, chefs and customers, hanging out in the kitchen.

Sip a perfectly iced Singha beer, so right for quelling chile pepper fires. While you wait for food to arrive, play the game of identifying some of the provisions that hang from bamboo rods around the edges of the kitchen—chile peppers, banana leaves, lotus flowers, tamarind. It's a nifty way to keep things tidy.

Start with tom yum gung, hot and sour lemongrass broth with fresh shrimp afloat (instead of the traditional dried shrimp) and well-seasoned with lime juice. The white Thai chicken soup, gai tom kha, made with coconut milk and bamboo shoots, was a good alternative.

A favorite starter with our crowd was Thai barbecued wings that could make you forget Buffalo. These crispy wings were marinated with lemongrass, chile, turmeric and garlic, and they had a more complex hotness than most hot wings about town. Both beef and chicken satay were good quality and came with an ultra-peanutty sauce and slightly sweet cucumber salad. Food here has more of the flavor punch that comes from passionate ingredients such as chile, lemongrass and coriander, to name just a few, and less of the cloying sweetness some other Thai restaurant owners seem to think customers want. An excellent case in point is pad Thai, the by-now-familiar rice noodles stir-fried in peanut sauce with shrimp, dried bean curd and sprouts. (In general, ever since I started adding the words "not too sweet" when ordering pad Thai, I have had better luck.) We also were smitten with kwaytio ki mow, broad rice noodles sautéed with tomatoes, basil, sweet soy sauce and bean sprouts.

Calamari salad, dressed with fish sauce and a squeeze of lime juice, was tossed peppers and mint leaves. Tod mun pla, the somewhat-chewy fish cakes, were served here with string beans and lime leaves; if you haven't tasted this type of fish cakes before, the texture may take some getting used to.

As long as we are talking string beans, they were sautéed with dried bean curd and goodly amounts of garlic for a winning vegetable dish. In season lately has been another knockout vegetable dish, flamed water spinach stir-fried with garlicky black bean sauce. Water spinach has broad leaves and seems more tender than the crinkly kind that we (here at BQ Eats) don't much like much anymore. Eggplant sautéed with black beans and lime leaves was also a treat; being a vegetarian here is easy. For a somewhat tamer dish, try kana namman hoi, Chinese broccoli steamed with sesame oil, shallots and a bit of garlic.

Lar nard, broad rice noodles stir-fried in soy sauce and topped with brown gravy, was a delightfully homey dish. We also liked khao goon chiang, rice fried with Chinese sausage and the mint fried rice tossed with chicken, mint and chile.

Vegetables, starters, rice and noodles were so appealing that entrées were almost an afterthought. But we can recommend green-curried chicken with basil and eggplant, and massaman kari, a coconut-milk curry built around chicken or beef with tamarind juice, peanuts, and, to soak up all those good flavors, potatoes. Then there's red beef curry made with coconut milk and coriander. Fish dishes we liked included pla jean, seared salmon burnished with a gingery coating, and pla lard prik, a crisp whole fish (though not the snapper the menu mentioned) well seasoned with chile, tamarind and garlic. Gai pad prik haeng, cashew chicken, was good, too. Be sure to order sticky rice and eat it as they do in Thailand, rolling a bite of it into a ball between your fingers.

After all these good things, dessert seemed silly, so we skipped it and abandoned our table to the next folks waiting in line.

LENTO'S PARK SLOPE
833 Union St.
Park Slope
(718) 399-8782

HOURS: Monday–Thursday, 11:30 a.m.–midnight; Friday–Saturday, 11:30 a.m.–1:30 a.m.; Sunday, noon–midnight.
PRICES: Entrées $9.50–$16.95; pasta $6.50–$8.50; appetizers $2.50–$7.25; pizza $8.50–$16. Lunch specials $6–$9. AE.
ACCESS: Wheelchair-accessible; restrooms equipped for disabled.
RESERVATIONS: Recommended for Friday–Sunday and for parties of six or more.
KIDS: No children's menu but will accommodate.
PARKING: Garage across from restaurant.
HOW TO FIND IT: Between Sixth and Seventh Avenues; subway line 2 to Grand Army Plaza/Prospect Park station or lines M, N or R to Union Street station; bus line B67 (on Seventh Avenue) or B71 (on Union Street, to 9 p.m.)

I'm having a hard time writing a full, fair, balanced review of Lento's Park Slope, because there's only one thing on my mind. It's pizza.

Lento's pizza is so outstanding that try as I might to order other things, I found myself always ordering more pizza instead. I took a hardy crew of eaters with me and tried to persaude them to order a wide array of other foods. They nibbled at pretty-good pasta and a delicious meatball hero, and even a chocolate-caramel Snickers pie, but once they tasted the pizza, they all wanted another pie, and I don't mean Snickers.

So this is about pizza, which is, after all, what made Lento's a legend. Here's how it happened.

In 1933, just after Prohibition, Eugene Lento (who came here from Calabria) and other Lento family members owned a small string of Brooklyn bars. The flagship was an old speakeasy on Third Avenue in Bay Ridge. After repeal, it was a bar again, an old, comfortable bar. And pizza (well, maybe beer, too) was the reason you went to the one remaining Lento's. Gene Conners, Eugene Lento's grandson, now owns Lento's Park Slope along with partners Arthur Della Croce, Chris Walsh and Greg Coyle. (Conners inherited part of the business from his father, Herbert Conners.)

Without any fancy equipment—no brick oven, no live coals—Eugene Lento figured out a way to make pizza crust that was exceedingly thin without being tough or too brittle. This is a trade secret, of course.

As a friend said upon tasting a Lento's (Park Slope) pizza for the first time, "This is the matzoh of pizzas," so thin and crisp is it.

Lento's partner Arthur Della Croce—he bought into the business about seven years ago—said it's hard for him and the other partners to relate to what it is that makes people so crazy about Lento's pies. "We've lived with it for so long," said Della Croce, a long-time family friend. "We are so accustomed to it being the way it is; we make a pizza pie the way you would make a cup of coffee."

That is part of the secret. When you make something every day, day in, day out, you get good at it. While Linda Calabrese, a granddaughter, manages the Bay Ridge location, chef John Jenkins and pizza makers Peter Della Croce (Arthur's son) and Peter Smith turn out the pies at the Park Slope. That's why you may notice subtle variations in the pie—the crust a bit browner, the blisters of cheese more prominent—but nothing that spoils the overall effect.

The exceedingly low amount of crust to cheese and sauce is part of what makes Lento's pizza special; because of the unusual ratio, the cheese (fresh mozzarella) and sauce (tangy but not acidic) meld into the pizza so that the one harmonious whole is achieved. Think about it—in all too many pizzerias elsewhere, the cheese and sauce sometimes peel away from the crust when you try to bite into a piece. At Lento's, this never, ever happens. The ingredients bond to one another.

The basic pizza ($8, no slices sold) is the best way to have a Lento's experience. I always like to add a few generous shakes of red pepper flakes.

To make a fitting setting for a pie of this caliber, Gene Conners, the elder Della Croce and other partners acquired a high-ceilinged old carriage house right across from the Park Slope Food Co-op and restored it themselves. The substantial old bar came from the now-defunct Dixie Tavern on Fifth Avenue and 20th Street in Brooklyn. The bar, at least 70 years old, was sanded, polished and cut down, all by hand, to fit the Lento's space. The original doors of the carriage house, too big and unwieldy to use as front doors, have become a decorative feature at the back of the spacious dining room.

Yes, you can have handsomely grilled pork chops ($10.95), good with a squeeze of lemon and some mashed potatoes. Yes, you can have Anchor Steam, Bass and Guinness stout on tap. The ravioli and the greens with garlic and olive oil are top-notch. But pizza, as the menu category says, is "how we built our reputation."

LOS MARIACHIS MEXICAN RESTAURANT
805 Coney Island Ave.
Midwood
(718) 826-3388

HOURS: Dinner Monday–Thursday, 2:30–11 p.m.; Friday–Sunday, 2:30 p.m.–1 a.m. Lunch Monday–Thursday, 10:30 a.m.–2:30 p.m.; Friday–Sunday, 10 a.m.–2:30 p.m.
PRICES: Entrées $6.95–$18.95; appetizers $1.50–$2.50. Lunch $3.95–$5.95. AE, DC, MC, V.
ACCESS: Dining area/restrooms wheelchair-accessible.
RESERVATIONS: Required for parties of 10 or more.
KIDS: Children's menu, $1.50–$3.95.
ENTERTAINMENT: Mariachi bands Fridays and on most holidays.
HOW TO FIND IT: Between Dorchester and Cortelyou Roads; subway line D to Cortelyou Road/East 16th Street station; bus lines B23, B68.

Manhattan has its share of both fancy Mexican restaurants and big-burrito bargains. But to find the real roll-up-your-sleeves, working-class Mexican restaurants, check out some of the Puebla-style Mexican eats in Brooklyn, where rents are often lower.

Los Mariachis, which opened about a year ago, is an example of the sort of Mexican restaurant that's somewhere between fancy and funky. Bright as a new penny and decked out in red poinsettias, it is decorated with vivid serapes and sombreros and staffed by waitresses wearing festive, traditional dresses of white, trimmed in red emboidery. The staff speaks Spanish, and that's a good sign, but one of the owners, Rosa Fuentes, is fluent in English as well. The good smells of steaming tamales and the large number of Mexican customers are other harbingers of happiness. So are the iced beer mugs that come with the Negra Medelo beer.

The down-to-earth food is the best news of all. Even before you order, you will be welcomed with an earthenware tray whose compartments are filled with a thin but snappy ranchero sauce, a mild green sauce, sour cream, guacamole and a generous batch of freshly made tortilla chips for dipping.

At lunchtime, wonderful tamales and soft, rolled tacos are only $1.50 each, and if at dinner you order other, more substantial platters of food besides, the chefs will let you have some then, too.

Pork-and-corn tamales, steamed inside cornhusks with a velvety, deeply satisfying red sauce were our personal favorites, but those prepared with a mild green tomatillo sauce were also first-rate. The red-colored "sweet" tamales were strange to us, more like dessert, but maybe we could learn to like them. Our pick of the soft tacos was shredded roasted pork with lots of crisp edges and chopped scallions.

No previous eating experience is needed to fall for the chorizo sandwich ($3), a bewitching combination of crumbled, browned Mexican sausage layered inside a sturdy bun with beans, jalapeños, guacamole, lettuce, tomato. These were so good that we always order a torta, or sandwich, as a kind of side dish to whatever else we are having.

At Los Mariachis, it seemed right to skip such nueva Mex fare as Mexican "pizza," though no doubt that dish would taste fine. Instead, we went for the cool, lime-tinged taste of seviche, shrimp tossed with chopped onion, cilantro, tomatoes and just enough fresh jalapeño pepper to jolt taste buds awake without setting them afire.

At my favorite Mexican hangouts, creamy refried beans come to the table unbidden, with baskets of warm, steamed tortillas, true daily bread. I like to slather the tortillas with beans, roll them up like small, cozy bean tacos and eat them in a few bites. Here, that is exactly the way it happened.

Standards such as chicken mole, a dark, rich sauce containing four kinds of peppers, are done very well indeed here. For chile relleños, vivacious red sauce blanketed chile peppers stuffed with white cheese. Sizzling shrimp fajitas with crisp onion were splendid one night, shrimp mildly fired with poblano peppers a good choice on another occasion.

Several menu items are unusual—in particular pork and zucchini slices stewed in a mellow pumpkin sauce. There's a homey chicken stew and sesina, well-seasoned steak, pounded thin and quickly grilled.

Thick, luscious papaya and mango shakes, served with fanciful straws, are good accompaniments to this cuisine if you don't care for beer or a decent margarita served in a wide, flat champagne glass. Jarrito, the long-necked Mexican soda, is available in such refreshing flavors as grapefruit and non-alcoholic, carbonated sangria. You can get Orange Crush in icy long-necked bottles, too.

For dessert, there's the usual flan and a sweetly old-fashioned treat, a banana split, really just bananas topped with vanilla ice cream, served in a genuine banana split dish. When I ate it, I realized that what I used to find excessive about banana splits was the syrup; the dish is better when it's simpler. This way, it's more like banana ice cream, a too-seldom-seen flavor. Or end a feast at Mariachis with a soothing cup of Café con leche, coffee with heated milk.

We'll be back on the weekend to try cabrito, barbecued goat served with chile-infused vinegar and a stack of warmed tortillas.

NEW CITY CAFÉ

246 DeKalb Ave.
(718) 622-5607

HOURS: Tuesday–Thursday, 5:30–10:30 p.m.; Friday–Saturday, 5:30–11 p.m.; Sunday, 4–9 p.m. Lunch Tuesday–Friday, noon–2:30 p.m.
PRICES: Entrées $17.50–$29; appetizers $4.50–$8.50; Sunday 5-course tasting $30. Lunch $10; 2-course tasting $15. AE, MC, V.
ACCESS: Three small steps down at entrance; dining area/restrooms wheelchair-accessible.
RESERVATIONS: Recommended.
KIDS: No children's menu but will accommodate.
HOW TO FIND IT: Near Vanderbilt Avenue; subway line G to Fulton/Lafayette Streets station; bus lines B25, B38, B69.

Do I have a sweet little restaurant for you! New City Café seats only 40 patrons at a time, and dinner there can turn an ordinary day into Valentine's Day.

New City, housed in the bottom of a landmark brownstone, circa early 1900s, has two fireplaces. Graceful white tulips, forced from bulbs, decorated the tables, and an antique Hoosier hutch was used as a sideboard. Every carefully selected plate at our table for four was different, and all were exquisite.

The menu is limited and will change with the seasons. Right now, it leans toward the French, with touches borrowed from Latin and Asian kitchens. The music leans toward Louis Armstrong and Billie Holiday, and that's all right with me.

Rebecca Scanlon, the twentysomething (well, almost 30) chef, studied at the French Culinary Institute. Raoul Richardson, her partner in the restaurant gig and in life, smoothly manages the front of the house while she cooks everything to order. Why, we asked Raoul, did you open in January, the month everyone has sky-high credit-card bills to pay? So we could practice, he answered.

As a starter, the salad of now-familiar but pristine "baby greens" hinted of spring in its lush vinaigrette subtly flavored with roasted garlic. Black bean soup had great depth of flavor and a fillip of fresh cilantro. When one diner in our party asked for chopped onion to put on top of the soup, Raoul demurred. "Taste it," he said. He was right.

Fresh vegetable-filled spring roll was formed into the shape of a playful miniature arch, encased in a thin, dainty wrapper and served with a few splashes of tomato-infused oil. Succulent pan-roasted shrimp were served with scallion cakes (too plain and too much like pancakes one night, better another) and not-quite-enough achiote sauce.

Scanlon has an imaginative flair not only with the entrées but with accompaniments as well. Her beautifully executed salmon, a juicy, pan-seared filet, was set over a bed of salsify and leeks with a citrus-tanged beurre blanc. One night, thin crisp rounds of lotus were served with it. Cornmeal-dusted catfish came with an earthy toss of black-eyed peas and barley and two tidy bundles of long-cooked (yet by no means overcooked) carrots. Chicken breast in a pan sauce that involved fresh thyme came with soothing whipped potatoes.

Slow cooking must be something of an article of faith here, for unless I miss my guess, wood-grilled breast of duck was treated to a long, slow cooking, which brought out subtleties of flavor so often missed. This handsomely browned duck was served with soft corn pudding and a sauce tinged with juniper berries and sage. Wood-grilling also gave wonderful flavor to a sirloin steak, served simply in a red wine sauce with pommes frites so thin they were like chips. A side dish of seasonal greens turned out to be perfectly sautéed spinach.

Though I'm seldom a fan of breads that are sweet alongside savory courses, all bets were off when it came to the thin slices of pecan-raisin bread that are one of the choices at New City Cafe. There were also well-made, properly crusty hard rolls from Eli's and slices of a moist, robust whole-grain loaf studded with a few caraway seeds.

Chocolate souffle was sweet bliss, served with a silver bowl of fresh whipped cream and chocolate sauce. House-made blackberry, raspberry and strawberry sorbets were refreshing, and lemon mousse had a lovely zest. Apple cobbler with vanilla ice cream was so good you wanted to ask for seconds. (Good espresso, too.)

NOODLE PUDDING
38 Henry St.
Brooklyn Heights
(718) 625-3737

HOURS: Tuesday–Saturday, 5:30–10:30 p.m.; Sunday, 4:30–9:30 p.m.
PRICES: Entrées $6–$12.

ACCESS: Dining area/restrooms wheelchair-accessible.
RESERVATIONS: Taken only for groups of 6 or more.
KIDS: No children's menu, but will accommodate.
HOW TO FIND IT: North of Cadman Plaza, between Middagh and Cranberry Streets; subway line A to High Street/Brooklyn Bridge station or line 2 to Clark Street/Brooklyn Heights station; bus lines B41 and B45.

The card for Noodle Pudding read "Col calore d'Ischia" (With the warmth of Ischia). I'd already eaten there before I picked up the business card. In fact, I'd blown in with a friend from the neighborhood without ever knowing the name of the place, and perhaps this was a good thing.

It was a good thing, because maybe I'd have passed up a place called Noodle Pudding, just because I wasn't in the mood for kugel. And I would have been wrong, so wrong. There is no kugel on this menu. Instead, it has a decidedly Italian bent, and it is a wonderful addition to the Heights.

Perhaps it was even for the best that I hadn't seen the card yet. I knew nothing about the Ischia connection, and if I had, I might have thought twice, for my memories of Ischia, the Italian island, were not wholly positive. To be specific, we visited Ischia so quickly we had no time for food.

Here's how it happened—and we'll get to the food of Ischia-in-Brooklyn in a moment. Ever the impressionable traveler, I had boned up on Italian islands. Ischia and Procida—both, like Capri, reachable from the Bay of Naples—sounded unspoiled and idyllic. The way I recall this book, it made Capri sound all tarted up and touristy. I wanted, of course, to go to Ischia, the less-spoiled island.

With my sweetheart and his daughter in tow, we set sail from Naples to Ischia. Once we arrived, we took some sort of jitney to a beach the book said was gorgeous. After one look, the daughter's chin began to quiver. This? This was one of Italy's finest beaches? her reproachful look said. The sand was black, the strip of beach was narrow, and it was crowded. She's a good sport, but, hey, once you've seen Jones Beach, Ischia loses its allure. Decisive action was called for. Before our blanket touched the sand, I swept it up and said, "We're leaving." No argument from my fellow travelers.

Via speed boats, we island-hopped to Procida. There wasn't much there to appeal to a teenager's fancy, either. Somehow, finally, that same day, we came to Capri. The sand was white and wide, though by now the sun was setting over it. We knew why people went to Capri, and we knew we ought to have gone there in the first place.

As for Noodle Pudding, the moral of the story is reversed. Don't try all the other places in the neighborhood first, just go to Noodle Pudding and be happy. It's a find.

In a formerly jinxed location decorated by satisfied eaters, the food is simple and well-made, but never boring. Alberto Yimgngz, known to family and friends as Pistolero, was a dishwasher who worked his way up to chef, working for owner Antonio Migliaccio at a restaurant he has since sold, Caffe Carciofo, on Court Street. (Migliaccio is, by the way, from Ischia.) Noodle Pudding is popular, but it feels more peaceful here than just across the water in Manhattan.

A hearty cream of mushroom and chicken soup was a robust beginning. Bruschetta alla Caprese (of Capri, that is) was three huge slabs of country bread (not the same one as in the basket, alas) topped with chopped tomato and basil. Baked out-of-season asparagus with fresh mozzarella could not have been lovelier, and at $5, it was a steal. The wild mushroom souffle was sort of mushy, not wholly successful, but it came with a red-pepper sauce that pepped things up.

Perhaps my favorite among the pastas was a soulfully simple sauce of sage and scallions in butter sauce, served with bucatini—the long pasta that's hollow in the center, to let the saged butter soak in. A few shavings of excellent aged Provolone, and it's a wrap. I imagine that's how pasta would have been in Ischia, if only I had had some. The sage sauce was a special that should maybe become a regular menu item, but angel-hair pasta bathed in a cozy sauce of fresh tomatoes and basil was perfection, too. And another special, radiattore, the pasta charmingly named for its radiatorlike squiggles, was divine with a rich sauce of gorgonzola and some small, light meatballs.

Tender lamb osso buco with red-wine sauce, a special, was a serendipitous match for peppered fettucine. Marinated loin of pork with broccoli rabe was robust with flavor. We asked for some polenta on the side, and that was simpatica with the bitter greens and the pork, too. Calves' liver alla Veneziana, with onions and pancetta, was not completely tender. But service was good, and we shrugged and started to think about next time: Pasta again? Always, with a perky arugula salad. Chicken scarpariello over linguine for $8? Sure thing.

We sipped good espresso, tasted a pal's good tirami su. We could not have been more contented on any island, not even one in Italy.

NORTHSIDE RESTAURANT
124 Bedford Ave.
Williamsburg
(718) 388-4200

HOURS: Tuesday–Sunday, noon–9:30 p.m.
PRICES: Entrées $3.50–$5.50; appetizers $3–$6.
ACCESS: Wheelchair-accessible; restrooms equipped for disabled.
KIDS: Children's menu, $3.
HOW TO FIND IT: At North 10th Street; subway line L to Bedford Avenue station; bus line B61.

It speaks well of a place when guys who make their living selling beer eat lunch there even though it doesn't serve beer—theirs, or any other brand. My pals from Brooklyn Beer eat lunch at the place they call Raymond's—proper name: Northside Restaurant—more days than not. Hot tea goes nicely with the sturdy Polish fare at the Northside, I think, but usually the fellows have coffee or just water.

The guys from Brooklyn Beer like to sit at the table in the corner by the pot-bellied stove, and so do I. Right now the stove is merely ornamental, but someday it may be hooked up to a chimney. There are a few other decorative touches—the sparkly little lights twined through greenery on one side of the room, the soft glow from a lamp over by the self-service counter.

In most ways, though, the Northside, run by Raymond Lesniewski, is all practicality. At this cozy eatery Raymond dishes up food that is warm, filling and inexpensive. Prices are so modest that even neighborhood folks who are on pinched budgets can afford to eat out here. They may not know just how lucky they are; I'd rather have crisp, thin potato pancakes instead of a fancy dining room any day, and Raymond's potato pancakes are topnotch. I'd rather tuck into a bowl of warm, tangy sour-grass soup (also known as schav) than gaze at paintings. (I'm told that sometimes a truck pulls up to unload that sour-grass by the bale.)

Some noontimes Raymond is as busy as the proverbial one-armed paper-hanger—ladling up generous portions of hot food, running back to the kitchen to give a pot a stir, sprinting across the floor to deliver a dish to a table. There's some help, but Raymond does have the knack of seeming to be everywhere at once.

And the remarkable Raymond serves remarkable soups: There's zesty and heartening borscht, mushroom-barley, robust tripe stew. Best of all, the bowls of soup all come with a side of fresh mashed potatoes scattered with bits of crisp bacon. This side dish is heaven to eat on its own, but it's really meant to be added by the spoonful, as desired, to the soups. This thickens the soups a bit more, should that be your goal, but it also adds nutrition. (Not long ago I learned in a careful perusal of the Ronniger's seed-potato catalog—these folks out in Idaho are to potatoes as Petrossian is to caviar—that 73 percent of a potato's protein is easily utilized by humans and only eggs rank higher, at 96 percent. But I digress, as I so often do when it comes to potatoes.)

After a bowl of soup and a generous helping of bread, you may feel almost too full for anything else. Press on for lightly breaded and greaselessly fried chicken or pork cutlets, dandy omelets made to order and served with stacks of crisp rye toast, hunks of fresh roast pork, homey liver and onions, big meatballs with gravy and other rotating specials.

With entrées you're apt to get more mashed spuds, this time with gravy over them. And, as with an old blue-plate lunch of times past, there are always some wintry salads—good coleslaw, delicious homemade pickled beets, a pile of lightly dressed carrot slivers. Perhaps Raymond makes all these things, things lots of restaurants get out of cans and frozen packets, because it is less expensive in terms of real cash, if not in terms of labor. It is also better, and lucky for the customers.

Raymond's potato-stuffed pierogi with sour cream and fried onions are out of this world, and his potato pancakes set an example for others. If it weren't for the thin, slightly crisp cheese blintzes—the triangular kind—scented with vanilla, I'd skip dessert in favor of another order of potato pancakes.

You can eat a balanced meal of meat, potato and something green or pickled, or you can choose what amounts to the potato sampler—soup with mashed on the side, pierogi and potato pancakes. Either way, you'll go away supremely well-fed.

I can't resist giving you my other favorite fact from the Ronniger's seed-potato people, who got it from In the Garden by Sylvia Thompson: High up in the Andes, where potatoes were the staff of life for centuries, "the Incan unit of time was as long as it took to cook a potato." You'll be back at the Northside, I wager, in scarcely more time than it takes Raymond to cook the next day's potatoes.

PLANET THAILAND

184 Bedford Ave.
Williamsburg
(718) 599-5758

HOURS: Monday–Saturday, 11:30 a.m.–11:30 p.m.; Sunday, 1–11:30 p.m. Brunch Sunday, 1–5 p.m.
PRICES: Entrées $6.95–$10; appetizers $1.95–$3.25; one menu with some specials.

ACCESS: Dining area wheelchair-accessible, restrooms are not.
ENTERTAINMENT: Live jazz during Sunday brunch.
HOW TO FIND IT: Between North 6th and North 7th Streets; subway line 7 to Bedford Avenue/North 7th Street station; bus line B61.

I tense up whenever I hear that the owner of a restaurant I know and love is opening a second place. That means that the owner will have to divide his attention between two places, and I worry that the quality of the food at both places will decline.

When David and Anna Popermhem opened Planet Thailand, an offshoot of their popular Thai Cafe, a few months ago, the place was overwhelmed by fans right away. Lanky David stood loyally at the stove behind the counter turning out delicious dishes as fast as he could, while Anna stood at the register ringing up absurdly low prices for it. It didn't seem as if they would ever catch up, what with a full restaurant and at least an hour's worth of takeout orders.

The good news was that I ate at the tiny Thai Cafe, on Manhattan Avenue near Kent Street, and at Planet Thailand, too, and the food at both restaurants showed the young couple's care and enthusiasm. David, the cooking half of the couple, seemed to dash back and forth between the two places cooking, prepping and making sure everything met his exacting standards. (The Popermhems met when both were working at Au Bar in Manhattan. In a nod to Anna's Italian ancestry, there are some Italian dishes on the menu at Thai Cafe.) The bad news was that at Planet Thailand, there were long waits for food.

Now, all the news is good. On two recent visits to Planet Thailand, we got served within a reasonable time, and the food was better than ever. (We went at 6 p.m. and at 7 p.m., instead of the prime time of 8:30 p.m., and that may have helped, too.) Quilted stainless steel gives Planet Thailand the look of a diner, sturdy and ready for action. There's seating at tables and at the counter, where you have a ringside view of the food being prepared. Usually there are a few blackboard specials.

A salad of crisp green papaya, tossed with shreds of carrot for color and tangy with citrus and fish sauce, is a wonderful way to begin any meal. I have never eaten at Planet Thailand without at least one order of this lovely salad. Other appetizing starters included David Popermhem's own version of fresh spring roll with a subtle apricot sauce, different and more delicate than some you may have encountered, and fresh, crisply fried calamari. You won't see sate on this menu, but small morsels of well grilled "chicken on skewer" with a hearty peanut sauce will satisfy a desire for that very item. A chile-fired shrimp soup was another fine choice. Steamed mussels fragrant with basil and lemongrass had only one drawback: There was no bread for mopping up the sauce, and no spoons for eating it like soup.

Room-temperature salads are perfect for entrées. Consider, for example, a handsome squid salad made with plenty of cilantro, lemon juice and onion, and a smattering of cucumber and tomato. And ground beef was pungent with basil, spicy with onion and chile pepper. There's a similar basil beef dish, made with sliced meat, and it was just as tasty.

I am powerless to resist David's robust, well made chicken massaman curry in a rich coconut-milk peanut sauce, with chunks of potato soaking up all the good curry and peanut flavors. If you thought you were tired of chicken, your appetite for it will revive here. Don't miss the grilled half chicken, marinated in a house mixture of herbs and lusciously juicy.

Nobody does a better pad Thai, the famous stir-fried noodle dish that may be ordered here with shrimp, chicken or vegetables. Just to try something different, we also ordered spicy noodles with seafood and were rewarded with a delectable toss of wide, soft noodles with vegetables and shrimp.

An utterly fresh whole sea bass was splendid in slightly gingery, garlicky sauce. The fish was so good that a Chinese friend reproached me for ordering sticky rice ($1 a bowl) before we finished it, admonishing that rice is only eaten last to fill in any hungry spots. I know, I know. It's just that I love the rice so.

Our busy waiter had no time for charm, but he was efficient and unflappable. Was he warming up to us when he offered us chopsticks? Perhaps. (I seldom ask for them; historically, Chinese conquerors brought chopsticks to Thailand and, traditionally, they are not used with Thai food.) Green tea ice cream made a refreshing dessert.

Months ago, a Greenpoint artist commented that it simply was not possible to feed the entire neighborhood of artists from two stoves, the ones at Thai Café and Planet Thailand. David Popermhem may be proving that it's not so impossible after all.

PRIMORSKI

282B Brighton Beach Ave.
Brighton Beach
(718) 891-3111

HOURS: Dinner Monday–Friday, 5 p.m.–2 a.m.; Saturday, 4 p.m.–2 a.m. Lunch Monday–Friday, 11 a.m.–5 p.m.; Saturday–Sunday, 11 a.m.–4 p.m.
PRICES: Complete dinners $20 Monday–Thursday, $25 Friday, $27 Saturday–Sunday. Lunch $3.99.
RESERVATIONS: Recommended.
ACCESS: Dining area wheelchair-accessible; restrooms downstairs.
ENTERTAINMENT: International caberet Sunday–Thursday, 8 p.m.; Friday–Saturday, 9 p.m.
HOW TO FIND IT: Between Brighton 2nd and 3rd Streets; subway line D to Ocean Parkway station; bus line B1.

We ordered the table to be spread, as my new friend Anya von Bremzen puts it, at Primorski last summer.

As is usual at Russian nightclubs, the table was crowded with the cold potato salad that has come to be known as Russian salad, garlicky eggplant salad, a salad of walnuts and red beans, cold smoked tongue and smoked fish, salmon caviar and what seemed like dozens more dishes. These were replaced with pelmeni, the Siberian dumplings filled with meat and sprinkled with dill. Then came several meats, fruit, and, finally, pastries. All this set us back $27 apiece. This abundance amply cushioned the shots of vodka, included along with music and dancing.

This was, I saw recently, a mere snack.

I saw this, because last week I went to Brighton Beach with Anya, who, with John Welchman, has just written a Russian cookbook called "Please to the Table," or, in the Soviet Union, prosim k stolu. It's like saying "Let's eat!" in Russian.

At lunch with Anya, grapey red Georgian wine and Marlboros accompanied the well-spread table. "The way you drink in Georgia," shrugged Anya, "you open the vat." She spoke a few words to Bubba, the bearlike and genial owner, and food appeared. It kept on appearing for hours. Misha Gulko, the energetic one-man band who plays at night, appeared and made an exception by doing a daytime medley. Then there were kisses—on both cheeks, of course—all around.

They were garlic-infused kisses, to be sure. By that time, Anya and I had feasted on mildly garlicky eggplant salad with mayonnaise; eggplant "caviar" zesty with garlic, red beans and walnuts; spinach with walnut and garlic sauce; mushrooms several ways; fresh broiled sturgeon; lamb shish kebab under tangles of onions and served with dill-flecked coleslaw and tkemali, a green plum sauce to mimic the Georgian version made of pomegranate juice, garlic, cilantro and hot pepper.

We liked savory pelmeni better than sour-cherry-stuffed vereneki; the pastry seemed a tad tough, but perhaps we were merely getting too full.

Did we want Stroganoff, asked Bubba, as we contentedly ate blini with sour cream and salmon caviar? No, we said. But we couldn't resist a few bites of coriander-scented, lamb-stuffed cabbage or nuggets of fried potato with garlic dill sauce.

And that's not all. We pretty well polished off a plate of marvelous, garlic-infused pickles: crunchy carrots, sprightly cabbage, tart watermelon. The watermelon is an Armenian treat, said Anya, the cabbage from Georgia, the whole pickled tomato traditional to the Ukraine. This is not Russian cooking, said Anya, but Soviet cooking.

Weakly, aided by strong dark coffee, we lifted forkfuls of kartoshka, a dense mixture of rum-soaked sponge cake, chocolate, butter and nuts. A mere bite was enough. Anya said it was all right to leave other desserts untouched. When your grandmother stands in line six hours to buy an orange, as happens in the Soviet Union, a refusal to eat it is a rejection of love, said Anya. But this is America, and you don't have to eat everything on your plate.

QUEEN ITALIAN RESTAURANT
84 Court St.
Brooklyn Heights
(718) 596-5954

HOURS: Monday, 11:30 a.m.–10:30 p.m.; Tuesday–Thursday, 11:30 a.m.–11 p.m.; Friday, 11:30 a.m.–midnight; Saturday, 2 p.m.–midnight; Sunday, 2–10 p.m.
PRICES: Entrées $11–$16; appetizers $6–$8.
ACCESS: Dining area wheelchair-accessible; restrooms equipped for disabled.
RESERVATIONS: Taken only for groups of eight or more.
KIDS: No children's menu but will accommodate.
HOW TO FIND IT: Between Schermerhorn and Livingston Streets. Subway lines 2, 4, N or A to Borough Hall station; bus lines B75, B41.

Queen is not just another Italian restaurant. The exuberant list of daily specials is so long that sometimes the restaurant's management is hard-pressed to fit it onto one sheet of paper, so they lengthen it by pasting it to a second sheet.

You may have been laboring under the delusion, as I was, that Queen is mostly a pizza parlor. Wrong. But that is a part of its history.

Anthony Vitiello founded the Queen at another Court Street location in 1958 as a pizza and hero shop. A few years later the store next door to the pizza ovens was, as the legend on the menu will tell you, made into "a white-tablecloth restaurant." Nearly three years ago the Queen moved to its current spot. Alas, not long afterward, the founder died. But sons Pasquino, who attended New York Institute of Technology's cooking school, and Vincent carry on. Old ways are treasured, new ones smoothly incorporated.

This is a rave. So I'll dispense with any attempt at fancy writing. Food such as this needs no embellishment.

Even the bread was unusual—homemade focaccia and flat, unleavened bread known as "music sheets."

Spiedini alla Romana, Italy's answer to grilled cheese, served with a savory anchovy sauce, proved that regular menu items can be as good as the specials. If further evidence had been needed, the extraordinary zucchini fritti would have provided it. Almost everything else we ate was a special.

"Where on earth do the Vitiello brothers get such incredible string beans, and how do they cook them so perfectly?" my friend Ted asked. He was eating some with sautéed Portobello mushrooms. (Although his question was mainly rhetorical, part of the answer is a pressurized steamer.)

Blood oranges have been on the menu lately, as part of a salad with fennel and red onions, as lovely to eat as it is to look at. Strips of endive were lightly marinated in vinaigrette (the quality of the olive oil is high at Queen), then served with fresh beets and meaty olives from Calabria.

Small, earthy Gaeta olives went into a dish of sautéed broccoli rabe with pine nuts one night, and just when we thought nothing on earth could taste better than that, we took a mouthful of outrageous escarole sautéed with potatoes and pancetta, the Italian bacon. To die. Tiny pastina-like pasta called acini di pepe was combined with lentils and broccoli rabe for a soup so satisfying it was difficult to share it.

One night there may be "candy wrappers," pasta twisted at the ends to resemble a candy wrapper, stuffed with escarole, mascarpone cheese and sun-dried tomatoes. (The hard, chewy knot at the twist is traditional.) There may be a light lasagna, with house-made noodles and filled with veal, or perhaps homemade gnocchi with zesty sausage (made here) and those fabulous string beans. And you haven't lived until you've tasted Queen's long fusilli with toasted bread crumbs and broccoli—simple but smashing.

Here are a few more perfect dishes to consider: tender, delicious osso bucco with peas and mushrooms, equally tender braised lamb shank with soft polenta, beef braciola with homemade gnocchi, homey veal stew with carrots, mushrooms, cream and toasty sticks of polenta. (Notice how side accompaniments change to suit the dish here.) Medallions of filet mignon with Barolo sauce were unearthly. We also liked linguine with baby artichokes, and a luscious chicken scaloppine with Gaeta olives, baby artichokes and fresh rosemary. And when there was a single thick veal chop left, we ordered it and exulted in our good fortune to be eating such excellent meat in rich brown natural gravy with thin-shaved Portobellos. There's a decent selection of wine at $13.25 to $24.75, with a few priced higher.

My 12-year-old pal Guy was enchanted to eat homemade ravioli for his main course, followed by warm chocolate raviolini filled with cannoli cream and served on a bed of crème anglaise with a chocolate tracery. Monte bianco, the chestnut purée, is sometimes on the menu here, and so is a creamy, cold zabaglione with blackberries. Chocolate mascarpone cheesecake was a dream, and cannoli filled with chocolate cream was a classic. Even spumoni and tortoni, the latter seemingly made of little more than almond-flavored heavy cream, were better than usual here. So was the espresso.

RASPUTIN
2670 Coney Island Ave.
Gravesend
(718) 332-8111

HOURS: Monday–Thursday, noon–11:30 p.m.; Friday–Sunday, 9 p.m.–3 a.m.
PRICES: Entrées $15–$22; appetizers $5–$12. AE, DC, MC, V.
ACCESS: Dining area/restrooms wheelchair-accessible (but steps at entrance; call ahead, staff will assist).
RESERVATIONS: Recommended for dinner.
KIDS: No menu but will accommodate.
ENTERTAINMENT: Friday–Sunday, 9 p.m. cabaret show.
HOW TO FIND IT: At Avenue X; subway line D to Neck Road station (then six blocks west); bus line B1.

Where do you begin? At the end of a rip-roaring Friday night at Rasputin, one of the more elegant Russian nightclubs, someone turned and asked me that question. Where, indeed?

There was the sumptuous spread of food—the blini with salmon caviar, the lush smoked sable and shad along with big bowls of perfectly boiled potatoes, the icy Absolut vodka and dozens of other good things to eat, not to mention the stellar service. We got clean plates at least 10 times, maybe more. There was the band, with Misha Botzman, a singer who belts out a tune in Italian as well as he does in Russian. There was the floor show, and maybe for the moment we'll just say ooh-la-la! (But keep on reading.)

To experience Rasputin at its most vibrant, go on a Friday or Saturday night, when both the kitchen and the entertainers pull out all the stops, and bring lots of friends.

You'll sit down to a feast of zakuska, the tidbits that make chilled vodka go down so well. (In the old country, some folks eat only black bread—which will be on Rasputin's table, too—or smell the sleeve of an old jacket when tossing back shots of vodka.) As Tatyana Tolstaya wrote recently in the New York Review of Books, reviewing an old Russian manual on cooking and housekeeping, vodka and zakuska are "indivisible. The word zakuska denotes specifically food that is eaten with vodka in order to temper the effect on the body." Vodka also paves the way for more food, and I have never really felt hung over from an evening of vodka and zakuska, followed by more food. (Nonetheless, you may want to designate a driver for the evening or call a car service.)

A handsome platter of smoked fish—silken salmon, plump sable, savory shad—was best eaten with the parsleyed potatoes. Help yourself to seconds from that platter instead of having the cold, sliced meats; tongue was too dry, and veal roast was nothing special. Gefilte fish was too dark and not top quality. But, oh! The pickles were wonderful—luscious hunks of salty watermelon pickle, big pickled tomatoes bursting with juice.

A tossed salad of tomatoes and onions was dressed in lively vinaigrette, and for a contrast note there also were bowls of Russian salad, the cold, mayonnaise-dressed vegetable salad that's on the order of a potato salad with peas. There were delicious thin blini with salmon caviar (fresher on a Friday than on a week-day night). Crowding the table in profusion were freshly grated purple horse-radish, white-radish salad, veal ribs with couscous, roasted meat and fowl and authentic, buttery chicken Kiev, mushrooms in a creamy sauce ("Four stars!" raved Gus, one of my favorite eaters.) A delightful creamy walnut sauce failed to hide the dryness of Georgian chicken. But if something isn't quite to your taste, just have another helping of something you do like; there's so much. Besides vodka, pitchers of seltzer, orange juice and cola with ice were available and were replenished frequently. (For an extra charge, juice is available, and you also can switch some or all of the vodka included in the prix fixe for wine or beer.)

Somewhere along about here in the meal, the band got very big, the strobes got dramatic, the dry-ice fog got very foggy—and out came high-kicking dancers with wig and costume changes galore. Not that there was that much to change, when it came to costumes as scanty (and glitzy) as these. The music careened wildly through many decades of American popular culture—class jazz stuff like Freddie Hubbard's waltz, "Up Jumped Spring," "Bei Mir Bist Du Schoen," the Yiddish song for which Sammy Kahn wrote the words and which the Andrews Sisters pop-ularized, on through pop clichés such as "New York, New York," complete with top hats for the dancers. The show goes on for hours, and afterward, there's danc-ing. Almost every table got at least one birthday cake, and the band played on.

And I do mean on. Eventually, we even got hungry again—should we have gotten a cake, too? Instead we picked at piles of grapes, oranges, melons and pastry.

On another night, we were happiest with the Russian items—pelmeni, dainty, well-made dumplings, pork chops, pickles and smoked fish. We did not hazard such faux French concoctions as filet mignon with dates and garlic, but we did try and regret a misguided risotto made with lobster and grapefruit. There is really no need to put on these airs when Rasputin's Russian fare is so good.

ST. MICHEL
7518 Third Ave.
Bay Ridge
(718) 748-4411

HOURS: Tuesday–Thursday, 5–10 p.m.; Friday–Saturday, 5:30–11 p.m.; Sunday, 4–9 p.m. Brunch Sunday, noon–3:30 p.m.
PRICES: Entrées $14–$21; appetizers $5–$7. Brunch $8–$13. AE, DS, MC, V.
ACCESS: Dining area wheelchair-accessible; restrooms downstairs.
RESERVATIONS: Recommended.
KIDS: No children's menu but will accommodate.
HOW TO FIND IT: Near 76th Street; subway line R to 77th Street/Fourth Avenue station; bus line B37.

St. Michel serves some of the best French food in any borough. The prices aren't low, but for food of this quality they are decent. St. Michel is elegant without being stuffy—none of that intimidating attitude that seems to come with certain French restaurants.

But will it play in Bay Ridge?

St. Michel is a high-ceilinged space with wide-plank oak floors, sconces shedding soft light, sheafs of wheat. The restaurant is a collaboration by chef Pascal Bettig, 35, and his brother Jacques, 31, former executive sous chef at The Water's Edge who manages the front of the house. The artistry is not so much on the walls as it is in the beautiful presentation of the food, easily a match for some of the finest plates and places in Manhattan. This is a celebratory Eats, with food that's a feast for the eyes and a carefully planned, yet affordable, wine list.

You will be welcomed with a basket of good bread; the warm onion bread was practically irresistible. Instead of butter or olive oil, help yourself to a savory vegetable spread, which changes according to the chef's whim. One spring night it was eggplant, red pepper, garlic and olives, and it was so delicious we asked for more.

The rest of the menu, which also changes from time to time, is quietly inventive. Who would think to serve carrot-crab soup? Yet the slight sweetness worked beautifully with the crab—no faux crab here. Lots of restaurants put crab cakes on the menu, but where else will you find beignets de crabe et de saumon—light, crisp crab and salmon cakes with corn, chopped plum tomatoes and chives. It wasn't a sauce, exactly, just an inspired combination.

Everybody puts a mix of mesclun, or tender baby greens, on the menu, but few balsamic vinaigrettes are as perfectly balanced as this one was. Endive salads are not uncommon, but St. Michel's was a whit different, with a crumbling of Roquefort and richly caramelized walnuts that reminded me of salads I've eaten in the Dordogne region of France, where walnuts are frequently used that way. An arugula salad, too, was perfectly dressed, tossed with truly red plum tomatoes and red onion. St. Michel's version of coquilles St. Jacques, the classic scallop dish, was a smooth, saffron-sauced rendition. Moules marinières were meticulously cleaned, simply steamed in white wine with garlic and shallots, perfect.

The item listed as crapaudine de poulet Cornique, $14, which, the menu was at pains to explain, would be "boneless Cornish hen [flattened with a brick] on wild rice, mushrooms, tomatoes, peas and natural juice," disappointed my friend Jonathan, who had hoped the brick would come on his dish. Even though it did not, this was one tasty little hen.

On a previous menu, handsome shrimp ($17) were sautéed with tomatoes, artichokes and basil and served with risotto. But perhaps I like the stunning current-menu version even better: shrimp grilled and marinated with lemongrass and served with slender asparagus and orange beurre blanc. I was even more partial to salmon steak roasted with baby leeks and served with a confit of tomatoes spiked with basil oil than I was to the heavier winter salmon medallions perched on green lentils with whole-grain mustard sauce. Seared tuna on a menu-described "mosaic" of roasted red pepper and black olives, with chive oil, a current menu item, was a delight. This is the type of restaurant where they'll ask you how you want your fish cooked; be brave, and go for medium-rare. It's not raw, and you won't regret it.

Savory, tender gigot de sept heures ($16), or leg of lamb, was braised for seven hours in a sauce of shiitake mushrooms and red wine and served over white beans. Steak au poivre, a prime shell and, at $19, the highest-priced item on the menu, was a classic, just right to go with a stack of slender shoestring fries. It's off the menu now that spring has arrived, but roast loin of pork served with mango sauce and mashed potatoes crowned with crisp-fried potato sticks was a winner earlier in the year. Always on the menu is half a comforting garlic-rubbed, rosemary roast chicken ($13) with mashed potatoes.

Desserts were lavish fun. Crème brûlée made with coconut might sound off-beat, but it was delicate. Banana and raspberry Napoleon, light as air, and vanilla bean ice cream with sour cherries in caramel sauce were different, yet familiar. Well-made chocolate mousse came with a saucy-looking almond "top hat," or flying saucer, and the faint flavor of Earl Grey in the accompanying crème Anglaise did nothing to detract. Skip nectarines poached in ginger-peach tea with more tea made into an ice; the sorbet assortment was better.

I kept looking around St. Michel, trying to get a fix on the customers. Who were they, and were they likely to return? Italian still holds sway in this neighborhood, but Bay Ridge's Third Avenue has become something of a Restaurant Row in recent years. There's room, I hope, for French.

SUN GARDEN SEAFOOD RESTAURANT
1241 Avenue U
Homecrest
(718) 375-3388

HOURS: Daily, 10 a.m.–10:30 p.m.
PRICES: Entrées up to $10.95; appetizers $1–$4.95; noodle dishes $3.50–$5. Lunch specials $3.50.
ACCESS: Street level, no barriers.
HOW TO FIND IT: Between Homecrest Avenue and East 13th Street; subway line D to Avenue U station; bus line B3 (on Avenue U)

Not least of the pleasures in discovering Sun Garden, one of a new cluster of Chinese restaurants and businesses in Brooklyn, is discovering the neighborhood.

Across the street is an Italian bakery. Beside it is a video store with what looks to be Russian lettering in the window. Best of all, perhaps, is the large fish store and pan-Asian supermarket within the same block as Sun Garden, and on the same side of the street. At V&H, which is the name of this establishment, there is a resplendent array of conch, fresh sardines and other seafood—perhaps some of the squid that was on our plate at Sun Garden came from here?—and fresh fruit and packaged items as well. Melamine dishes in a Chinese pattern? You'll find them here. Seeds for growing luffa sponges? V&H stocks them. Here, too, in season, you will find huge, smelly rambutans, fruits that are an acquired taste and that may be ordered with shrimp at Sun Garden. For future reference, V&H is at 1237 Avenue U, (718) 382-8889 or (718) 382-6906.

But I digress; back to lunch—or dinner.

The tout who clued me in about Sun Garden praised the Hong Kong cuisine in general and in particular a dish of shrimp with honeyed walnuts and mayonnaise. This dish sounded offbeat—mayonnaise in Chinese food?—but, hey, years back I stopped being surprised to see black pepper in Chinese dishes. Why not mayonnaise?

In fact, the ultra-fresh jumbo shrimp were excellent. So were other dishes we tried. One lunchtime, we liked Buddha vegetable rolls, a special, wonton skins stuffed with an assortment of mushrooms and flat-leaf spinach, pan-fried and served with lush brown gravy. Surely, this dish was blessed. It may not be the food I grew up on, but I know comfort food when I see it, and Buddha's vegetable rolls fill the bill. (Speaking of Buddha, piles of fruit were heaped before the small, lighted religious shrine at the back of the dining room.)

Another day, there were fresh seafood rolls, which we had crisply deep-fried instead of pan-fried for a change, and they were almost as good as vegetable rolls. Two pan-fried noodle dishes were hearty and satisfying; after having high-quality, tender beef with scallions in a dish of flat rice noodles, we tried black bean and beef sauce over the noodles next time, with equal pleasure.

Lunches are a particularly good buy; small servings of slightly chewy squid in black bean sauce and delicate shrimp in "egg" sauce (what used to be called lobster sauce), with a pile of fluffy, carefully cooked rice, cost only $3.50. We also liked a delicious, spicy assorted vegetable "combination platter," $6.50, which came with good fried rice and an egg roll that was nothing to write home about. But the vegetables—broccoli, water chestnuts, wood-ear mushrooms, baby corn, bamboo shoots and pea pods—were terrific in a sauce that surely contained star anise as well as pepper.

Salt-baked chicken—which isn't salty, never fear, because moist salt encases it while it is being baked and then is broken off—was succulent. Water spinach in garlic sauce was a fine substitute for the pea pod leaves we just missed; another day, we saw fresh ones being stripped from their stems and then forgot to order them.

Appetizing, burnished chickens and ducks "country-style" hang in the windows, but waiters and waitresses are not eager to let non-Chinese order them, fearing they will complain about the layer of fat between the skin and the meat. We didn't push it, but then, it's difficult to get these good-hearted folks to let you order more of anything beyond a certain point. "Too much for you," one waiter insisted, although we pleaded that our friend Regina, despite her tiny size, was the woman who made all-you-can-eat buffets lose money.

Even with her along, we had to pass up a lot at Sun Garden. I lusted after fish congee, thinking how lovely it would have been to have some when, earlier that day, I'd been home holding ice to an aching tooth. I wished, too, that we had been able to sample lobster, right now at the special price of two for $20, in any of several appealing ways, including with ginger and scallion and also with black bean sauce and pepper. Next time.

The tea was good and fresh, and dessert consisted, properly, of orange wedges and a fortune cookie. Mine contained happy news: "The star of riches is shining on you."

Here's another review by Suzanne Curley, who finds authentic cooking, whatever the cuisine.

TACI'S BEYTI I
1955 Coney Island Ave.
Midwood
(718) 627-5750

HOURS: Daily, noon–11 p.m.
PRICES: Entrées $7–$13.50; appetizers $3–$4.

ACCESS: Dining area/restrooms wheelchair-accessible.
RESERVATIONS: Required for weekends.
HOW TO FIND IT: Between Avenue P and Quentin Road; subway line D to King's Highway station (then 4 blocks west); bus lines B2, B5, B7, B31, B68.

In Turkish, beyti translates as "homemade." But this eatery owned by a former Turkish sportswriter and his brother bring the meaning closer to "made in heaven." The cooking is done by a gifted chef (the aforementioned brother).

Turkey's highly sophisticated cuisine owes much of its raison d'etre to the rich tastes of the sultans of centuries past. In acknowledgment, perhaps, of that heavy historical debt, the original Taci's Beyti is decorated with framed scenes from the heyday of the sultans. Lending a touch of modernity, however, is the background music, tapes of such pop tunes as "Strangers in the Night" and "Delilah" sung in Turkish.

Taci's II, down the road a piece, is more spacious and somewhat fancier, with an eclectic decor that includes such things as '50s-style wall plaques of Caribbean bongo-drummers. Taking up nearly half a city block, the newer restaurant is housed in what appears to be a former diner, flanked by its own parking lot. It's at 2718 Coney Island Ave. (between Avenues X and Y), Sheepshead Bay, (718) 615-0700.

Contrary to popular belief, Turkish cuisine hasn't borrowed from but has rather inspired the cooking of neighbors, such as Greece. Other countries benefited as well. The Russian pirog, for instance, is a stepchild of the Turkish borek, a pastry or pie, a good example of which is the flaky, golden and freshly baked spinach pie that is one of Taci's glorious meze, or appetizers. Others include the truly fine yalanci dolma, spicy rice-stuffed grape-leaf rolls, and two kinds of bean "stew"—white or red kidney beans cooked in olive oil, onion and lemon juice, sprinkled with fresh parsley and served cold.

The versatile eggplant, or patlican, must surely have been one of the sultans' favorite vegetables. Here it appears in two delicious guises: either puréed with garlic and parsley, to be dipped into with slices of pita bread, or sliced, pan-fried and served cold with yogurt-garlic sauce. There's also pastirma, the Turkish version of pastrami, pungent strips of air-dried beef flavored with cumin, garlic and paprika. Or you can begin your meal with what a large party of Turkish diners next to us were having, a fruit platter consisting of huge slices of cantaloupe, watermelon and other seasonal fruits.

But our favorite meze proved to be the one we tried only out of a sense of duty—pan-fried liver cubes. This dish bears no relation whatsoever to the greasy and leathery liver-and-onions dish served by many overzealous American homemakers in the '50s. Here the liver is diced small, fried quickly so as not to lose any tenderness and served side-by-side with sliced raw onions sprinkled with powdered sumac. (Sumac, a seasoning sometimes used on pita bread, is made from the Vitamin C-rich berries of weedy trees that line roadways in this country, and is not to be confused with poison sumac, another plant entirely.)

Overriding our sense of duty, this time, we passed on the beef tripe soup, in favor of the delightfully refreshing chilled cucumber-yogurt soup flavored with garlic, fresh dill and mint. The latter is a perfect choice as a first course if you hope to have an appetite for Taci's good and hefty entrées, which are mainly a wide range of kebobs: lamb skewered in half a dozen different forms, marinated chicken or calf's liver en brochette, as well as baby lamb chops and a mixed grill.

Bring your own wine or beer, if you like, to either restaurant. Or drink ayran, a salty yogurt drink, with your meal and follow it with some of the thick, sweet coffee that is one of the crowning achievements of the Turkish kitchen. Desserts here are not compelling, being the usual pastries such as kadaif, ladyfingers or baklava. Chances are, that after sampling all those meze, you won't have room for them anyhow.

TAQUERIA EL PAISANO
4010 Fifth Ave.
Sunset Park
(718) 871-3469

HOURS: Friday–Monday, 10 a.m.–1 a.m.; Tuesday–Thursday, 10 a.m.–midnight.
PRICES: Platillos $8.50; enchiladas $7.50; frajitas $8.50–$9; burritos $6.50; tacos $2; sandwiches $3.50; salads/soups/appetizers $3–$7.
ACCESS: Wheelchair-accessible; restrooms equipped for disabled.
RESERVATIONS: Recommended for weekends.
KIDS: No children's menu but will accommodate.
ENTERTAINMENT: Mariachi band Saturday–Sunday starting at 3 p.m.
HOW TO FIND IT: Between 40th and 41st Streets, near Sunset Park; subway lines R, N or B to 36th Street/Fourth Avenue station; bus lines B35, B63

Taquerias are opening all over Manhattan nowadays, but for the true taqueria you must travel to Brooklyn.

Richie, my tipster on this one, is from California, but his parents were from Mexico, so when he mentioned that he drives out of his way to go to Taqueria El Paisano, I went on immediate Taco Alert. (Taco Alert is the name of a file folder in which, aided and abetted by my friend Taco Fred, I keep valuable information about really down-home taco joints.)

I was expecting no-frills at Taqueria El Paisano. In fact, I was hoping for that. Plainness bodes well when it comes to taquerias. Not much English was spoken here, which made Paisano seem even more likely to be authentic. Eagerness and helpfulness sometimes speak louder than words.

But one member of my party looked around and said, "Should we get takeout?"

No, I said, I wanted to eat right there, next to a cold case full of beer and Jarrito sodas on one pale blue wall and the Virgin of Guadalupe on another. The chairs are covered in red vinyl. That was plenty of atmosphere for me. So what if it was a little drafty at Paisano? We had our coats.

And we had food to keep us warm. Such food!

Taqueria El Paisano's menu is based on soft tacos, not the brittle-fried, pseudo-tacos northerners first knew, made of corn tortillas. These fresh, earthy tortillas are wrapped around a number of fillings for tacos, and they are fried crisp for tostados. Oh, sure, they have flour tortillas for making burritos, too, but when I can have corn tacos as good as these, I lose interest in the wheat-flour model.

Stringing together a few of my Spanish nouns (as Calvin Trillin said of French, I don't do verbs), I was able to get moist steamed chicken tacos, fried pork tacos, and tacos de lengua delivered to our table. This last, tongue tacos, may sound off-putting, but the meat was tender and delicious.

That was true of almost everything we sampled at Paisano. At too many other taquerias the meats are not really simmered into submission, but at Paisano, somebody has the patience to do it right.

The steamed (al vapor) chicken was especially juicy, but my favorite was the pork taco, pieces of pulled pork showered with scallions and fresh coriander. A tostado carnitas was made with crispy little crumbles of pork and a garnish of good guacamole.

Soups were substantial enough to serve as main dishes on a wintry night. There's menudo, or tripe soup, alleged to cure hangovers. Instead, since none of us had overindulged the night before, we ordered caldo de cameron, a robust, soulful red shrimp broth. Posole, the pork and hominy soup, was satisfying, too. A simple avocado salad that included truly red tomatoes and radishes was perfect with a squeeze of lemon and a splash of oil.

Cheese enchiladas—soft corn tortillas rolled around queso blanco—were wonderful under a blanket of tangy green sauce, made with tomatillos. All of us tried to sneak limp, savory onions away from the man who ordered bistec encebollado, or beefsteak with onions, at our table. Chicken fajitas were terrific, too. We even liked the vegetable burrito, generous with mushrooms and a bit of a stretch in a place like Paisano. Long-simmered red beans, yellow rice and some guacamole came with platters such as these.

Fiery, thin homemade salsa, added judiciously, improved these already good things. At so many taco eateries, you need to pour on the heat just to make the food taste like something, but not here.

In the drawing on the back of the menu, two gents wearing sombreros sleep, sitting on benches. They snooze away right in front of a sign that says "Mexican Food." I didn't go to sleep right away after eating at Paisano, but I did share their contented mood. It's easy to imagine that this sleepy duo had just availed themselves of the toothpicks that are thoughtfully provided.

This food is elemental. It might be what I would want if I were stranded on a desert island, along with some cold cerveza, of course. (Corona and Tecate are on hand at Paisano, as well as Heineken and Bud.) If the gringo in The Milagros Beanfield Wars had brought the saint an offering of Paisano's tacos, he could have gotten any favor he wanted right away, for sure.

VERACRUZ
195 Bedford Ave.
Williamsburg
(718) 599-7914

HOURS: Tuesday–Sunday, 4–11:30 p.m. Lunch Monday–Friday, noon–4 p.m. Brunch Saturday–Sunday, noon–4 p.m.
PRICES: Entrées $6–$15; appetizers $1.50–$4.25. Lunch $4.50–$7. Brunch $4.95–$6.95. AE.

ACCESS: Wheelchair-accessible; restrooms equipped for disabled.
RESERVATIONS: Taken for groups of four or more.
KIDS: No children's menu, but will accommodate.
HOW TO FIND IT: Between North 6th and North 7th Streets; subway line L to Bedford Avenue station; bus line B61.

Chino, which is the nickname artist Jaime Palacios goes by, went to rent a space that he and his partner Richard Ampudia thought would be perfect for a restaurant.

The man he had to see was Kevin Nealis, who owned the former shoe store he was trying to rent. "He told me he was looking for a partner to start a Mexican restaurant," said Palacios, "and I said, 'Here I am.'"

But it was Chino's dream that shaped the place. He did not want the stereo-typical Mexican restaurant: "We didn't want to get caught up in the mariachi thing."

For months before Veracruz opened, anticipation was high on this stretch of Bedford Avenue. Neighborhood artists who frequent Planet Thailand, the excellent Thai Café across the street, kept peeking to see how Veracruz was coming along. When at last it opened, it was easy to see what had taken so long. Chino did a bang-up job of decorating the restaurant, with many personal touches.

A big gob of wires and junk at the top of a pillar, for example, was turned into a bright mosaic. But mostly, the space is understated, with soft colors and touches such as mirrors and mantels salvaged from old brownstones. The idea, Chino said, was to evoke the '40s and '50s, an "elegant period" in Latin American restaurants both in Mexico and here in New York, where the chic were hanging out at the Copacabana.

As for the food, Chino hired a chef, Alfredo Peco, who hails from Puebla, Mexico. Smart move.

I say this because one day when we were raving about how tasty and creamy Peco's refried beans were, Chino confided that he makes refries out of a can. Refried frijoles made out of canned beans may be better than nothing, but they're not better than beans made the old-fashioned way, simmered a long time and then hand-mashed as they fry. Peco is capable of food much more elegant, too. The dinner menu, which I have yet to try, lists such delights as grilled rib-eye steak in chipotle-mushroom cream sauce, grilled seasonal vegetables with chile butter and homemade mole. As an antojito, or first course, the menu now lists grilled cactus and grilled corn on the cob with mayonnaise, chile piquin and queso fresco. Now that's worth a trip to Brooklyn from another borough.

Peco cooked at Carmine's in Manhattan but took a pay cut to join the Veracruz team. "It is so hard to find a Mexican chef who can cook Mexican," said Chino happily. "Usually they are cooking Italian."

The best of Veracruz' food is akin to those beans, simple and satisfying. Everyone in our crowd liked the jalapeño peppers stuffed with shrimp and cheese so well that we ordered a couple of plates of them as first courses and then more to eat with our main courses. Quesadillas, made with corn tortillas (which we prefer) instead of flour, were tasty stuffed with cheese and epazote, the corn fungus, or mushrooms. Best of all, there were potato quesadillas—perhaps in tribute to Brooklyn's Polish flavor and potato pierogis? We were also partial to flautas de pollo, crisp little chicken tacos with sour cream and salsa.

The rest of the lunch lineup is what you imagine it might be in an artist-hang-out-cum-Mexican-restaurant: the ever-popular enchiladas suizas, stuffed with chicken and served under tomatillo-based green salsa, good beef in enchiladas al tajin with both red and green salsas, a perky house salad with jicama, a classic Caesar salad, burritos and tacos. All are satisfactory, if not always exactly made the way you would expect to find them back home in Puebla—or Veracruz, either. For dessert, there's good fried ice cream and generous servings of the obligatory flan.

Jarrito-brand Mexican sodas in long-necked bottles—lime, tamarind, sangria—are available. Once summer comes, there will be that huge, inviting garden in back.

QUEENS

ARIGATO

221-02 Horace Harding Expressway
Bayside
(718) 423-2888

HOURS: Monday–Saturday, 3–11 p.m.; Sunday, 2–11 p.m. Lunch Monday–Saturday, 11 a.m.–3 p.m.
PRICES: Entrées $7.95–$19.95; appetizers and soups $1.50–$7. Lunch $5.95–$7.50. AE, DC, MC, V.
ACCESS: Dining area/restrooms wheelchair-accessible.
RESERVATIONS: Recommended, but not required.
HOW TO FIND IT: On Long Island Expressway south service road, just east of Springfield Boulevard; subway line E to Jamaica Center/Parsons Boulevard station then bus Q30; bus lines Q27, Q30.

Arigato unites Japan and Korea with enough skill to make the United Nations envious. It's a successful alliance.

Although these cuisines have few genuine similarities, Arigato handles the two of them with equal dexterity. Still, the place is primarily a Japanese restaurant, with 103 of the 122 selections ranging from suimono to chicken katsu.

Arigato is situated just east of Springfield Boulevard and slightly west of Slim's Bialys, in case you have to stock up for later. The slice of an eatery is no wider than a couple of bowling lanes. But there's height to help compensate victims of claustrophobia.

Indeed, the exposed ductwork probably contributes to the decoration as much as anything else does. Most diners will have a good view of the large-screen TV. Others may just study the familiar prints, deco-style sconces, sushi charts or, for that matter, the very beige color scheme.

You're not here for the visuals.

That is, unless you're concentrating on your plates. The sushi chef is deft, and the kitchen is consistent. During recent visits almost every choice was a winner. Arigato's Korean specialties are tingling and diverting, the Japanese more familiar by now, but prepared with equal care.

Sushi and sashimi, the uncooked gems of Japanese cuisine, are essential. The sashimi is pristine and glistening. Try the conical, sushi hand rolls. And combination rolls are pleasing, though they sometimes veer too far from the sea and into curiosity.

The "birthday roll," for example, includes cream cheese and onion, scallion, salmon and avocado. Maybe it's the influence of Slim's. Smoked salmon enters the Alaska roll, along with avocado and cucumber. Better than these are the deeply flavored salmon skin roll, and the delicate rolls containing eel, vegetables, the buttery yellowtail and the tuna.

Ordering a la carte will let you be specific and avoid the unwanted that may land on your assortments. If you're addicted to spectacle, however, Arigato prepares shiploads of sushi and sashimi: the wooden trays, shaped like boats, with enough cargo to feed you and all the fishermen you know.

The cooked Japanese fare is generally fine. Start with gyoza, the crisp, meat-filled half-moon dumplings. Agedashi-tofu, little deep-fried bricklets of bean curd, are light and right.

Arigato's tempura, while not an ornate filigree, is greaseless, crunchy and recommended, whether you like the vegetables, shellfish or chicken.

Sautéed chicken is close to deep-fried and golden. Pork katsu is essentially the same presentation, and just as tasty. Arigato also sends out satisfying teriyaki, led by a neatly lacquered fillet of salmon. But beef negimaki, rolled around scallion, is tough.

Fat udon noodles and the slim soba noodles both are excellent, particularly the cold soba. Only the tempura paired with udon and broth disappoint, and that's simply because the crispness vanishes faster than you can eat.

You'll like the traditional, cloudy miso soup and the clear, fish-based soup. The clam soup, however, is watery, and the solitary, whole shelled clam has a rubbery texture.

The Korean dishes have spark. Kimchi jee gae, a fiery, crimson casserole, has sliced pork and vegetables along with the pungent fermented cabbage. A plate of the condiment, which may be made with turnips, too, arrives in case you want to intensify the heat. The entrée is an invitation to consume rice.

Yuk gae jang translates into a scarlet-tinted stew of tender shredded beef with noodles and vegetables over rice. It's guaranteed to increase the BTUs, though not to as high a level as the kimchi does.

Kal bi gui is perhaps the most familiar of the Korean courses, juicy short ribs that have been marinated and broiled. The meat is peeled off the bone, and it's delectable, requiring neither sauces nor seasonings.

Stewed monkfish, or agu jjim, is, by contrast, work-intensive. These are bony rounds of the fish, finished with soy beans and bean sprouts. If you'd rather have more exotic stuff, there's ox tripe in beef broth.

Arigato turns minimalist at dessert, with a scoop of green tea ice cream or a fruit plate, lately some unripe honeydew, a sliced orange and red grapes.

But you could go around the corner, onto Springfield Boulevard, and notice a Carvel ice cream shop.

After all, Arigato does like to diversify.

—Gianotti

ARUNEE
37-68 79th St.
Jackson Heights
(718) 397-0808

HOURS: Dinner Wednesday–Monday, 4–10:30 p.m. Lunch 11 a.m.–4 p.m. Closed Tuesdays.
PRICES: Entrées $4.50–$9.95; appetizers $4.50–$6.25. Lunch $4.95–$5.95.
RESERVATIONS: Recommended.

ACCESS: Dining room wheelchair-accessible, restrooms are not.
HOW TO FIND IT: Just off Roosevelt Avenue; subway line 7 to 82nd Street/Jackson Heights station; bus Q32.

The menu at this little spot carries 100-plus dishes and about 30 asterisks. The stars denote spice. And Arunee means it.

This can be high-voltage cookery, fully flavored and almost always compelling. If you want the heat, you'll get enough to turn incandescent. But don't conclude that eating here merely approximates toying with electricity.

At Arunee, Thai fare is an assured balance of the saline, sweet, sour and spicy. It can be as soothing as it is incendiary. The kitchen combines chiles, coconut milk, peanuts, lemongrass, basil, mint, ginger, coriander, tamarind. The result: delightful.

The arresting stuff is prepared in a small, very informal space just off Roosevelt Avenue, identified by a blue canopy. Inside, the restaurant is plain and neat. Travel posters provide splashes of color. It's the kind of dining room where the television could act as a centerpiece.

Mainly, Arunee is neutral in everything save the food. Behind a facade that looks like the work of Flintstone & Rubble P.C. is a consistent and subtle kitchen.

Start with the elemental satay, made with either pork or beef. The skewered, marinated meat has a hint of curry. It's ready for the excellent peanut dipping sauce and the familiar cucumber salad.

Contrast the satay with the crunch of koong hom pa, a deep-fried dumpling filled with shrimp and boosted by a diverting sweet-and-sour sauce. Nuea tod, or sliced marinated beef, will test your jaw but is worth the exercise.

Arunee's salads are mandatory courses. They're certain to ignite your appetite. Larb, with chopped pork, chicken or beef, is intensely seasoned and coated with fired-up lime juice. Yum pla krob translates into ultracrisp pieces of fish spiked with an invigorating sauce defined by chiles, onion and cashews. The heat rises slowly and then just takes over.

Mee krob, the sweetish, crackling rice noodles, are presented with shrimp, bean sprouts and green onion. Broad noodles with broccoli and either pork, beef, chicken or shrimp almost rival them. Spicier is guay tieow kie mao, thin noodles with ground beef, chiles, tomato and garlic.

Soups are available for two. Kang jeud pug is a calm one, combining chicken and vegetables. Tom yum nuea mixes beef with lemongrass, lime juice, chiles and straw mushrooms, but it's a mellow number, too.

Red snapper receives deluxe treatment, whether in a light ginger sauce with onions and mushrooms; or fiery amalgam of chile, garlic and hot and sour sauce. The union of stir-fried bean sprouts, bean curd and salted fish also is recommended.

Panang, meat or poultry in a sauce of red curry and coconut milk, is accurately listed under "traditional favorites." So's sliced, grilled duck finished in coconut milk, basil, red curry and tomato.

Have Thai beer, as a complement and a coolant. There are no desserts. Scout around, because depending on what you've consumed, you may be in the mood for ice cream.

Two scoops, minimum.

—Gianotti

BAHAR

82-19 Queens Blvd.
Elmhurst
(718) 335-6828

HOURS: Daily, noon–midnight.
PRICES: Entrées $4–$11.95; appetizers $4–$5. DS, MC, V.
ACCESS: Dining area wheelchair-accessible, restrooms are not.
HOW TO FIND IT: Near 51st Avenue; subway lines G or R to Grand Avenue/Newtown station; bus line Q-60.

SPEEN GAR

40-09 69th St.
Woodside
(718) 426-8850

HOURS: Sunday–Thursday, 12:30–11 p.m.; Friday–Saturday, 12:30 p.m.–midnight.
PRICES: Entrées $3–$11.95; appetizers $4–$5. DC.
ACCESS: Dining area wheelchair-accessible, restrooms are not.
HOW TO FIND IT: At Corner of Roosevelt Avenue; subway line 7 to 69th Street/ Fisk Avenue station; bus lines Q32, Q45.

Eat enough Afghan food, and you'll have a skewered view of the cuisine. That makes sense.

In this kitchen, the kebob is king, whether you want to impale lamb, beef, chicken or fish. Rice is a staple. The influences are many.

Bahar and Speen Gar, which, in full, are billed as shish kebob houses, stick to the basics. The prices at these related eateries are remarkably modest, and the meal is invariably hearty.

The newer of the two is Bahar, situated opposite the Elks lodge on Queens Boulevard. It's a friendly, bright and spare kind of place, with pine chairs and faux-brick walls. The artwork portrays life in the countryside. There's a poster that says bluntly, "Free Afghanistan."

At the Woodside venue, the looks are sufficiently informal to make Bahar seem the spot to seek for a haute time. You pass the grill en route to small tables in a windowless rear space, where the Free Afghanistan theme extends to an oriental carpet, wherein the imagery is a battle with the then-Soviet army.

Politics aside, the fare is sturdy, unyielding and there's plenty of it.

Bahar, in particular, sends out excellent manto, delicate homemade dumplings filled with beef. They're capped with a lively sauce of minted yogurt and tomato.

Bolani gandana is another winner. The fried turnovers are packed with scallions and herbs, for a savory starter. Bolani kadu is filled with pumpkin. These turnovers arrive with a minted yogurt sauce. So does the bolani katchaloo, which has a satisfying filling of potatoes, herbs and spices.

The influence of India is evident in the tasty samosas, generously packed fried turnovers that hold beef, onions and spices. Lighter, and just as good, is aushak, boiled scallion dumplings amply herbed and spiced.

From these appetizers, you move onto kebobs, chalows and palows, and some fine vegetarian entrées.

The kebobs themselves are well-charred, and offered with basmati rice, a salad and Afghan bread. The rice is first-rate, the bread isn't. The main courses generally are blunt and flavorful.

Marinated slices of filet mignon are especially tender. Kabab e sultani refers to a combo platter of the filet mignon and spiced ground beef. The mixed grill of ground beef, boneless chicken breast and lamb is right, too. Tandoori chicken is available for the less adventurous.

Kalbi palow translates into basmati brown rice with raisins and carrots, plus a side order of lamb curry. The lamb is a bit gamey, but this is a diverting dish. Naringe palow adds almonds and strips of orange peel to the rice, and chunks of lamb.

Favorites among the vegetable entrées are led by lentils and white basmati rice. Badenjan burani, or sautéed eggplant with fresh tomatoes, onions and spices, is worth selecting, for one or for the table. Bamia, or whole okra, in a similar preparation may test your fondness for the vegetable's texture.

Speen Gar has a kindred menu. The bolani with scallion or potato is easily recommended. So's the crisp, appealing samosa with meat and onions.

The house's version of aushak (or, here, ashack) is workmanlike and tasty. Manto is on a par with Bahar's rendition. The eggplant and okra are about the meal, too.

Morgh kebob, the boneless chicken, with rice, salad or both is elemental and definitely fuel for a chilly night. Corma palow, brown rice with a side of lamb curry, is on the greasy side. Instead, stay with the range of kebobs.

They include the tika kebob, or leg of lamb; keema, with grilled ground beef; chabi, with sautéed ground beef; lamb chops, and kingfish.

Both Bahar and Speen Gar serve halal meat, adhering to Muslim dietary laws. There is no pork. And no alcohol.

Desserts are limited to one or two on any given day. Firny, a milk pudding, may remind you of facial cream. A multi-layered baklava, heady with honey and nuts, is a better finale, and may be ordered at Bahar. But it has a chilly center.

After all that rice, you may have little room left. Besides, you know you're not coming here for dessert. Just keep that "natural charcoal" hot and those skewers turning.

—Gianotti

CABANA
107-10 70th Rd.
Forest Hills
(718) 263-3600

HOURS: Dinner Sunday–Thursday, 3–10:30 p.m.; Friday–Saturday, 3 p.m.–2 a.m. Lunch Monday–Saturday, noon–3 p.m.
PRICES: Entrées $6.95–$14.95; appetizers $2.95–$9.95. Lunch entrées $6.95; sandwiches $5.75–$6.50. AE, MC, V.
RESERVATIONS: Recommended for Friday–Saturday.
ACCESS: Ramp at entrance, dining area wheelchair-accessible; restrooms equipped for disabled.
ENTERTAINMENT: Live music occasionally (call).

PARKING: Two pay lots on same street.
HOW TO FIND IT: Subway line E to Continental Avenue/71st Avenue station; bus lines Q23, Q60.

With a whimsical burst of gold and blue, Cabana celebrates the cooking of the sun and the sea. All it needs is a tanning salon.

The playful, noisy and very, very bright eatery is a spirited addition to the neighborhood and the borough. It's definitely unlike any restaurant in the vicinity.

And, given the lighthearted decor and the partying mood in the dining room, it differs markedly from most of the Queens eateries that evoke the Caribbean. Cabana doesn't have the edge of authenticity. But the place is fun, and the food often is good. This is the Caribbean for vacationers.

The walls are a brilliant hue of yellow headed for gilding. The ceiling suggests a dreamy color for the sky, even though ductwork interrupts the hallucination.

You can forgo the margarita and go the colada route, or stay with any of the beers. They've got slushy, nonalcoholic drinks with flavors such as coconut and banana, too.

For a starter with verve, try the spicy chicken wings. They're dubbed Jamaica jerk, as if to ensure that you don't mistake them for expatriates from Buffalo. The meaty wings are marinated and grilled, slathered with a jazzy barbecue sauce.

Coconut-crusted shrimp are considerably milder and sweeter. The shellfish also are short on crunch. Instead, sample baccalaitos, or light codfish cakes paired with a tasty avocado salsa. The Bahamanian conch fritters are the size of small zeppoles, battered and accompanied by a peppery dipping sauce.

Vegetable fritters are paired with a dipping sauce that's spiked with cilantro. But the dish is a little limp. Jamaican beef patties, which contain ground, spiced beef, have a fine filling but the pastry is pasty.

The house's chicken soup is generous with white meat and vegetables, in a fragrant broth. Heartier is the meaty, reddened conch soup.

A serving of long-cut plantain chips goes with the drinks. Have them immediately, because the crispiness vanishes faster than a bottle of Dos Equis after you've accidentally downed a Scotch bonnet pepper.

Those incendiaries are part of the cooking here. Ask for the full blast and you're likely to get it in the Jamaican jerked chicken and jerked pork, two husky and tingling entrées.

Ropa vieja, the shredded skirt steak stewed with tomatoes, peppers and onions, is ample and very good. But churrasco, a thin, grilled tenderloin, charred outside and red within, is even better. The beef is marinated with plenty of garlic and herbs. Sancocho translates into a gutsy beef stew, thick with fresh yucca, corn and yams. It's one of Cabana's entrées to hold in reserve for a chilly evening.

Chicharrones de pollo, or deep-fried chunks of chicken, are hefty but could be crunchier. Coco Cabana chicken means white meat in coconut milk, spiked with curry and hot peppers. The two flavors are surprisingly mild. But it's good chicken.

The fish of the day may be salmon, glossed with a tangerine glaze. The salmon steak is moist and flavorful, and the citric accent is restrained. The slab is on a mound of sweetish coconut rice. Have the finfish before diving into the house production of paella or the jumbo shrimp simmered in wine and garlic.

Salads are pleasing alternatives to the appetizers, or sides to the main courses.

The Cabana salad adds hearts of palm, red onions, tomatoes and queso blanco to mixed greens before the black-bean vinaigrette goes on. The jerked chicken salad is a sensible lunch choice.

Asombroso is a lively lunch choice, with grilled chorizo sausage, sautéed onions, and sweet and hot peppers. The sandwiches are flanked with either sweet potato fries or plantain chips.

Maduros, or fried sweet and ripe plantains, are commendable with most of the main courses. Likewise, the rice seasoned with coconut milk, and the vegetarian black beans. Arepas con queso, or grilled cornmeal cakes with cheese, are dry.

Dessert means a wobby, chilly flan. Or mango ice cream. The coconut cake and the coffee cheesecake are dull numbers. Stick with those fruit drinks. And think of summer breezes and a gentle surf.

—*Gianotti*

CAFFE ON THE GREEN
201-10 Cross Island Pkwy.
Bayside
(718) 423-7272

HOURS: Tuesday–Thursday, noon–10 p.m.; Friday, noon–11 p.m.; Saturday, 5–11 p.m.; Sunday, 3–9:30 p.m.
PRICES: Entrées $9.50–$19.50; appetizers $4.50–$6.50. Lunch $9.50–$15.50. AE, MC, V.
RESERVATIONS: Recommended.
ACCESS: Wheelchair-accessible; restrooms equipped for disabled.
ENTERTAINMENT: Pianist Monday–Saturday.
PARKING: Lot on premises.
HOW TO FIND IT: At corner of 201st Street, next to Clearview Golf Course; subway line 7 to Main Street/Flushing station then take the Q16; bus line Q16.

At the entrance to Caffe on the Green is a sign advising visitors that Valentino used to reside here. And the food could be described as son of the chic.

This Caffe is a bright, starry spot. The interior is airy. Outside, there are twinkling lights, perhaps to evoke another establishment on another green. And greenery abounds, whether in the dining areas or just beyond the door. It's a verdant patch near the Throgs Neck Bridge.

The shade is off-white. Mirrored walls and windows are interrupted by exposed brick. Neo-something reliefs rim the room just south of the ceiling. A soft-hued painting that pleasantly suggests Impressionism by numbers indicates you're en route to a lovely garden.

Which is reason enough to pick the fine minestrone, a springtime-red-tinted soup full of vegetables and tubettini pasta. The lone competitor is pasta e fagioli.

A thinly sliced disc of mozzarella threaded with smoked salmon is a diverting opening number, with the fish where you usually find prosciutto. The round is flanked by good, bitter greens. Better is the spiedino, which looks like a golden bread loaf, full of molten mozzarella. It's boosted by a spirited tomato sauce accented with anchovy. Fried zucchini is pretty limp.

Pastas may be ordered as appetizers. Especially recommended is a savory special that's a thin version of linguine. The strands are tossed with a thick sauce generous with tomato and eggplant, capped with a dollop of ricotta.

Gilded soft-shell crabs are finished aromatically with Pernod. The crabs are meaty and crunchy. Red snapper in a deft, crimson sauce is an adroit, traditional entrée, garnished with clams and mussels. You've had it before. Chopped tomato and onion are the mantle for herbaceous, moist grilled swordfish, a more enticing selection.

Chicken scarpariello is very good, with tender chunks of meat on the bone and fennel sausage. It could use an edge of vinegar. Chicken, sausage and veal are paired with peppers and mushrooms, and set on broccoli rabe for a production number that's hearty, but a surprisingly quieter alternative to the robust scarpariello.

Veal giardiniera translates into a tender, pounded, breaded cut of veal that's fried till crisp and then topped with a chopped salad. The warm-cool contrast is terrific, and the veal doesn't turn soggy. The juicy, grilled shell steak under a hillock of caramelized onions, also is excellent.

Caffe on the Green has a respectable wine list. The 1991 Palladino Gavi di Gavi ($24) is a dry, attractive white. Nino Negri's 1988 Sassella ($22) is a sturdy, no-nonsense red.

You'll receive a separate dessert menu, complete with color photos. Tirami su is best, with a distinctive espresso taste. It's followed by the eggy cheesecake.

Service is accommodating—you won't be rushed. The sunny mood of the restaurant is part of its attraction. In this part of northeastern Queens, Caffe on the Green is an oasis. Rudy would approve.

—Gianotti

CHADA THAI
81-44 Lefferts Blvd.
Kew Gardens
(718) 846-9226

HOURS: Tuesday–Thursday and Sunday, 4–10 p.m.; Friday–Saturday, 4–11 p.m.; closed Monday.
PRICES: Entrées $3.95–$14.95. AE, DC.
RESERVATIONS: Recommended.
ACCESS: Dining area wheelchair-accessible, restroonms are not.
HOW TO FIND IT: Near Cuthbert Street; subway line E to Union Turnpike station or A to Lefferts Boulevard/Liberty Avenue station then take bus Q10 at either stop; bus line Q10.

So, last night's dinner was as exciting as watching tableware tarnish. You can't look at another metallic tomato sauce, watery soup, or incinerated hamburger.

And, in search of that elusive tingle, you're willing to take the pothole plunge on Lefferts Boulevard.

Think Chada.

You arrive at an operation the neat but plain appearance of which has no bearing on the marvelous food therein. Chada is a little star. The dining room looks like a transformed luncheonette given an injection of Art Deco. Stools are ready to spin at the counter. Tables are tight and the woodwork is lacquered black. The other main shades are gray and white.

The modest appointments ensure you're not distracted from the vivid food and the sunny personalities of the staff. On all counts, Chada is the kind of place that's guaranteed to make you smile, enjoy a thoroughly satisfying dinner, and keep finances in order.

Thai cookery is a vibrant union of Southeast Asian ingredients, with touches from China and India. It can be hot, hot, hot; tart; soothing; saline; sweet. Rice is the centerpiece, but then come the accents. Chada's kitchen generously uses curries, coconut milk, peanuts; tangy tamarind and incendiary chile peppers; bean curd, fish sauce, ginger, potent basil, mint, lemongrass. The flavors meld.

At the Thai table, everything appears at the same time, generally at room temperature, and you pick whatever you want whenever you want it. No rules about appetizers and entrées. You can do the same at Chada or stick with the three-or-four-course approach.

Pad Thai, a savory sauté of rice noodles, bean sprouts, tofu, ground peanuts, egg and shrimp, is satisfying, as a starter or side dish. And try the excellent chicken saté: striplets marinated in coconut cream, curry and coriander. They're grilled and paired with a lush peanut sauce and a refreshing cucumber salad.

Mee krob, the ultracrisp rice vermicelli, is sweet and flecked with shrimp and pork. Shrimp stuffed with seasoned pork and wrapped tightly in flaky spring-roll skin continues the theme of crunchiness.

An invigorating starter is yum nuea, or tender, grilled beef emboldened with Thai herbs, peppers, onions and a shot of lime juice. Naem sohd complements it: minced pork that has been marinated in lemon juice and finished with a serious ginger, peanuts and shallots.

Yum pla merk translates into broiled squid, which is a bit chewy, in a lively combination of red onions, chile paste, pepper and lime juice. You may have the squid in 10 other preparations from a "create your own" list. The beef, pork and chicken options are better, especially when either sautéed with ginger, onion and black bean sauce.

The house's curries have bite, but you may order any of them mild, too. Gang ped, or pork simmered with red curry, coconut milk and bamboo shoots, comes up slowly and then grabs you. Mussamun curry, with chicken, tamarind, peanuts and onion, rivals it.

Chada's seafood is led by a quartette of deep-fried red snappers. Pla lad-prig, or the whole fish capped with garlic and a sweet-spicy sauce, is recommended. Blunt garlic sauce, curry paste and a ginger-onion-scallion number are the alternatives.

At some point, you must sample Chada's soups. The "chicken in spicy coconut soup," silky and rich, could wake up the most jaded diner. The thinner hot-and-sour chicken soup, spurred by sourish lemongrass, merits its adjectives. You can have it with shrimp, too. A soup of shrimp, meats and Chinese cabbage seems ordinary by comparison.

They don't serve alcoholic beverages here. And soft drinks aren't always up to the job.

Desserts are either a custard or ice cream. They provide an easygoing, back-to-basics return from your palate's adventure in the land of smiles.

But you may want to stay.

—Gianotti

COOKING WITH JAZZ

12-01 154th St.
Whitestone
(718) 767-6979

HOURS: Monday and Wednesday–Thursday, 5–10 p.m.; Friday–Saturday, 5–11 p.m.; Sunday, 4–10 p.m. Closed Tuesday.
PRICES: Entrées $10–$20; appetizers $2–$8. DS, MC, V.
RESERVATIONS: Strongly recommended.
ACCESS: One step at entrance. Dining area wheelchair-accessible, restrooms not accessible.
KIDS: Children's menu, $5.
PARKING: Small lot on premises.
HOW TO FIND IT: At corner of 12th Avenue; subway line 7 to Main Street/Flushing then take bus Q15; bus line Q15.

Cooking With Jazz is closed on Tuesdays. But it always seems like Mardi Gras. The Cajun food tingles on cue and makes you want to raise a glass of Dixie beer.

For those whose memory of the cuisine is smoke detectors gone wild, Cooking with Jazz is both heartening and refreshing. Diners should find the opening as welcome as Café du Monde's mail-order coffee.

Attribute the efforts at authenticity to an enthusiastic and ambitious chef, Steven Van Gelder. His resume, not surprisingly, includes a three-year stint with chef Paul Prudhomme, still the unabashed, unofficial spokesman for the culinarily Cajun.

What you'll visit is a 50-seat spot that can get pretty tight. The walls are gray and the banquettes teal. And there are the expected posters of crayfish and how to eat them, plus those of contented chefs. Van Gelder occasionally pops out of the kitchen to chat with customers.

The primary reason to eat here is the Cajun and Creole cooking. But half the menu is headlined "Not So Cajun," as if to ensure that the wary will find a hamburger or a Caesar salad while the bold dive headlong into red beans and rice. Enjoy the peppered cornbread and the rest of the breadbasket, and your decision will be made swiftly.

Chicken and andouille sausage gumbo is a smoky, intense, brown-broth number, generous with rice. The flavors are true and the effect is bracing. You also may sample a slightly milder gumbo with seafood, okra, tomatoes and rice.

Shrimp remoulade is modest, with medium-size shellfish and a lively, thick sauce. The shrimp are preferable to the stuffed eggplant. You get crisp discs, capped with a seafood-and-cornbread dressing, in addition to buttercream sauce with shrimp.

Ravioli filled with shrimp and tasso, the highly seasoned smoked ham, benefits from a delectable pink sauce. For a pasta with no Cajun connection, try the zesty penne glossed with olive oil and tossed with roasted peppers, onions, garlic and sun-dried tomatoes.

Jambalaya is a mainstay of Creole cooking that stars rice with plenty of hearty ingredients. Typically, they include onions, peppers, tomatoes and shellfish, meat or poultry. Here it's chicken with andouille sausage and smoky bacon. And for the addicted the peppery production is terrific.

Humbler but equally tasty is red beans and rice. Andouille, cornbread and a cut of well-spiced blackened chicken finish it. Buttermilk-battered chicken, southern-style frying matched with biscuits, is a straightforward, meaty, moist and crispy delight.

The charcoal-grilled, herbed chicken is blunt and appealing. Van Gelder sends out a lively version of the classic Big Easy entrée, chicken Tchoupitoulas. The tender, peppery boneless chicken is finished with bearnaise sauce and paired with diced tasso and fried potatoes.

Blackened swordfish has the obligatory kick from its buttery, seared-spice coating. Seafood Big Mamou, a name apparently taken from a Cajun tune, refers to moist and tasty finfish and shellfish in a sweet-hot tomato sauce, atop corkscrew pasta.

Crayfish étouffée may be a special when you go. If so, order it. The crayfish are sweet and delicious, the sauce brown and biting. The menu could use more crayfish dishes. The lighter poached salmon arrives in an artichoke broth, spurred by fennel and tomato. A whole, peeled fresh artichoke heart and the petals surround the perfectly cooked fish.

At dessert, pick bananas Foster, a spin on the rich, brown sugar-and-booze sauté with vanilla ice cream that originated at Brennan's restaurant in New Orleans. Pecan-and-sweet-potato pie will lure you, too.

Sip café au lait. And let the bon temps rouler.

—Gianotti

DELI MASTERS
184-02 Horace Harding Expwy.
Fresh Meadows
(718) 353-3030

HOURS: Daily, 9 a.m.–9 p.m.
PRICES: Entrées $9.95–$12.95; sandwiches $5.95–$8.95; appetizers $2–$5.75. AE, DC, MC, V.
ACCESS: Dining area wheelchair-accessible, restrooms are not.
KIDS: Children's menu, $6.50.
HOW TO FIND IT: At corner of 184th Street; subway line 7 to Main Street/Flushing station then take the Q17; bus lines Q17, Q30, Q88.

In Mondo Deli, what's better than a nice sandwich is a nice, very big sandwich. And at Deli Masters, it's fressermania.

This tribute to Formica, marbleized glass, paneling and Hebrew National's greatest hits does a good job of balancing portion, quality and price. You won't leave either hungry or poor.

And when you do depart, it probably will be with a take-home order.

Deli Masters has enough hard surfaces to bruise the noise level. The interior has touches of deli, diner and assorted hybrids, all of which owe a debt to a designer whose primary concern was function.

The staff gingerly fits in, with some amiable talk before the rush of food comes out. It's an eclectic selection, from what are billed as Israeli vegetarian dishes to burgers, salads, omelets, soups, and a series of appetizers and main courses guaranteed to brace you for everything except dieter's guilt.

Admittedly, it's hard to pass up the first thing you see, which is a sizzling frankfurter. Have a couple on your way out, with hearty mustard and good sauerkraut that allow you to forget the limp buns.

At table, after the preliminary and obligatory mouthful of coleslaw and bite of pickle, you're advised to sample the essential chicken soup. It's presented with noodles, rice or matzoh balls that don't masquerade as exiles from a tennis court.

The stuffed cabbage, approximately the size of a can of soup, has a significant shot of sweetness and an old-fashioned style. You can skip the chopped liver, a scoop with a stuffed green olive at the center, flanked by lettuce, tomatoes and onions. It's on the dry side. Stuffed derma defines density. It's described on the menu as, with "gravy like grandma's but no heartburn." That's partially accurate.

The baked potato knish is a warm, soft heavyweight and more satisfying than the merely weighty fried rendition. You must be totally devoted to the subtleties of the kasha knish to enjoy it. Chicken fricassee, ably stewed, requires less allegiance.

And chicken in a pot simply asks for an appetite. The meat is tender, with a supporting entourage of peas, carrots, noodle and a matzoh ball just in case. The production is a little bland, but that's not really a deterrent. Flanken in a pot continues the theme.

It's tough going with the rib steak, a leathery slab that underscores why the prime attractions at Deli Masters are the "triple-decker skyscrapers," 11 constructs on rye that may not rise to that old Carnegie Deli height, but will surely test your ability to bite.

Pick at random. The favorite here is named PLT Special: a reckless pile of fried pastrami, corned beef and salami that's given a healthier tone with lettuce, tomato and onion—none of which is necessary for any reason except the title.

The hot union of brisket of beef, corned beef and pastrami is the runner-up. You'll be content with corned beef, pastrami and salami, too. Or hard salami, "wide" salami and bologna.

There are many permutations in the sandwich area. "Build your own" is a heading you'll appreciate. For those frightened by pastrami overload, fine white meat turkey is available. And it's better on the sandwich than as part of the hot turkey dinner. Warm, open-faced sandwiches are the compromise. A husky potato pancake goes with any of this. A side order of kasha varnishkes works, too.

In the vegetarian arena, Deli Masters has sensible tahini, the sesame sauce that's offered with pita bread. Tasty hummus, the chickpea spread with sesame sauce; and two eggplant salads also have their appeal.

Naturally, you drink Dr. Brown's: cel-ray tonic or cream soda, depending on the meal, the mood and the state of your insides. They have other sodas, including Snapple and, if you'll pardon the expression in a piece about deli, Best Health. But it wouldn't be right. The one-liter bottle is $2.50.

For dessert, Deli Masters has a seven-layer, bakery-level chocolate cake, apple strudel that could be flakier, marble cake, chocolate blackout cake. Or you may be drawn to the baked apple and the rugelach ("4 pc."). Watermelon is "seasonal." Jell-O isn't.

Either way, it's unlikely that you'll linger here, unless your next destination inspires delay. A deli dinner requires a dash of frenzy, just for seasoning. In the meantime, eat, eat.

DOCKERS SEAFOOD GRILL
110-74 Queens Blvd.
Forest Hills
(718) 263-7411

HOURS: Dinner Monday–Thursday, 5–10 p.m.; Friday–Saturday, 5–11 p.m.; Sunday, 4–10 p.m. Lunch daily, noon–3 p.m.
PRICES: Entrées $10.95–$17.95; appetizers $3.50–$5.95. Lunch $6.95– $11.95. AE, DC, MC, V.
ACCESS: Dining area wheelchair-accessible, restrooms are not.
RESERVATIONS: Recommended.
HOW TO FIND IT: Between Ascan Avenue and 73th Road; subway line E to 71st Avenue/Continental Avenue station; bus line Q23.

In the parlance of restaurants, Dockers has perfect syntax. This star of Queens Boulevard specializes in fish and shellfish, grilled and otherwise. And besides, the name reminds you of comfortable pants, too.

You could find a score of grills without much effort throughout the city, and most of them will offer some sort of seafood to toss unadorned on the grids.

What sets Dockers apart from the usual run of these joints, and from the standard-issue fish houses that populate Queens, is the eye-catching spareness of the operation. The absence of seafood kitsch is refreshing. You'll have to go elsewhere for a harpoon or nets or mounted marlins.

You'll choose from a couple of soups and salads, a half-dozen appetizers, 10 specialties and a listing of finfish and scallops available broiled, grilled or fried. And you've paid twice as much elsewhere for this quality.

Dockers' New England clam chowder is a distinctive production, fragrant, herbaceous and far from the ultra-thick bowls of paste that pass for this classic. It's more milky than creamy, and not devoted primarily to potatoes. The herbed cream soup with seafood isn't as flavorful, but it's generous with shrimps and scallops.

During recent visits, the raw bar offered littleneck clams, bluepoint oysters and Malpeques, the luscious, coppery Canadian oysters. They arrive with shallot vinegar and the familiar red cocktail sauce.

Ordinarily, the shrimp cocktail is a pedestrian affair. Dockers sells the shrimp by the pound, with one-third pound going for $5.95. These are plump shellfish, artfully arranged at attention, tails high, surrounded by squiggles of tasty sauce that hint of mustard and tomato.

The salmon and tuna tartare is an elegant little tower, coral on top and rosy below, rimmed by a border of thinly sliced cucumber. Lemon pepper is the spark, but the mild marine taste is what lingers. It's an excellent starter, whether you're a fan of the raw or the cooked.

Cornmeal-coated fried calamari are tender, but could use more crunch, too. The marinara sauce for dipping lacks the advertised spiciness; it's more of a mellow companion that doesn't get in the way. Caesar salad also tends toward the unassertive, with good whole leaves of romaine, shavings of Parmesan cheese and a singular absence of anchovy. If one did visit, it didn't stay long.

The finfish available daily are tuna, salmon, swordfish, lemon sole and red snapper. They're all fine, particularly the snapper. But that fish is best finished in a crispy potato "vermicelli" crust and set on savory eggplant.

Broiled red snapper is moist and to the point. The plain grilled tuna tastes right, but it's better when capped with a trio of pepper purées that form a three-tier rainbow on the steak. Broiled salmon is appealing, but the pan-roasted salmon with tomato salsa and potatoes accented with white wine has more verve. Grilled swordfish is blunt and first-rate, with an evergreen of rosemary sprouting from the two slabs.

Sea scallops, fat and peppered, are sweet but carry a current of welcome heat. Fried sole is elemental and satisfying. And if you need pasta, try the linguine marinara with cuts of finfish and shellfish that have been sautéed with garlic and olive oil.

Meat-eaters will like the tender loin veal chop with wild mushrooms. The grilled shell steak is juicy, but the roasted garlic and shallots really are what make the entrée essential. You could have a side dish of them with anything. Main courses are served with a choice of potato or rice, and a julienne of vegetables.

Desserts are led by a fragile and flaky apple strudel that's boosted by a lush vanilla sauce. The crème brûlée also is a winner, crackling and rich.

Dockers fills up quickly. It's a winner, in any language.

—Gianotti

DON PELAYO
39-20 Queens Blvd.
Long Island City
(718) 784-4700

HOURS: Sunday–Thursday, 5–11 p.m.; Friday–Saturday, 5 p.m.–2 a.m.
PRICES: Entrées $8.95–$22.95; appetizers $5.50–$7.50. AE, DC, DS, MC, V.
RESERVATIONS: Recommended.
ACCESS: One step into dining area, otherwise wheelchair-accessible; only men's restroom on same level.
ENTERTAINMENT: Pianist Friday–Sunday.
HOW TO FIND IT: At corner of 39th Place; subway line 7 to 40th Street/Lowery Street; bus lines Q32, Q60.

Tapas are the addictive appetizers of Spain. At barside, you can make a meal of these mouthfuls, accompanied by some sherry. Or, have them to jump-start a more elaborate meal.

In Queens, Don Pelayo is the king of tapas.

This Spanish star has been here for years. After a couple of visits, you'll know why. It's easy to become a regular, nibbling away season after season, as the menus change.

Don Pelayo is sufficiently kitschy in decor to suggest a Spanish courtyard situated a mere sidewalk away from Queens Boulevard—"El Cid" by way of the IRT. But tastefully done.

The familiar, soulful strains of Rodrigo's "Concierto de Aranjuez" periodically may be heard in the background. The second movement will protect you from the evening rush of buses visible through a small window.

You enter the dining room from the bar, passing under a stucco arch. The stucco is heavy-duty, akin to terrified icing. Tile is on the wall and colorful, assorted stone set in the floor. Service is genial and attentive. You may be guided gingerly through the evening's tapas, which in a gesture of accommodation are available both at the bar and in the dining room.

A suggestion: Order them first, then peruse the formal menu of chef Jose Menendez.

His tapas change regularly. They may include stuff simple as salami with green olives toothpicked to a crust of bread, or wedges of fluffy, inch-high egg-and-potato omelet. Both, of course, mandate another bite. Singularly garlicky shrimp and cool mussels vinaigrette are standard fare.

But the kitchen definitely gets going with the zesty, pinky-size sausages that look like cheroots; and the vivid rounds of chorizo sausage with peppers. Stewed tripe with tomatoes is tender and terrific.

A union of warm tomatoes and cool potatoes, potent blue cheese, and clams in garlic sauce all are sturdy, mandating another sherry. A quartered Portobello mushroom cap topped with delicate smoked salmon and some cheese is mandatory.

The husky Galician soup rife with greens, caldo gallego, will ensure you leave winter smiling. The garlic and clam soup is equally fortifying. Chicken consommé sparked with sherry is, by contrast, an also-ran.

Don Pelayo's entrées are a lively intro to Spanish cuisine. The standout is perhaps the most rustic choice, fabada Asturiana y campagna: a thick, hearty, warming white-bean pottage heady with Spanish sausages and meats. It's nearly rivaled by ropa vieja, a bracing stew of shredded beef and vegetables.

Diverting and different: sweet red peppers stuffed with duck breast, finished in a light, orange sauce; and stuffed turkey breast, a ring of white meat around ground veal flecked with olives, peppers, and prunes, in brown sauce. Capon with almonds in an aromatic saffron sauce is a winner, too.

The rack of lamb for one is tender and flavorful, accented with mustard and herbs. The prime rib is a blunt choice, generous and to the point. But it's not the classic steak-house variety. Pasta with almonds, onions, peppers, eggs and prunes, plus tomato, is over-orchestrated.

Sample the merluza, two discs of snowy fish, in an herbaceous, brothy green sauce. The cuts of fish are flanked by spears of asparagus. Paella Valenciana, the great saffron-rice dish with sausages and chicken, receives its due at Don Pelayo.

The wine list has variety, from venerable Spanish reservas to the ever-present pitcher of sangria. If you don't feel like reliving freshman year with the latter or entering middle age with the former, there's lighthearted, low-octane sparkling apple cider. And the essential sherry.

Desserts are comparatively few. The basic flan can be rubbery or right, depending on the night. Better is a lush variation on créme brûlée, spiked with hazelnut liqueur. The house's syrupy spin on French toast, flamed at tableside with brandy and strewn with sliced almonds, is a showy sweet.

Anyway, these finales aren't the reasons to dine here. Don Pelayo itself really is an appetizer: a restaurant that makes you want to eat. And then, have some more.

—*Gianotti*

EAST LAKE
42-33 Main St.
Flushing
(718) 539-8532

HOURS: Daily, 8 a.m.–2 a.m.
PRICES: Dinner entrées, $7.50–$30; lunch $3.95–$11.95.

ACCESS: Steps at entrance; dining area tight, difficult to manuever.
PARKING: Small lot at restaurant.
HOW TO FIND IT: Near Franklin Avenue; subway line 7 to Main Street/Flushing station; bus lines Q17, Q27, Q44.

In the tradition of Mott, Pell and Bayard is Main. And one of its liveliest destinations is East Lake.

This noisy establishment used to be the site of a fondly remembered diner. The transformation isn't entirely complete except on the menu. You'll still get a dose of old-time glitter, and the exterior has a style bridging the '50s and '60s. Sharks' fins now have a more direct meaning here.

What must be a display of them is positioned in a case above the cashier. You know what you're eating at East Lake, from the moment you enter the spot. Several tanks at the entrance hold finfish, shrimp, lobsters, crabs and eel.

The color scheme indoors is green and red. Marble wainscoting, a gold dragon and phoenix, some etched glass, a long framed mural of a bucolic Chinese scene, in big letters the word "welcome"—it's all diverting. So's the food.

What's certain to lure you to East Lake is the marvelous dim sum, and the delicate preparation of both the familiar and the unusual.

Dim sum translates from the Cantonese as heart's delight. And when done as skillfully as at East Lake, it lives up to the definition. Dim sum also means variety: small, tempting dumplings, rolls, buns, pastries, steamed and fried. Have it when East Lake is bustling at midday.

The place fills unto chaos, wagons of the dim sum bump into each other. Indeed, English can seem a second language here. But dim sum requires merely that you point. Each plate, based on size, is duly recorded on your tab with a little stamp.

Shrimp dumplings, steamed or fried, are first-rate. But the pork buns are delectable and essential fare. The chicken pie, fragrant and neatly crusted, should be chosen, too. You can fill yourself rapidly, so be selective. It's hard.

Main dishes at lunch can be less inviting. The pork chop with chili and spicy salt on rice is very dry. But sliced flounder with vegetables is sweetly moist. Pan-fried noodles with chicken or beef are satisfying, as is the fried vermicelli with beef and a nutty satay sauce.

Kam lo wonton, a frying of shrimp, roast pork, chicken and squid, is paired with pineapple and tasty, but marred by a sweet-sour sauce that's thick.

Among the stellar entrées is barbecued beef with black pepper. The filet mignon is presented on skewers, with only a tantalizing hint of the expected heat. Another winner is intensely smoked salmon trout, capped with a top-browned, lush cream sauce. Steamed chicken topped with striplets of ham is a fine contrast in texture and taste.

East Lake's minced lobster in a lettuce leaf, a rich spin on a preparation that frequently stars chicken, could use a dab of hoisin, but is light and appealing. Shrimp with asparagus and crabmeat sauce is its equal. Baked crabs with ginger and scallions and fried crabs with black bean sauce are strong competition.

The adventurous will be drawn toward unusual items: frogs' legs wrapped in lotus leaves, smoked boneless pig's feet with jellyfish, braised abalone with oyster sauce, preserved duck egg, and more.

They're available for takeout on a listing that doesn't exclude subgum wonton soup, egg drop, and shrimp fried rice. But your host will state adamantly that they don't have either ice cream or fortune cookies, to go or to stay. There's enough of that in Flushing and everywhere else. The almond cookie will do. Fresh orange slices and, if you insist, litchis will complete dessert.

The next time someone recommends a trip to Chinatown, suggest visiting the authentic one. It's in Queens.

—Gianotti

EAST RIVER GRILL
44-02 Vernon Blvd.
Long Island City
(718) 937-3001

HOURS: Memorial day–Labor Day, outdoor dinner dining (weather permitting) daily, 5:30–10 p.m. Lunch indoors Monday–Friday only, 11:30 a.m.–5:30 p.m. Labor Day–Memorial Day, indoor dining Monday–Friday only, 11:30 a.m.–10 p.m. (closed Saturday–Sunday).
PRICES: Entrées $9.95–$15.95; appetizers $3.95–$5.95. AE, DC, MC, V.
RESERVATIONS: Recommended.
ACCESS: Not wheelchair-accessible.
ENTERTAINMENT: Live jazz Friday nights.
PARKING: Lot on premises.
HOW TO FIND IT: At corner of 44th Road; subway line E to 23rd Street station or line G to 21st Street station; bus lines Q103, Q104.

The view from the East River Grill is so grand that you feel almost exhilarated enough to order something caught in the nearby waters.

But the choices here are considerably better than that. The seafood and the grillings satisfy. And, on a clear night, the restaurant itself becomes the main course.

This place is perched perfectly. Your perspective on Manhattan is interrupted only by the southern tip of Roosevelt Island. But, add illumination for mood or for a sound-and-light show, and the ruins there would have a certain charm, too.

East River Grill is in the East River Tennis Club. The entrance is marked by columns whose original purpose could have been exhaust pipes. They're turned vertical, into a hybrid of rococo and high-tech.

By the time you get to the eatery's white plastic tables and chairs, you've passed through the club's sitting room, observed assorted courts in action and skirted the swimming pool.

The pungent aroma of chlorine fades quickly as you reach the much-used, lopsided boardwalk leading to the dining area. It's replaced by the scent of garlic and of meat on the grill. Fortunately, these days the river isn't contributing any aromatics.

You'll be seated alfresco somewhere between Citicorp and the U.N. At nightfall, you have a terrific angle on the tiara atop the Chrysler Building. East River Grill could make a lifelong New Yorker smile like a first-time tourist.

The key factor in all this is the weather. The locale of the East River Grill embodies summertime, cloudless skies, a gentle breeze, outtakes from a Woody Allen movie. Try not to notice the ants that inevitably find your table and the more advanced wildlife that keeps a polite distance.

It's likely that you'll have plenty of time to survey the restaurant and the skyline, since service can be exceedingly slow and erratic. But when the cooling, soothing gazpacho materializes, that becomes a minor complaint. The soup is heady with the taste of peppers.

A duet of crabcakes is flaky and flavorful, but does seem to overdo the breading. Coconut shrimp are encrusted with sweetness, and the coating flakes off rapidly. But the shrimp are fat. The vegetable quesadilla is a zesty starter filled with a julienne of zucchini and carrot.

East River Grill offers two pizzas daily. The vegetable pie has a generous coverlet from the garden, but the thin crust lacks the necessary crispness. Black pasta, a cousin of linguine, arrives squid-inked, with a pile of calamari rings and tentacles on it, plus a dose of respectable tomato sauce.

You may have an expertly grilled tuna steak, paired with a savory relish of roasted red pepper and tomato. Moist, delicate, seared salmon has a crunchy coat, and a black-bean-and-corn accompaniment.

Soft-shell crabs receive a semolina dusting and are fried till they are crunchy at the center and brittle at the tips. They rim a disc of mellow, grilled polenta, which should support other entrées. It's better than most of the potatoes.

Barbecued chicken has a gentle bite. The grilled chicken breast on a bed of greens is tender and should lure purists. The grilled sirloin is cooked precisely and arrives with wedges of corn fritter. The hamburger is a husky, thick affair, with a pleasing char.

East River Grill's arugula salad has some unwanted graininess, as if the last washing didn't entirely succeed. The Caesar salad bears a fleeting resemblance to the real thing; there's a touch of lemon, but the pet anchovy apparently didn't deign to make its cameo appearance.

The 1990 Sonoma-Cutter Russian River Ranches Chardonnay ($19.50) is typically citric and reliable, a fine white to complement a lot of the menu. The 1991 Morgan Sauvignon Blanc ($14.50) is an uncomplicated, herbaceous alternative. For a red, try the soft 1989 Clos du Bois Merlot ($22).

Chocolate cake, flanked by clouds of whipped cream, is basic and appealing. Cheescake is creamy and light. The apple cake is a bit dense; the pecan pie, an improvement. You'll like the lopsided multi-berry tart instead of the metallic lemon number.

A tennis match, or some laps, will take care of the accumulated calories. The East River Grill is easy on your appetite—and your eyes.

—Gianotti

EL REY MEXICAN RESTAURANT
25-21 Astoria Blvd.
Astoria
(718) 545-2292

HOURS: Daily, dinner 5:30 p.m.–1 a.m. Lunch, noon–5:30 p.m.; breakfast, 9 a.m.–noon.
PRICES: Entrées $8.50–$12.50; appetizers $3.25–$4.25. Lunch $7.50–$8.25. AE, MC, V.
ACCESS: Dining area wheelchair-accessible, restrooms are not.
HOW TO FIND IT: Near 27th Street; subway line N to Astoria Boulevard/Hoyt Avenue station; bus lines Q19, M60.

Just remembering last night at El Rey gives me a case of instant nostalgia. It's late now, too late for even El Rey, which closes at 1 a.m. And I'm nowhere near Astoria.

Yet, my craving for the earthy, satisfying food of El Rey is so powerful that I walked over to the vending machine just now and bought a bag of corn chips.

These corn chips are but a pathetic substitute for El Rey's homemade ones and the thin but hot salsa. Oh, how I'd like to be there now, biting into the steamed white corn of a tamale, through to its meaty, mellow inside, washing it down with a Negra Modelo.

For the moment, I can only imagine. I'd walk in hungry. I'd want to eat at least two pork tamales, one with zesty green tomatilla salsa and one with red salsa. I'd rather not share those with anyone, but maybe I could bear to divide my next pork course, which would be a torta—pounded, breaded pork cutlet on a Mexican bun—with a friend. Or maybe not.

I'd want to bring scads of people, actually, so we could make it a real fandango and share lots and lots of things. At El Rey, I never want to stop eating; that's how spectacular the food is.

Even burritos are a marvel here. Usually, I don't order burritos, because I am bored with the big ones stuffed with mostly rice; here, a vegetable version did burritos proud. Quesadillas may be nice enough elsewhere, but often they are sort of anemic; at El Rey, the quesadillas are voluptuous—moist foundations of sturdy corncake topped with meat of your choice, shredded lettuce, bits of avocado. A few of these would make a mini-meal of great substance.

All soft tacos were peak experiences; pork, chorizo, chicken and beef tongue or lengua, which all the really down-home Mexican places serve. Don't knock it until you've tried it. There's not much of any way you can go wrong here. Crispy tostados filled with either pork or chicken and deep-fried flautas stuffed with chicken were both wonderful.

All the aforementioned foodstuffs are some of the best Mexican victuals you'll find in any borough. But plan on repeat visits to El Rey to sample all its delights.

At too many Mexican places, big platters of food are desultory assortments that seem calculated to please non-Mexicans. At El Rey, the platters were superb, works of art in the medium of food. We could scarcely get enough of the pollo al jalapeño, made with goodly quantities of garlic and enough pepper to make it tasty, not tear-provoking. Shrimp a la Veracruzana was a tangy, bright melange of shellfish with strips of red and green peppers and a bit of garlic. Flavorful steak was served beneath a vivid mixture of jalapeño peppers, tomato and onion.

Enchiladas El Rey consisted of the freshest of flour tortillas wrapped around savory chicken and served with a restrained creamy cheese sauce. What could have been overkill was instead just right. Only molé poblano, the sauce made from nuts and chocolate and served over chicken, seemed just this side of bitter. It goes almost without saying that the refried beans are cooked to a fine creaminess and the yellow rice is fine.

It's hard to dredge up any complaints. The guacamole might have been a little bit salty, but just about everything else was primo.

Still, more exploration may be required. I haven't had the chiles rellenos, and surely the cheese-filled poblano peppers would be perfection here. I haven't tried the comidas Americano, such as hamburguesas, either.

I'll just have to go back, and often. Let's see, could I get there for desayunos?

(That's breakfast.) And I've never had dessert, unless you count the homemade limonada.

Pale pink walls and the usual bright serapes and sombreros are the decor, and everything is tidy as the proverbial pin. There are booths along one long, narrow wall, and there's a garden out back, though I think only regulars are allowed to sit in it. Our waitress was patient and kind, but some knowledge of Spanish may prove helpful.

—Gianotti

ENOTECA TOSCANA
234-19 41st Ave.
Douglaston
(718) 631-0600

HOURS: Tuesday–Sunday, 5–10 p.m. Lunch Tuesday–Friday, noon–3 p.m.
PRICES: Entrées $16.50–$22.50; appetizers $6.50–$15. Lunch $6.50–$12. AE, MC, V.
RESERVATIONS: Recommended for weekends.
ACCESS: One step at entrance. Dining area/restrooms wheelchair-accessible.
PARKING: Lot at station (free weekdays, fee weekends).
HOW TO FIND IT: Between 234th and 235th Streets, across from Douglaston LIRR station; subway line 7 to Main Street/Flushing station, then take bus Q12; bus line Q12.

The Douglaston station of the Long Island Rail Road should be your new stop. Enoteca Toscana, a work-in-progress on the north side, is open for breakfast, lunch and dinner. And it will charm you any time of day.

It's a multi-ethnic enjoyment, despite the Italianate name, decor and connection with Il Toscano restaurant on the other side of the tracks. Yes, you'll pass posters, photos and examples of things Italian, from images of Venice and Siena to herbed olive oil and cookbooks, en route to the upper deck. It's an airy, spare space, marked by pastels and shiny dark wood, deco fixtures and a skylight.

Tall, round-top windows look onto the station plaza. A dumbwaiter adjoining it spares the genial, knowledgeable fellow on duty from wearing out the stairway. He'll cite several invariably catchy specials. The regular menu is no cliché, either. Chef Matthew Reis must be having a good time.

That's clear with the apple-and-walnut soup, creamy and sweetish, which could double as a modest dessert. He must have figured it's too tasty and you shouldn't wait. The split-pea soup contains cuts of shiitake mushroom, and is savory, hearty stuff.

Crunchy, shrimp-filled wontons float in a pungent, nutty and citric broth. Lemon and oregano embolden a sauce for rigatoni that's tossed with full-flavored black olives, red peppers and plump capers. The sauce for light, inviting angel hair with salmon, cabbage and chives carries the tint of saffron.

Wilted arugula is a slightly peppery foil for goat cheese and shrimp in a lively salad course. A sliced Portobello mushroom, doused with balsamic vinegar is, by now, routine. But devotees of the tart-sweet will overdose contentedly.

An entrée of grilled chicken breast is paired with a chicken leg that, in turn, is stuffed with well-seasoned chicken mousse. This three-way bird is juicy, playful food, served with a zucchini-and-bean timbale. It's better than the surprisingly bland grilled chicken on a layer of braised lentils and caramelized pearl onions.

The sesame-crusted filet of beef has no such problem, especially because of an invigorating vinaigrette with Thai spices. The double-cut, grilled pork chop also makes a vivid entrance atop apple-braised cabbage and potato cakes spiked with blue cheese. The heavyweight chop is glossed with a sauce defined by red plum. But those assertive, crisp, cheese-shot triangles won't be disguised.

An ample slab of salmon, rosy at the center, arrives capped by an equally high horseradish crust. Salmon caviar is the decoration. And the entire enterprise is alternately potent and mellow. Milder and lighter is a terrific, snowy red snapper in fennel broth.

Desserts are showy and assured. Chocolate ravioli translates into fragile half-moons of molten richness. Raspberries finish it. Assorted berries bound with gelatin may sound like a '50s kiddie sweet, but there's more to it, from sweet cream to wedges of banana nut bread. Grand Marnier glâcé has the impact of velvety ice cream, with thin white-chocolate striplets finishing the black-plate production. A turret-like "napoleon" of sweet potato-and-maple mousse sandwiched between molasses snap cookies rises above a peanut-and-coconut sauce.

So, Enoteca sometimes overdoes it. But when too many others are taking safe routes, this place goes another way. It's never boring.

Check the schedule, yours and theirs.

—Gianotti

GATEWAY OF INDIA
138-31 Queens Blvd.
Briarwood
(718) 657-3600

HOURS: Daily, dinner 5:30–11 p.m. Lunch Monday–Friday, 11:30 a.m.–3 p.m.; Saturday–Sunday, 11:30 a.m.–3:30 p.m.
PRICES: Entrées $7.95–$18.95, appetizers $3–$5. Lunch buffet $6.95 weekdays, $8.95 weekends. AE, DC, DS, MC, V.
RESERVATIONS: Recommended.
ACCESS: Dining area/restrooms wheelchair-accessible.
PARKING: For dinner, indoor lot half-block west of restaurant.
HOW TO FIND IT: Between Main Street and Hillside Avenue; subway line E to Union Turnpike/Kew Gardens station then take bus Q46; bus line Q3, Q17, Q46.

Gateway of India provides entry into the spice trade. Here's a kitchen that tingles.

That doesn't mean the new Indian eatery is exclusively for asbestos palates. The chefs season to your wishes. But when you want it hot, you get it hot. And, at a time when blandness is rising, it's a refreshing experience.

This Gateway is situated between Hillside Avenue and the Van Wyck Expressway, turf that hasn't been fruitful for lively dining. But Gateway immediately changes that.

It's a traditional Indian restaurant that's comparatively restrained, short on the wail of the sitar and devoid of beaded curtains. There are, however, a few paintings that suggest the artist was influenced less by the Taj Mahal than the beer named after it.

Mirrors enlarge the place. And you may peer through a round-top window to observe the kitchen at work. What comes out is consistently good, often better.

The familiar appetizers are easily recommended. The pyramid-shaped vegetable samosa, a crisp and greaseless pastry, is filled with potatoes and peas for a homey opener. The vegetable pakoras, or fritters, also are fine starters. Chicken pakoras, dipped in chickpea flour, are modestly spiced and tasty.

Small, lentil-flour "doughnuts," which resemble popped holes instead, are delectable, alongside a mound of grated radish. Mango chutney goes well with them, too.

Shami kabab refers to a hamburger of sorts, made with ground lamb and lentils. These discs tend to be dry. You'll have to boost them with the assorted condiments that arrive with the gratis papadum, the zesty lentil wafer.

Alu papri means crunchy crackers paired with potatoes, then coated with whipped yogurt and a sweet-sour sauce. After a few of the preceding appetizers, it's an invigorating contrast. Bhel poori has the same effect, with noodles finished with sweet and sour chutneys.

Gateway offers two soups, each typical and each flavorful. The mulligatawny number, with lentils, mild spices and the suggestion of coconut, floats a wedge of lemon, which gives it added zip. Subz shorba, billed as vegetable soup, is intensely peppery, to the point that you think it's the main ingredient. They can tone it down.

Vegetarians should enjoy Gateway of India. The cuisine is loaded with vegetarian delights and so is this particular menu. Especially worthwhile are dal makhani, lentils with cream, bolstered by spices, and fried, and masala gobi, or cauliflower in a hearty onion sauce.

Chole peshawari, or chickpeas and diced potatoes, has a savory kick. Likewise, mattar saag paneer, or a variation on cottage cheese with spinach and green peas. Kadai paneer adds ginger, chiles and tomatoes to the homemade cheese.

Tandoori dishes, cooked in the clay oven, are moist and true. The tandoori chicken, in a shade beyond burnt orange, is juicy. So's murg ka tikka, boneless pieces of chicken prepared on a skewer. The tandoori lobster is ample and highly seasoned.

Shrimp bhuna, accented with ginger and garlic, has a gently herbaceous flavor and the shellfish resist turning tough. An alternative is shrimp kabab masala, skewered and completed in the tandoor.

Chicken curry is oniony and doesn't have the spark frequently associated with the production. Chicken tikka masala, boneless and buttery, has the company of tomatoes and "green spices." It's fine.

You can ignite your palate with lamb vindaloo, the vinegary and sharp concoction that improves as the BTUs go up. Rogan josh, the crimson lamb stew here spiked with almonds, cream and yogurt, provides keen competition.

All of Gateway's breads are first-rate and essential. Try the whole-wheat bread seasoned with fenugreek leaves, or the onion kulcha, a white bread packed with onions. Alu paratha, an unleavened whole-wheat bread filled with potatoes, is another winner. Poori, the puffed-up, deep-fried whole-wheat bread, offers a pleasant contrast to those baked in the tandoor.

Beer is the right drink with the hotter foods, and Gateway has the two well-known Indian brews, Taj Mahal and Kingfisher. Lassi, the yogurt beverage, is an excellent coolant, and when flavored with mango, could double as dessert.

The sweets here are led by a spin on carrot cake and pudding. It's a crumbly, diverting finale, with raisins and nuts. A dish of mango or vanilla ice cream is an obligatory accompaniment.

Rasmalai, the rounds of sweetened cheese; a grainy kheer, or rice pudding; and kulfi, a conical cut of Indian ice cream, follow in that order. They put out any lingering fires.

—Gianotti

GOODY'S
94-03B 63rd Dr.
Rego Park
(718) 896-7159

HOURS: Daily, 3–10:30 p.m. Lunch 11:30 a.m.–3 p.m.
PRICES: Entrées $7.50–$15.95; appetizers 95 cents–$6.50. Lunch $4.25– $5.50.
ACCESS: Dining area wheelchair-accessible; restrooms not accessible.
HOW TO FIND IT: Between Saunders and Booth Streets; subway line R to 63rd Drive/Rego Park station; bus line Q60.

From the outside, Goody's could be mistaken for the executive entrance to an adjoining fruit market. The canopied storefront, about a bowling alley long and two wide, hasn't been designated a local landmark yet.

Except by those who've eaten here.

For appetites made weary by the company of shrimp fried rice and subgum lo mein, Goody's can be much more than a sliver of Chinatown East.

Yes, you'll get plenty of the standard stuff. A lot of the regular menu is devoted to it. But ask for dishes from the single-sheet, typed menu. The hostess will note that these are recent translations from the house's Chinese-language list.

You'll be dining in a convivial atmosphere where decor is an afterthought. Some posters highlight calligraphy. A mirrored wall tries to enlarge the premises.

Table tops are leaning against the entryway, ready for a big party. In case it's raining, you may put your umbrella in a plastic bucket once used for pasteurized liquid egg whites.

A crackling, seasoned turnip pastry competes with pork-filled steamed buns and crabmeat buns fragrant with ginger to start your meal. Both are winners. Vegetarian duck, looking very much like a slablet of strudel, also is a singular number that will allow you to forget mock productions elsewhere.

Assertive, cool and spicy pickled cabbage can become addictive. Pair it with the intensely nutty cold noodles in sesame sauce. The refreshing, shredded, dried bean-curd salad fits in neatly, too. Subtler is the spongy Shanghai bean curd with mushrooms.

Wine chicken is exactly that: tender white meat with a singularly vinous kick. Seafood fried dumplings and the familiar fried pork dumplings are good. Boiled pork dumplings, however, are pretty pasty.

Soups range from the standard to the diverting. You can sample the regular wonton or egg drop soup. But not at the expense of the tangy union of watercress and bean curd, Shanghai-style.

Or the striking "salty egg and mustard cabbage" alliance that's sure to vanish, despite the unpleasant-sounding description. Devotees of hot and sour soup will be delighted by the gutsy rendition at Goody's.

Main courses generally are an invigorating group that will lure you away from moo shu pork or chicken with peanuts, which are available, too. Especially recommended: fried cuts of moist, snowy yellow fish in a batter flecked with seaweed.

Almost as enticing is carp in a minced chili sauce, light in texture and the shade of burnt orange. Crispy shrimp are a little limp and the sauce not spicy enough to merit an asterisk. Have the sauté of baby shrimp instead.

And definitely have the braised pork shoulder: a memorable, terrific dish. Flaky, luscious and unusual, it's a mandatory pick. You'll be tempted to consume it all, the thick layer of fat included. Complement it with the marvelous mincing of dried bean curd and jalapeños, handily the hottest mouthful during recent visits. The "spiced salt pork chop" has compelling taste. Sweet and sour sauce is offered with it, but stick to the thinly cut, saline pork unadorned.

General Tso's chicken, the standby, earns a salute for its crunch, tenderness and afterglow. Steamed chicken with ginger and scallions is moist and mellow. Diners who'd like the chef's crispy chicken will have to order the bird, either whole or one-half, a day in advance.

The trio of desserts is candied and sliced lotus root with sticky rice, a fried crêpe filled with red bean paste, and fried banana with the bean paste. No ice cream.

You won't mind. Besides, you can pick up a few oranges on the way home.

—Gianotti

GREEK CAPTAIN FISH MARKET
32-10 36th Ave.
Long Island City
(718) 786-6015

HOURS: Daily, 11 a.m.–1 a.m.
PRICES: Entrées $7–$16; one menu.
ACCESS: Dining area wheelchair-accessible, restrooms are not.
RESERVATIONS: Recommended for weekends.
HOW TO FIND IT: Near 32nd Street; subway line N to 36th Avenue/Washington Avenue station; bus line Q102 (on 31st Street).

From the moment I walked into the Greek Captain Fish Market, I loved it. Piles of beautiful, fresh seafood were nestled on ice. The pert whiting gleamed, the fresh snapper blushed with good health, the whole porgies had a silvery glow. I fell in love with this unpretentious place even before I ate a single bite.

All this truly fresh seafood, along with scads of lemons and Greek salad and garlic bread, is pretty much my idea of heaven. Tiny, twinkly lights in a shade that must be Aegean blue decked the room. The aroma of retsina and cigarette smoke mingled with the smell of toasting bread, browning potatoes and broiling fish.

Simple the Greek Captain may be, but it's cosmopolitan, too. At just the few tables we were within earshot of, we could hear Greek, Italian and Spanish being spoken. In fact, the menu is given in both English and Spanish, instead of Greek. On the cover is a picture of proprietor Angelo Skentzos, looking appropriately crusty in his Greek fisherman's cap. Skentzos started with a fish market in Corona and eventually added a couple of tables. That was a few years ago. Then, about a year back, with partner Barbara Tzoulis, he opened Greek Captain in Long Island City.

Greek Captain II, as we might call it, is as notable for what the kitchen does not do as for what it does. There's no hummus, no taramasalata, no dessert and coffee.

All meals follow a similar pattern, and there's something comforting about not having to make too many decisions. Do you want plain bread or garlic? (Take the garlic.) Do you want feta cheese and everything in your Greek salad? (Yes.) Do you want house wine, the most expensive bottle of wine ($10) or the second-most expensive bottle ($8)? (We splurged on the pleasant, slightly fruity $10 bottle of white.) Do you want your fish fried or broiled; your potatoes baked, french fried or Greek-style? (Take the Greek potatoes, which are like thick, delicious home-made potato chips, and eat them lickety-split, while they're still crisp.) You don't have to ask for more lemon; here, a lavishly large pile of lemon wedges arrived without our asking. They're good squeezed on salad, in soup or on seafood.

If you crave a first course other than soup and salad, take a look at those handsome fish up front and choose some small ones to have fried, though none are listed as appetizers. We had a heap of fried marida (a phonetic spelling of the Greek word for spearing), not quite crispy enough. A platter of slightly chewy fried calamari fared better in the fry kettle. Some days smelts (another size of marida) or mullets may be available. The fish stew was a homey concoction that needed a bit of oomph from the lemon and a dash of salt and pepper.

There are two kinds of seafood—broiled and fried. We enjoyed crisply fried scallops, but a fried porgy was too long on the fire and somewhat dry. Simply broiled porgy was nice and juicy, though. Ditto for beautifully fresh red snapper. A $10.99 broiled lobster special came with some savory stuffing, though a small lobster does dry out a bit when broiled; perhaps it would have been better to ask for it steamed. The Greek Captain combo, which included crab legs, was not noteworthy except for more of the tangy stuffing.

The waitresses are no-nonsense but take a great deal of trouble to make sure you get what you want and don't pay too much for it. (We felt almost embarrassed about getting the $10 wine; probably the $8 wine would have been perfectly fine.) They seem to want to save you money, an exceptionally rare attitude in restaurants nowadays.

You'll linger, elbows on the blue-and-white-checked oilcloth, to drink another glass of wine and nibble at the last of the thin, good French fries. You'll start to plan your next meal at Greek Captain—fried shrimp, perhaps, for only $8.50? No, maybe fish and chips, just $5.99. And eventually, you'll go for coffee at one of Astoria's Greek cafes. (My fave: Lefkos Pirgos, 22–85 31st St.; (718) 932-4423.)

HAPPY DUMPLING
135-29 40th Rd.
Flushing
(718) 445-2163 or 445-2164

HOURS: Daily, 11 a.m.–10 p.m.
PRICES: Entrées $7–$11; appetizers $2.50–$4.25. MC, V.
RESERVATIONS: Recommended, especially during dinner hours.

ACCESS: Dining area wheelchair accessible, restrooms are not.
HOW TO FIND IT: Near Main Street; subway line 7 to Main Street/Flushing station; bus lines Q12, Q13, Q15, Q16, Q17, Q20, Q26, Q27, Q28, Q44, Q48, Q58, Q55.

OK, maybe there is a noodle shop on every other corner in Manhattan nowadays. But Flushing is still the true noodle central, the place that is the cutting-edge standard for noodles and dumplings and salt-baked chicken and all manner of authentic Chinese fare.

Happy Dumpling, a narrow but prettily decked-out space on a side street, is so good you'll want to go there from Manhattan. Scott, who works in Manhattan and lives in the 516 area code, makes this place a stop between the two, and after one visit, we saw why.

We had a delicious dish of noodles with meat and bean sauce and lively eggplant in garlic sauce. We liked bean curd with black mushrooms, spicy prawns and a fine whole crisp fish with chili sauce. (Sea bass was on the menu, but beautifully fresh pompano was available when we asked.) Scallion pancakes were thick and hearty but just as tasty in their own way as the usual thin version. Yet it was none of these, commendable though they were, that completely sold us on Happy Dumpling; it was the remarkable vegetable dumplings.

Steamed vegetable dumplings are not even on the menu, not unless you count the somewhat vague entry "home made dumplings [12 pieces]." They probably can be any kind of dumplings you want them to be. One bite of these ambrosial morsels and we were in heaven. Whisper-thin dough was stuffed loosely with bits of scallion and bean curd, without cellophane noodles or other filler.

Next time, in search of more ambrosia, we went with Scott, who obviously is a favored customer. When he shows up at your table, you get little extras, such as a plate of fresh, addictively good salted peanuts and a bowlful of delicious cold, roasted fava beans. There's a menu category called snacks, and although neither of these treats was listed, they fit the spirit perfectly.

From that section of the menu, we ordered steamed corn bun, like a kind of airy cornbread. We ate lovely pan-fried noodles, subtle cold sesame noodles, a cold jellyfish salad that was good considering that it's an acquired taste, and cold, plump chicken marinated in wine. As more and more courses arrived, clean plates were offered with them. We heartily recommend chicken with garlic shoots as well as vegetarian bean-curd chicken in a cold, soy-accented sauce. Once in a while, in this feastlike array, a dish stood out as even more special than the others; mustard greens in a sauce of pungent dried scallops was such a standout.

At Scott's urging, we even tried sea cucumbers in brown sauce. These delicacies are sometimes inelegantly known as sea slugs and in modern-day China, as hi-shen, or ginseng of the sea, for their aphrodisiac powers. Sea cucumbers do soak up seasoning with zest, and this brown sauce was so tasty that it could win you over.

A few dishes were not such happy tastes: Tangerine beef was too fatty, and Szechuan cabbage and tripe soup seemed bland. These were exceptions. And even the tea was uncommonly good, always fresh and never bitter.

Our good fortune was just to discover Happy Dumpling. But if more was needed, the fortune inside the cookie couldn't have been sweeter. "One who admires you greatly," it read, "is hidden before your eyes."

INDIAN TAJ
37-25 74th St.
Jackson Heights
(718) 651-4187

HOURS: Daily, dinner 5–11 p.m. Lunch 11 a.m.–5 p.m.
PRICES: Entrées 6.95–$10.95; appetizers $1.50–$3.95; roti $1.45–$3. Lunch $3.95–$4.95. DC, MC, V.
ACCESS: Dining area wheelchair-accessible; restrooms equipped for disabled.
RESERVATIONS: Recommended for weekends.
KIDS: Children's menu, $3.95–$4.95.
HOW TO FIND IT: Between Roosevelt and 37th Avenues; subway line 7 to 74th Street/Broadway station or line E to Roosevelt Avenue/Broadway station; bus line Q45.

JACKSON DINER
37-03 74th St.
Jackson Heights
(718) 672-1232

HOURS: Sunday–Thursday, 11:30 a.m.–10 p.m.; Friday–Saturday, 11:30 a.m.–10:30 p.m.
PRICES: Entrées $7–$9; appetizers $1.75–$5.25. Lunch buffet $4.99, specials $4.50–$5.95, Monday–Friday; lunch buffet $6.99 Saturday–Sunday. AE, MC, V.
ACCESS: Dining area/restrooms wheelchair-accessible.

KWALITY RESTAURANT
37-13 74th St.
Jackson Heights
(718) 779-1513

HOURS: Sunday–Thursday, noon–10 p.m.; Friday–Saturday, noon–10:30 p.m.
PRICES: Entrées $10–$15; appetizers $2–$3.75; lunch buffet $4.50 weekdays, $6.50 weekends. AE, MC, V.
ACCESS: Not wheelchair-accessible.

I call it the street of saris. All along this stretch of 74th street there are windows of bright silks, saris for sale. By the front doors of fabric stores, boxes filled with remnants entice. Who can resist the acquisition of a yard of fluttery yellow print that might be hemmed for a scarf?

On a recent snowy afternoon, a band of five intrepid eaters set out to sample the amazing Indian buffets of Jackson Heights. I say amazing because the prices are so low and the food is so good. Can you believe $4.95 for a feast? $4.50? Dessert is included, but tea is extra. How do they do it?

One unusually communicative waiter clued us in to the fact that his bosses were making only approximately 20 cents on each customer. But, he said, they have to compete.

Maybe these bargains won't last forever, but while they do, eat up.

One rule: Don't ask for a doggy bag. Think about it; if you were allowed to take the buffet food home for a later meal, there's no way they could make even a slim profit.

Our first stop was an old favorite, Jackson Diner, where the buffet is $4.95. Other restaurants may have attractive decor (the Diner has no decor to speak of), but they can't beat the Diner for earthy tastes and the atmosphere that loyal customers bring with them. We were especially lucky this day because there was a large, festive, Indian wedding party, the bride dressed in a red sari and other women dressed in vivid silks, too. Many smiles, much picture taking.

Each buffet featured something that set it apart from the others, and in the case of Jackson Diner, savory cheese balls made with lentil flour were one of the most unusual and delicious items. The steam trays held paneer, homemade cheese cooked with spinach; chicken curry; deeply tangy, long-marinated tandoori chicken; mixed vegetable curry, chick-pea curry and beautifully cooked white and yellow rice. Everything was spicy enough to warm toes wet from the slush. There was salad, and there were breads (nan and utthapam, a kind of pancake with peas) and chutneys, and rasmalai, the sweet cheese balls, besides. There is no license for wine or beer, so we ordered tea and coffee. (After all, this was our breakfast, in a way.)

Kwality, the Punjabi restaurant that came to this block about a year ago, has gone Jackson Diner one better by serving its buffet for the rock-bottom price of $4.50. And instead of being skimpy, it is lavish. The array of sweet, brightly colored Indian confections available at the restaurant's own shop, practically next door, was the most generous dessert we found anywhere. But first things first.

This is an elegant-looking room with a mauve-and-gilt color scheme, and here we could order big bottles of icy Taj Mahal beer to share. In a way, we felt guilty for liking this buffet as much as we did, because we are so loyal to the Jackson Diner.

But we did love it. Indian breads are best consumed straight from the oven, so none are left out on the buffet, but you may order delicious, puffy nan for no extra charge. The meats in chicken and goat curries were tender, and the dishes seemed particularly fresh. Corn curry was wonderful. Tandoori chicken had an almost delicate quality. We learned that the cooks at Kwality blend their own tamarind sauce, chat masala (red chile powder) and other condiments. This attention to detail gives Kwality an edge, no doubt about it.

Ask about anything you don't understand. We sampled a luscious dish, new to us, called bhel puri. You mix it yourself, first taking from the buffet table a mixture of almonds, chopped onions and potatoes, puffed rice, coriander and chick-peas. Then you add chutney sauce, and, last, homemade yogurt.

Dessert is divine; small syrup-soaked cakes made of semolina flour, a coconut confection so sweet it is like candy, a not-so-sweet candy made mostly of cooked-down heavy cream and pistachios. You'll feel like lingering over tea.

At Indian Taj, the third buffet, we must admit to having lacked a hale and hearty appetite. So it was a tribute to the good cooking that we were able to eat anything at all. (We'll be back to try the 15-course weekend buffet, $5.95.) Both the chicken tikka masala, tandoori chicken bathed in a rich tomato-cream sauce, and the chickpea curry were excellent. The fluffy white basamati rice was scattered with hot pepper, more as a garnish than as a flavor component, and the menu promises: "Don't think Indian food is always spicy. We will prepare to your taste." Well, we like spicy, and this food was tasty enough to win our crowd's thumbs-up. We couldn't manage more dessert, but we sipped milky masala (or spiced) tea gratefully.

JEAN'S
188-36 Linden Blvd.
St. Albans
(718) 525-3069 or 525-2333

HOURS: Lunch/dinner Monday–Saturday, 11 a.m.–11 p.m. Breakfast 7–11 a.m.
PRICES: Entrées $6.75–$9. Breakfast $5.
ACCESS: Dining area wheelchair-accessible, restrooms are not.
RESERVATIONS: Accepted only for large groups.
KIDS: No children's menu but will accommodate.
HOW TO FIND IT: At Farmers Boulevard; subway line E to Jamaica Center/Parsons Boulevard station, then take bus Q4; bus line Q4.

Remember the old song, "Sugar in the mornin', sugar in the evenin', sugar at suppertime"?

Well, at Jean's Jamaican eatery, the word Jean could substitute for sugar, because owner Jean Chisholm is ready to feed you three times a day, and you wouldn't mind eating there that often. How sweet it is to eat at Jean's.

Jean's is an unassuming little storefront decorated with a few posters of Jamaican food and a bulletin board thickly covered with business cards.

Jean's gets a steady stream of savvy customers. The regulars seem to follow a pattern, so that some folks come for dinner at 7 p.m., others at 8 p.m. or later, and the tables are nearly always full.

Savory, tender curried goat was the dish that convinced my friend Esther to tell me about Jean's, but there's a lot of other good food, too. Braised oxtails in their own rich brown gravy were a match for the goat. Spirited escoveche—a marinade based on onions and peppers—was a delicious treatment of snapper, and it would probably be equally fine on other fish. None of them, though, can beat the sassy jerk chicken, made with fiery Scotch bonnet peppers.

Almost all these entrées came with "peas and rice," though to the uninitiated, this dish will seem like beans and rice. The peas and rice are served somewhat dry, the better to soak up the peppery gravies and good juices of the meat and chicken. Most dishes also came with plantains or "provisions," an assortment of boiled root vegetables such as yucca and cassava, plus some boiled plaintain. The vegetables are bland by themselves, but with the spicy meats and stews, they're a perfect counterpoint.

"Mornin' time," though, is perhaps my favorite time at Jean's. The strong coffee was good enough to drink black, the way I like it. The home-fried potatoes, one of many American touches, were oniony and brown. The ackee with salt fish was indeed, as the song would have it, "nice." Calaloo, tender young leaves of plants such as taro, was cooked with salt cod, too, and made a delightful, if unusual, breakfast. Frizzled ham was top-notch quality and would be dandy as a side dish with any breakfast. Care had also been taken with grits, so that they were not too thick and pasty as they often are in restaurants. (The secret is to add extra water, and don't try to hurry the grits up, either.)

Beverages included the always-popular sorrel and ginger beer, and "Roots," a small bottle of a strengthening potion that tasted more than a little like medicine.

Luckily, Jean's offers the perfect chaser, Taste the Tropics' incredible ice cream in irresistible flavors—butter pecan, rum raisin, cherry vanilla. And don't knock "great nuts," which really is made with Grape Nuts, until you try it. It is great, honest.

JOE'S SHANGHAI
136-21 37th Ave.
Flushing
(718) 539-3838

HOURS: Sunday–Thursday, 11 a.m.–10 p.m.; Friday–Saturday 11 a.m.–10:30 p.m.
PRICES: Entrées $7.95–$14.95; appetizers $3.95–$6.95.
RESERVATIONS: Taken only for parties of 10 or more.
ACCESS: Dining area/restrooms wheelchair-accessible.
KIDS: No children's menu but will accomodate.
HOW TO FIND IT: Near Main Street; subway line 7 to Main Street/Flushing station; bus lines Q17, Q27, Q44.

Three rows of chairs are jammed together at the entrance to Joe's Shanghai. It's the waiting room. Stick around.

With an ever-rising noise level and crowds that threaten to spill out and annex another restaurant, Joe's Shanghai practically pulsates.

You half-expect the stacked cases of soda to topple because of the vibrations, the continuous movement, the errant elbow. This is dining out at full speed, where the suggestion that you take part in communal seating is a practical matter.

No one is late for his or her next appointment.

Your lingering impression here is fast food in the best sense. There's almost nothing in the decor that stays in your memory, save for a fish tank whose temporary residents don't seem there only for show.

Shanghai is the food capital of eastern China. The cuisine is well-represented at Joe's, with assorted steamings, noodles and dumplings. But the kitchen does venture elsewhere with skill and refinement.

You'll enjoy the minced chicken and corn soup, the shredded pork and pickled cabbage combo, the hot-and-sour, and the watercress and bean curd union. Bean curd with pickled cabbage and noodles also is tangy and good.

Fried pork-and-chive dumplings are crisp and flavorful. You may have these either boiled or steamed, too. Crabmeat-filled steamed buns burst with a bite and are salty, soupy delights. They're distinctive and enticing.

The familiar scallion pancake is a fragrant, crunchy disc. Smoked fish shouldn't be confused with the sort that goes well with a bagel. These mouthfuls are bony and crusty stuff, on the sweet side.

Recommended cold appetizers include the sliced, pickled cabbage and the braised pork. If you have a taste for the unusual, some starters to consider are duck's web with celery, sliced kidneys with mixed vegetables and the ever-popular jellyfish.

Seafood naturally dominates at Joe's Shanghai. The "crispy whole yellow fish" is fine, though you'll need a surgeon's dexterity to debone it. Yellow fish is prepared in various guises. You may choose among yellow fish casserole in broth, steamed or braised yellowfish, sweet-and-sour yellow fish and "crispy yellowfish fingers with seaweed."

Unshelled prawns with spicy pepper salt require labor and deft decapitation. But the shellfish are vibrantly saline and strewn with tiny ringlets of jalapeño.

The competition for these salty celebrities ranges from spirited prawns in chili sauce to the more challenging prawns with braised sea cucumbers. The most expensive item on the menu is straightforward enough: shrimp with large sea slugs. Maybe next time.

Joe's Shanghai sends out a glossy sauté of chicken with hot peppers, and a lively, crisp "pepperskin duckling." The standard General Tso's chicken and the sesame chicken are worthwhile alternatives.

Forget about dessert. No need to dawdle. Besides, your seat already has been reserved.

—Gianotti

JUST LIKE MOTHER'S
110-60 Queens Blvd.
Forest Hills
(718) 544-3294

HOURS: Monday–Thursday, 7 a.m.–10 p.m.; Friday–Saturday, 7 a.m.–11 p.m.; Sunday, 7:30 a.m.–10 p.m.
PRICES: Entrées $5.95–$10.75; soups $2.50–$3.50; breakfast $2.25–$6.95. MC, V.
ACCESS: Dining area wheelchair-accessible; restrooms equipped for disabled.
HOW TO FIND IT: Between Ascan Avenue and 73rd Road; subway line E to 71st Avenue/Continental Avenue station; bus lines Q23, Q60.

The name Just Like Mother's is a challenge that invites comparison. Not Almost Like Mother's, but Just Like Mother's. (Then again, maybe your mother was a bad cook.)

"Do you think these latkes are better than Grandma's?" one woman who was breakfasting at Just Like Mother's asked her slender husband.

"Don't ever, ever tell her this," he replied, "but these are better. These are so thin." He tasted a crispy edge of potato pancake appreciatively.

This is a man I can trust, but, to protect the guilty, I won't tell you his name. I will tell you, though, that this lean New York Marathon runner has been known to polish off most of a platter of babka-French toast and some latkes, not to mention a side of grilled kielbasa, all at one sitting. He has been known to start the day with latkes, banana pancakes, a couple of slices of toast and, for good measure, a double side order of bacon. If breakfast is this fellow's favorite meal, latkes are arguably his favorite breakfast. He never breakfasts at Just Like Mother's without them. Yet none of this matters; this guy seems to get thinner every time I see him.

I share his passion for the light, oniony latkes (with a side of applesauce, please) at Just Like Mother's. And, like him, I find it hard to decide what I want most, so I order a surfeit of food.

Cheese blintzes were light, scented with vanilla and prettily sprinkled with powdered sugar. Scrambled eggs came with fresh, nicely browned home fries and delicious grilled kielbasa. Banana pancakes—the banana is in the batter—were excellent. Orange juice and carrot juice were freshly squeezed.

For those concerned with life beyond breakfast, soup is a good lunch or, at supper, a first course. Try white cabbage borscht enlivened with bits of spicy kielbasa, thick mushroom barley and hearty tripe soup. Big rollmops—one rollmop, actually, as our waitress pointed out—was a rollup of satisfying pickled herring with pickles and vinegared cucumber inside.

Or start with pierogies, top-notch either boiled or fried; besides the usual sauerkraut and mushroom, fluffy potato and farmer-cheese flavors, you can get spinach pierogies here, or even little dumplings stuffed with cheddar cheese. (We skipped cheddar, preferring the classic mushroom and sauerkraut. It's enough just to know that cheddar pierogies exist.)

One untraditional item we can heartily recommend at Just Like Mother's is the "Hungarian pie," which turned out, happily, to be based on latkes—two potato pancakes with savory beef goulash in between. With a side dish of something pleasantly tart, such as cucumber salad or red cabbage, the Hungarian pie would make a dandy meal.

Most of the Polish-Hungarian favorites are to be found here. Bigos, the mixture of sauerkraut and bits of meat, with a boiled potato showered with fresh dill on the side, was lackluster. But chicken Kiev, handsome and properly buttery, was a treat. It was emphatically not the dreaded chicken Kiev seen on so many menus, the one that comes from a central frozen-food factory unimaginably far away.

Chicken in the pot, boiled fowl with an assortment of root vegetables, might be the perfect restorative when you're feeling under the weather. Cabbage was lightly stuffed and tasty. Most entrées came with two vegetables chosen from an array that included the aforementioned boiled potato, mashed potatoes (here, homemade, of course), kasha, red cabbage, beets, or that sprightly cucumber salad. Beets, cabbage and other vegetables with a tart tang provide just the right contrast with megadoses of meat and potatoes. To drink, you might want to try kompot, the refreshing homemade fruit beverage.

Apple fritters, a sweet version of potato pancakes dusted with powdered sugar, were all the dessert we could manage. But based on a taste of the breakfast devotee's babka, we can recommend a slice of it with a cup of tea.

As the story ends, we leave the breakfast-meister despairing over his generous serving of French-toast babka. "This is like eating a whole loaf of bread for breakfast," he muttered, clearly distressed that he was not even going to be able to tackle the home fries on someone else's plate. "This is lunch, too," he rationalized, lifting just one more forkful. Still, he had that hungry, hollow-cheeked look.

Jim Morrison and The Doors, a group that probably reached Poland late, are a favorite tape at this bright little eatery. Perhaps the words of "The End" should be, here, "Meal That Never Ends."

—Gianotti

KHAYAM
248-25 Northern Blvd.
Little Neck
(718) 281-0706

HOURS: Sunday–Thursday, 11 a.m.–10 p.m.; Friday, 11 a.m.–midnight; Saturday, 11 a.m.–1 a.m.
PRICES: Entrées $9–$17; appetizers $3–$4.50; lunch special $7.95. AE, DC, DS, MC, V.

RESERVATIONS: Required for dinner.
ACCESS: Dining area/restrooms wheelchair-accessible.
KIDS: No children's menu but will accommodate.
ENTERTAINMENT: Friday–Saturday live music with belly dancer, 9 p.m.
PARKING: Indoor/outdoor parking area.
HOW TO FIND IT: Near 248th Street, in Little Neck Shopping Plaza; subway line 7 to Main Street/Flushing ,then take bus Q12; bus line Q12.

The twain meet at Khayam.

Khayam has straightforward and flavorful Persian fare. But there's an alliance with Eurofood to make the United Nations envious. Khayam brings together several cuisines.

Khayam's color scheme is pink and mauve, with accents of chrome. Not a grand carpet in sight. But it's definitely the decorative and architectural highlight of a little shopping center that also includes a pharmacy and a pizzeria. Service is halting and unfailingly polite. Very accommodating, too.

Start with halim bademjan, a deftly seasoned union of "smashed" eggplant, garlic and tomato sauce. The savory spread may be slathered on warm pita bread, or just taken straight.

Just as invigorating, and similar in other ways, too, is the vibrant kashk bademjan, that smashed eggplant with copious amounts of garlic and a sauce made with yogurt. An essential opener, or at least a garnish for other dishes, is dubbed must and mousir, which is translated accurately as yogurt and garlic.

Hummus, the crushed chickpea dip, is more grainy than creamy, dabbed with lemon juice and olive oil. The thick sauce is best on the pita bread, and tasty with olives.

Most of the salads are good. The combo of diced potatoes, eggs, chicken, lemon juice and mayo is a Middle Eastern riff on chicken salad, calling for whole-wheat toast more than the pita. But it's satisfying. Diced tomato, cucumbers and onions have the spark of mint before the oil and vinegar take over.

Lentil soup is warming and true, floating some carrots. The house's pleasing borscht has enough tomato and assorted vegetables to do double duty as minestrone.

If these appetizers seem headed in one direction, be assured that you may have a shrimp cocktail. And, if you want to continue a western ride, the "European entrées" are reliable.

Wiener schnitzel, the Viennese cutlet of French origin, here is sautéed, golden and greaseless. You could move on to steak au poivre, chicken Française or Chateaubriand.

The broiled salmon kebob is excellent, dotted with minced dill. Or try ample kebobs of char-broiled beef, seasoned ground beef and meaty Cornish hen: all tender, moist, recommended. Better than these is khoresht rooz, a hearty beef stew with beans and tomato.

There are three desserts, each equally honeyed. The two that aren't baklava are not that far removed from it. A swirl of fried dough and balls of it the size of walnuts are very sweet and sure to prompt you to sample the Middle Eastern coffee.

If that's not your favorite beverage, they have espresso and cappuccino, too.

—Gianotti

LA BARAKA
255-09 Northern Blvd.
Little Neck
(718) 428-1461

HOURS: Dinner Monday–Friday, 5–9:30 p.m.; Saturday, 5–10:30 p.m.; Sunday, 4:30–9:30 p.m. Lunch Monday–Friday, 11:30 a.m.–2:30 p.m.
PRICES: Entrées $18.95–$25.95; appetizers $3.95–$9.95; early dinners (5–7 p.m. Monday–Friday, 5–6:30 p.m. Saturday) $15.95 and $18.95. Lunch buffet $8.95; a la carte dishes $6.95–$16.95. AE, DC, DS, MC, V.
ACCESS: Dining area wheelchair-accessible, restrooms are not.
RESERVATIONS: Recommended, especially on weekends.
KIDS: No children's menu but will accommodate.
HOW TO FIND IT: Three blocks east of Little Neck Parkway; subway line 7 to Main Street/Flushing station, then take Q12 bus; bus line Q12.

There are so few grand cru French restaurants in Queens that you half expect any one you see to be a mirage. But, close to the borough's eastern border is an oasis.

For years, La Baraka has been an essential stop along Northern Boulevard. And it's still a charmer, with full-flavored food, genial personality and a level of popularity proving all tricolors don't need arugula.

La Baraka's dining room is a warm, stuccoed affair. Vivid posters herald Lillet, Piper Champagne, Bieres de la Meuse, the Palais de Glace. At least one image evokes Toulouse-Lautrec; another, Mucha. Copper pots are part of the decor. So is a coffee grinder, a yoke that could suit husky plow-pullers and pretty old clocks.

La Baraka turns back the hands.

This is de Gaulle's France. Go elsewhere for nouvelleties, meals minceur and things that taste as if they haven't been cooked. And start here with snails.

Escargots often are rubbery excuses to dive into butter and garlic. The plump, tender fellows at La Baraka receive fragrant, tasty treatment. You'll be using bread as a sponge.

The pâtés here vary, but an exceptional one is made with goose liver: smooth, silken, recklessly rich and finished with a bull's eye of sweet meat. Diners in a mellower, nostalgic mood may sample the high, light quiche Lorraine, or the quiche with spinach.

Bestel refers to a flaky, baked pastry holding a savory union of potato and ground beef. It arrives quartered, cutting down on the fragmentation and making it easier for your companions to steal a piece.

Of course, there's onion soup and it's the classic gratinée. Striking and unexpected is an import from the French Quarter—vibrant, thick and smoky gumbo, heady with sausage and okra. The eatery's mushroom soup, however, stresses creamy texture rather than earthiness. It's routine. The lentil soup has deeper flavor.

Entrées are a familiar, and welcome, group of Gallic specialties. But there's a definite standout, a dish that distinguishes La Baraka from other local French establishments. This is where you go for couscous.

This is the grainy semolina that's basic to North African cooking. Traditionally, it's steamed and served with meats and poultry, a regional spin on the boiled dinner that knows no borders.

La Baraka has a fiery sauce on the side, as well as some fine bouillon. The couscous, studded with chickpeas, is at the center of your plate. The blond mound is surrounded and topped by cubes of lamb on a skewer with onions and peppers, a chicken breast, breakaway tender beef flanken, and a zesty sausage of lamb and beef. The result is terrific. If you have one meal here, the "couscous royal" should be it.

Lamb chops with parsley are a juicy and first-rate alternative, down to the little panty on the bone. Shell steak in red wine sauce; chunks of beef in a kindred, vinous sauce, and filet mignon with peppercorn sauce provide some competition.

Likewise the big broiled veal chop, under an irresistible mantle of bacon and onions. Veal Normande translates into a brandy-and-cream sauce, with sliced mushrooms, atop tender scallops of meat.

Another winner is chicken with mustard sauce. And the roast duck is crispy and moist, recommended with any of the three deftly done sauces: orange, raspberry or peach. The rind-threaded orange sauce is especially good.

Tuna Provençal, a slab capped with a sauce of tomatoes, peppers and capers, is rosy and right. Or you could move on to trout amandine or frogs' legs with garlic and parsley.

A bottle of Jadot's fruity, firm 1992 Moulin-a-Vent ($22.50) suits La Baraka. And Jolivet's 1990 Sancerre ($27), while not as youthful and fresh a sauvignon blanc as you'd like, has body left.

Naturally, you may conclude with chocolate mousse. Crème caramel wobbles on cue. Pear Helène is devoted to chocolate. And the profiteroles, filled with ice cream, have a charming time-capsule quality.

So does La Baraka. Rub your eyes and open the door.

—Gianotti

LA ESPIGA BAKERY II
32-44 31st St.
Astoria
(718) 777-1993

HOURS: Daily, 7 a.m.–10 p.m.
PRICES: Entrées $3–$5.50; breakfast $3–$3.75. AE, DC, DS, MC, V.
ACCESS: Wheelchair-accessible; no restrooms.
PARKING: Municipal lot nearby.
HOW TO FIND IT: Near Broadway; subway line N to Broadway/31st Street station; bus lines Q102, Q104.

"We ain't just bread" is the motto of La Espiga Bakery II, borrowing a line from the Martin's paint ad. In fact, they might go even further and say bread is the least of what they do.

This is not to belittle the daily bread—tortillas—at La Espiga. The tortillas are delicious, all right. It is to say that tortillas are but a component of the wonderful food available here. Tortillas are, after all, the foundation for tacos made of crispy bits of pork, the perfect accompaniment to "beans of the pot."

And then there are the sandwiches, or tortas, made of three gorgeous cheeses and sandwiches made of spicy Mexican sausage, or chorizo. Sit down on one of the nine or so stools haphazardly arranged around the counter, sip a Mexican Coca-Cola or a Jarrito soft drink (my favorite is the grapefruit flavor) and gaze around this busy bakery. Just breathing in the appetizing smells of pinto beans simmering and tortillas toasting on the griddle is a peak experience. But you also can start to do your shopping.

I would rather eat here, or get takeout, than take home these alluring ingredients, however, for the simple reason that the guys at La Espiga's grill know a lot more than I do about making Mexican food. Sitting at the counter on a Friday afternoon, you can watch as a skilled craftsman uses an old, seemingly handmade wooden press to stamp out wide, oval-shaped tortillas for a special recipe. You can ask for salsa to spice up your cheese torta and be rewarded with a molcajete (that's a stone mortar-and-pestle affair) filled with a coarse, homey sauce that is little more than crushed chile. You can watch as bakers carry trays of sugary, puffy cookies and sweets high aloft toward a display case near the door.

I almost protested that I didn't want any enchiladas suizas, or "Swiss enchiladas," having been a victim of too many gloppy, Americanized versions of that dish in what I now think of as my early and unenlightened days as a Mexican food eater. But when my pal Jim said not to miss them, I took his advice and was glad I did. These enchiladas, stuffed with savory chicken, luxurious with cheese and napped with green sauce, must be the best I ever tasted. Like everything else here, they are made to order, carefully, expertly.

La Espiga's three-cheese super-torta crowds cheese, beans and pickled jalapeño onto a light, yeasty house-made sandwich bun. The grill man smushed a bit of creamy pinto beans onto the cut side of the bun he was warming on the griddle. (This is standard procedure for tortas here, and it is one of the touches that sets La Espiga's tortas apart.) The three cheeses, by the way, include one from Oaxaca, one that is surely the Mexican version of mozzarella, another (the grilled cheese) that is like muenster, only better. Super torta is not hyperbole when it comes to this sandwich.

Panbasos, which the menu translates simply as special fried Mexican sandwich, was a savory combination of potatoes, garlic and cheeses, this time with beans smeared on the outside as well as the inside of the sandwich, and with the bun toasted. It's a lot more special than the vague name implies. And chorizo, or sausage, torta, spicy and melding with the beans, was not to be missed. For those seeking a triple shot of protein, there's the Francesa, made of stewed chicken, ham and more glorious cheese.

Don't neglect the tacos, the soft sort that are authentically Mexican. Two soft corn tacos were wrapped around tender, deep-fried carnitas, small tidbits of pork (and yes, some bits of fat, too) along with a generous scattering of cilantro and onion. Al pastor, chile-soaked pork, also made a fine soft taco.

Craving tamales, we called to see whether there were some one fin de semana (weekend), but there were none. Other specials that may, or may not, be available on the weekend included barbecued goat, goat soup and beef tripe soup. Never mind; I'm happy enough with the everyday eating at La Espiga.

No, solo vendemos pan; no, it ain't just bread, not by a long shot.

LATERNA
47-20 Bell Blvd.
Bayside
(718) 423-1245

HOURS: Daily, dinner 3 p.m.–midnight; lunch 11 a.m.–3 p.m.

PRICES: Complete dinner $9.95–$11.95, 3 p.m.–7 p.m. daily. Lunch $3.75–$7.50. AE, DC, DS, MC, V.
ACCESS: Dining area/restrooms wheelchair-accessible.
RESERVATIONS: Suggested for weekends.
KIDS: No children's menu but will accommodate.
ENTERTAINMENT: Friday–Sunday, live Greek music, 7 p.m.
HOW TO FIND IT: Between 47th and 48th Avenues; subway line 7 to Main Street/Flushing station, then take bus Q13; bus line Q13.

Laterna applies the new Grecian formula. It's sleek and definitely not gray. Here's the taverna turned modern, with much space and light, plus a charcoal grill working overtime.

Outside, the colors are familiar blue and white—except, recently, for a rainbow of tulips painted along the floor-to-ceiling windows. Once indoors, Laterna is all earth tones, from the polished wood floor to the beiges and greens along the walls and tables.

Your table is covered with a sheet of glass. Atop that is a paper placemat that could double as an elementary crib sheet. It has a map of Greece, an image of the flag, a guide to Corinthian, Doric and Ionic columns, a sketch of the Parthenon and boxes that provide capsule history and a quick intro to the geography and the economy.

All this, and no mention yet of moussaka.

Indeed, the regular menu doesn't include either that or pastitsio. But don't be alarmed. Recently, they were among the daily specials.

Avgolemono soup, with its citric edge, rice and chicken, tends to be the soup of the day. And it's a respectable version. But Laterna lures you with most of its hot and cold appetizers. You could make a savory meal of them.

Fried eggplant arrives as well-seasoned oval slices, about $1/4$ inch thick. They're matched by the crisply fried zucchini. Make it a trio with long, oily, fried peppers under a shower of oregano.

Spanakopita, the spinach pie, also is pleasing. Likewise, saganaki, the hot plate of bubbling cheese. Diners who turn away at the mention of octopus should sample the charcoal grilled production here: tender, smoky, sweet.

Keftedakia are little, fried meatballs, which the menu quickly adds are "without tomato sauce." The football-shaped mouthfuls are crunchy and filling. They benefit from the company of tzatziki, a refreshing yogurt and cucumber dip.

The house's cold appetizers are the Greek classics: taramasalata, the roe spread with bread, olive and lemon; melitzanosalata, the vivid eggplant purée, and skordalia, the elemental and intense garlic dip. Slather them on the sturdy bread. And be sure you have a drink at hand. Kefalograviera, a plate of tangy strips of the cheese, neatly completes the group.

For main courses, the charcoal-grilled fish are recommended, particularly the meaty and snowy red snapper. Porgies undergo the same preparation. But a cut of swordfish is, despite the modest price, on the thin side. An assertive, flavorful choice is dubbed bakalarios skordalia. It's two large pieces of fried codfish complemented by the garlicky accompaniment. And the "seasoned chicken on the spit," a cousin of shish kebob, has some spark. The straightforward shish kebob of chicken is ample, alternating with peppers and onions.

Moussaka and pastitsio are big slabs, multi-layered, and more than enough to feed two. The moussaka, with its ground meat, eggplant and cloud of béchamel is rich and hearty stuff. The pastitsio, with its layer of macaroni, is equally large and well-seasoned.

It's hard to resist a wine named Aphrodite. The nonvintage Keo wine from Cyprus is $13. For a red: 1990 Naoussa Boutari ($15).

Recently, Laterna had two desserts. The official baklava, when fresh, is first-rate. The rice pudding, with a cinnamon dusting, is creamy and fine. And you may return immediately to tradition with a very grainy, very sweet Greek coffee.

—*Gianotti*

LITTLE NECK FISH AND GRILL
254-16 Northern Blvd.
Little Neck
(718) 631-3474

HOURS: Sunday–Thursday, 5–9 p.m.; Friday–Saturday, 5–10:30 p.m.
PRICES: Entrées $16–$19.50; appetizers $4.50–$8.50. AE, MC, V.
RESERVATIONS: Recommended, especially for Friday–Saturday.
ACCESS: Wheelchair-accessible; restrooms equipped for disabled.
HOW TO FIND IT: Block and a half east of Little Neck Parkway; subway line 7 to Main Street/Flushing station, then take bus Q12; bus line Q12.

Little Neck Fish & Grill, is a major catch in Queens.

The handsome restaurant has refined its cuisine and turned almost every entrée into a visual delight. Under chef Kevin Kessler, the place shows plenty of potential and delivers on a lot of it, too.

It's the good-looking, bright establishment you'll remember. The decor is dominated by posters and artwork immortalizing venerable ships and lines, with the Art Deco image of the Normandie still the favorite.

Recently, you could start with a sampler of raw oysters: Malpeques, Hood Canal, bluepoints, flowers, all perfect. Or equally pristine cherrystones and, of course, littleneck clams. The seafood platter is a briny, sweet cross-section.

Going from the raw to the cooked, sample the generous and satisfying crab and sweet corn chowder. It's an elemental, rich soup regardless of the season.

The crab and shiitake mushroom spring roll is terrific: a diagonally cut duet forming a mini-skyline of flavors. This architectural appetizer is spiked with a well-spiced carrot sauce dubbed Thai. Fried calamari, not the standard pile of tentacles, is crisp, greaseless and sent out with a diverting roasted tomato-and-smoked chili mayonnaise.

A holdover from the early days is the smoked seafood plate, now holding trout, salmon, shrimp and marvelous, peppered bluefish. You'll enjoy these morsels unadorned, but the horseradish-and-caper dressing does have spark.

Eggplant "caviar," shaped much like a precisely formed, thick hamburger, is accompanied by two discs of tangy goat cheese, with roasted peppers and a subtle complement of balsamic vinegar syrup and basil-infused oil. Refreshing stuff. A fine entrée of grilled salmon is set on some of that eggplant mash, a variation on caponata featuring sun-dried tomatoes.

If none of the sturdier starters appeals to you, the kitchen makes a good

Caesar salad, ironically one that hides the anchovy, and an ample salad of flavorful young greens.

The vigorous, peppery seared tuna has a keen edge. The main course is capped with a thatch of fried potatoes that rises high enough to warrant a zoning challenge. It's the unofficial, eastern Queens entry in the tall food Olympics.

Striped bass is topped with an energizing horseradish crust. The tasty dish is completed with cucumber "vermicelli" and a modest spin on risotto with shrimp. The pan-roasted red snapper is a delicate counterpoint, encased in scales of potato and enriched by a merlot wine sauce.

The meat-eaters at your table will do with the Cajun grilled rib-eye steak, which is halved and forms a small arch above garlicky mashed potatoes. The beef is excellent. Grilled, French-cut chicken is packed with goat cheese and herbs, and flanked by white beans and broccoli rabe. It's moist and right.

Little Neck Fish & Grill has respectable wines by the glass. Among them are the 1992 Rosemount Shiraz and the 1992 Dry Creek Fume Blanc. By the bottle, wines are $17, $23 or $29. The less-expensive ones include the 1992 Pierre Sparr Riesling and 1992 Jadot Beaujolais Villages.

Little Neck Fish & Grill already has improved things for anyone seeking quality seafood east of Manhattan and west of Montauk.

—*Gianotti*

LONDON LENNIE'S
63-88 Woodhaven Blvd.
Rego Park
(718) 894-8084

HOURS: Dinner Monday–Friday, 3–10 p.m.; Saturday, 4–11 p.m.; Sunday, 2–9 p.m. Lunch Monday–Friday, noon–3 p.m.
PRICES: Entrées $14.95–22.95; appetizers $5–$10. Lunch $6.95–$10.95. AE, MC, V.
RESERVATIONS: Taken for groups of 6 or more Monday–Thursday, 8 or more Friday–Sunday.
ACCESS: Dining area/restrooms wheelchair-accessible.
KIDS: Children's menu, $6.50.
PARKING: Small lot behind restaurant, valet parking during lunch hours.
HOW TO FIND IT: Opposite 63rd Drive; subway line G or R to 63rd Drive/Rego Park station, then take bus Q38 or Q53; bus lines Q11, Q38, Q53.

L ondon Lennie's, a staple on Woodhaven Boulevard for three decades, is one of the borough's best seafood restaurants.

They take reservations only for six or more, so you may have a brief wait. Look around the place. The walls carry maps of the Central and Bakerloo lines from London's underground, posters of the horse guards and other very British images, plus a lot of fish art.

The menu poses the question "What makes a Cockney?" and offers appropriate translations. And you're advised about Lennie's voyage from four fish 'n' chips stands in London to this more-ambitious colonial outpost, thereby becoming the fish king of Queens.

The varieties of oyster available have included Glidden Bay and Spinney Creek, Hama-Hama and Martha's Vineyard, Pearl Bay and Fanny Bay, Virginicia and, of course, Bluepoint. A mixed platter is an ideal way to begin.

Try the fried shrimp dumplings, crisp and flavorful mouthfuls, with an Asian accent. A special of "halibut nuggets" is deftly fried chunks of the fish almost the size of a Twinkie. It's a very satisfying appetizer of the firm, mild fish that could do double duty as a small main course.

The hillock of tasty fried calamari, accompanied by a cup of tomato sauce, offers more conventional competition. The addictive frying continues with expertly done onion rings.

New England clam chowder and Manhattan clam chowder both emphasize the shellfish instead of the supporting cast.

Your lobster may be steamed or broiled, with the former definitely preferable. The lobsters lately have been up to four pounds, $15 per. They're perfectly cooked and need neither the drawn butter nor the lemon to distract from their elemental sweetness.

The preparations of finfish usually are first-rate. If you've been after fish and chips, this is the place to have it. A single golden slab of scrod, not a stack of morsels or a pile of fingers, is the centerpiece. This is blunt and simple food, skillfully and greaselessly prepared. Just ask for the malt vinegar, and resist the temptation to eat the fish with your fingers off a newspaper, Londoner style, rather than knife and fork.

Sheepshead, a member of the porgy clan from Florida, arrives in a ribbonlike potato crust, flanked by a cabernet glaze. This spin on a nouveau classic is workmanlike and to the point.

Sautéed medallions of monkfish are complemented by a sauce hinting of balsamic vinegar, for a diverting entrée. The mashed potatoes have a hint of sesame. Broiled salmon and lemon sole, grilled tuna with a honey-mustard sauce, and sautéed skate in a tarragon beurre blanc add to the worthwhile selections.

For the diner who ends up here and can't abide seafood, London Lennie's juicy, fibrous and neatly charred T-bone steak is a solid alternative. They also have sirloin and filet mignon. The straightforward grilled chicken is satisfactory, too.

Desserts are led by a lush, genuine strawberry shortcake, a serious banana cream pie and a playful turn on the English trifle. The pear-and-apple strudel is flaky, fragile and appealing.

Customers often leave with leftovers, if not a purchase for tomorrow. Contented faces abound.

—Gianotti

MANDUCATIS
13-27 Jackson Ave.
Long Island City
(718) 729-4602

HOURS: Dinner Monday–Friday, 5–10 p.m.; Saturday, 5–11 p.m.; Sunday, 2–8:30 p.m. (closed Sundays in July-August). Lunch Monday–Friday, noon–3 p.m.
PRICES: Entrées $9–$18; appetizers $5–$7. Lunch $7–$15. AE, DC, MC, V.
ACCESS: Dining area wheelchair-accessible; restrooms equipped for disabled.

RESERVATIONS: Recommended for weekends.
KIDS: No children's menu but will accommodate.
HOW TO FIND IT: At corner of 47th Avenue; subway line 7 to Vernon Avenue/
Jackson Avenue station or line G to 21st Street (Van Alst) station; bus line B61.

This is not a review. It is the story of a love affair.

A dozen years ago, on an intrepid search for fresh eggs, I found myself in a red brick light-bulb factory in Long Island City. Sources had told me that the folks at the factory sold eggs from upstate farms, and this turned out to be true. The factory was an offbeat place in other ways—the owners had brought a perfectly swell upright piano in off the street, and one of them played it—and I spent a few happy hours there. These people handed me a card with the name Manducatis on it. This card would change my life.

On a first visit to the then-modest-looking restaurant, my friends and I knew we had stumbled into the presence of genius. It was not that the menu looked different from many another Italian menu; it didn't. But what came out of the kitchen was different. Lasagne had never tasted this good, and neither had canneloni. Somehow, we were able to keep eating this almost-delicate food long after we usually would have felt too full. Partly, this was because of chef Ida Cerbone's light hand and her insistence on fresh ingredients. Partly, perhaps, it was because she sent us a wonderful salad at the end of the meal, Italian style, "to help push things down."

On our second visit, somebody had spilled the beans, and Ida and her husband Vincenzo Cerbone—Vincent to most customers—knew we were from a newspaper. That was election night in 1980 (when Jimmy Carter lost to Ronald Reagan), and after the Cerbones had given us wine and bread, they came to the table, coats on, and asked us to excuse them while they voted. A good review was not more important to them than exercising that American right.

Over the years, I have come to know Ida and Vincent's four children and now two grandchildren: Anthony, Joseph, Piero, Gianna, Angela and Vincenzo, named for his grandpa. Their friends and family are mine, now, too. We have visited Ida's home village near Monte Cassino in Italy, eaten figs from her family's trees, strolled to the bottom of the hill to fetch water from Ida's spring, eaten pizza made from flour milled at Ida's brother's mill. Our bond has little to do with restaurants and much to do with the fact that we both were once farm girls.

In Ida's case, that meant carrying a bucket of milk to the family of a baker on the way to school each morning. At 10 or 11, she noticed a handsome young man, the baker's son, 10 years or more older than she "I had my eye on Vincent even then," Ida said lightly. He paid her no attention.

Many years passed; she was 19, and he was more than 30, and both, unbeknownst to one another, were in America. They met at a party, and both broke off their engagements to other people. It sounds corny to mention it, but Ida and Vincent are still crazy about each other, and you can see it when they are together.

Memories crowd each other, jostling for space. Should I reminisce about the time Vincent and I sang too much with the accordion player on New Year's Eve, which is also Vincent's birthday? Or about the time I was in the hospital and Ida, forever thin and young, showed up wearing gorgeous suede boots, bearing pastries and looking like a movie star? Then there was the morning I found an antique wooden ironing board on the street and brought it to Ida. There were mornings we three sat in the sunny front room of the now-expanded Maducatis and drank coffee together before the restaurant opened. Or should I tell you Vincent's story about Al Capone, a story I can follow even in Italian, for I have heard it so many times at my own request that I know it by heart?

No, there is no space for all that. You want to know about food, because this is a space where food is the important part. Before Manhattan restaurants had New Zealand mussels and flown-in buffalo-milk mozzarella, I had them at Ida's, our name for this place. Long before it became the craze, she filled small bowls with privately imported "liquid gold" olive oil for bread dipping. Chefs from Manhattan come to her for ideas. I, too, try to make things taste "like Ida's." Ida makes her own arugula pasta, roasts succulent little pigs in winter, lets white beans simmer by a wood fire overnight for soup. We yearn for her greens when we have done without them too long.

When tomatoes are at their peak, Ida not only jars all the tomatoes used all year in the restaurant, she sometimes goes to a cousin's farm upstate to help gather the tomatoes! This is uncommon in the extreme, but Ida does it as if it is a perfectly ordinary way to run a restaurant. We never consult the menu now, we just ask Vincent. Vincent tends a fine collection of wine, stories and friends, and he knows how to cure proscuitto and make wine with great finesse.

One night, missing someone, I went into Ida's kitchen and saw an appealing dish of tomatoes and rice. "I want that," I said. But there was a pasta I coveted that evening, too. Ida sent the two starch courses to me, one after the other, and she said, "Tell Sylvia this is pasta with love."

This is a Valentine for Ida and Vincent, with love.

MOMOYAMA
136-17 41st Ave.
Flushing
(718) 762-9516 or 939-4082

HOURS: Dinner 4–10 p.m. daily. Lunch Monday–Friday, 11:30 a.m.–4 p.m.
PRICES: Entrées, $6.50–$25; multi-course tasting dinners, $35 and $45; appetizers, $3–$8; sushi, $1.50–$3. Lunch special, $6.50–$7.50. AE, MC, V.
RESERVATIONS: Recommended for weekends.
ACCESS: Steps at entrance; dining area/restrooms wheelchair-accessible.
PARKING: Commercial lot with half-price discount for patrons.
HOW TO FIND IT: Just east of Main Street, on the north side; subway line 7 to Main Street/Flushing station; bus lines Q12, Q15, Q17, Q44.

Momoyama has become one of the leading Japanese restaurants in a neighborhood where the cuisines of Asia abound with flavor and flair. Look for the vertical neon sign illuminating SUSHI. The word is across from another lit with equal wattage: Budweiser.

Flushing is a destination for many New Yorkers who've reached their capacity for neutralized Chinese and Japanese fare. It's also the closest community for consistently good Korean meals, an intro to Vietnamese cooking, and assorted forays to Malaysia, Pakistan, India and points beyond.

You begin with a couple of free appetizers. Perhaps a whole, silvery, assertive grilled mackerel. Or chawanmushi, a delicate, steamed egg custard with a nugget of seafood inside. The menu at Momoyama takes in the traditional array of starters, soups and entrées, at fair prices.

And the restaurant fashions a superb omakase, or chef's choice dinner. This is a grand, pricey multi-course affair, a degustation refined and invigorating. Kaiseki, an artful, ceremonial tasting meal, also is prepared, here covering some of the same, plus sushi.

What you'll receive is a survey of Japanese dining, a stirring procession of dishes bringing together the various forms of cookery that define the cuisine: assorted appetizers, clear soup, lustrous sashimi, an intermezzo, grilled food, deep-fried fare, a vinegared dish, a simmered one, pickles and, at least at Momoyama, dessert.

If you order the designated "dinner box," you'll get tempura, broiled fish, a salad, raw fish, rice and soup. It adds up to a satisfying package deal.

You may, of course, fashion abbreviated versions of the omakase, the dinner box, or whatever, from the menu or by request. They're accommodating.

For a fine rendition of a dish too-often wrecked, sample the negimaki, or velvety rolled beef around scallion. Yakitori are tender chunks of skewered chicken, in a slightly sweet sauce. Deep-fried bean curd: terrific. The house's gyoza, or crispy grilled shrimp dumplings, are marvelous. Tempura, whether shrimp or vegetables, is filigreed, crunchy and greaseless.

A sashimi of fluke, arranged like the pearlized petals of a flower on a blue-on-blue plate, is perfect. All the raw fish sampled at Momoyama was outstanding, whether pristinely as sashimi or as sushi, the fish with vinegared rice.

Favorites during recent visits: a lush, conical hand roll of fatty tuna; another of buttery yellowtail; a third of toasty, slightly sweet eel. The rainbow roll is a multi-hued concoction, with beefy red tuna at its center. The seductive salmon-skin roll and a roll containing soft-shell crab are diverting and delectable.

Among the special main courses at Momoyama is a superlative shabu-shabu. It's thin slices of well-marbled beef quickly cooked in broth at your table. A staff member does the work. But you may participate when the place is crowded. In go the vegetables, then the meat. You may choose to spike the beef with a zesty dipping sauce.

The ever-present miso soup is fragrant and first-rate, preferable to the dull clear soups with shrimp or with a clam better suited for chowder.

Dessert is the standard red bean or green tea ice cream, both satisfactory if not exactly exciting.

But you're in Flushing. Walk around. The choices are many.

—Gianotti

PARK SIDE
107-01 51st Ave.
Corona
(718) 271-9871

HOURS: Daily, noon–11:30 p.m.
PRICES: Entrées $10–$20; appetizers $3–$8. AE, DC, MC, V.
RESERVATIONS: Recommended.
ACCESS: First-floor dining area wheelchair-accessible (second floor not accessible); restrooms downstairs.
PARKING: Valet parking next to restaurant.

HOW TO FIND IT: Corner of 108th Street and 51st Avenue; subway line 7 to 103rd Street/Corona Plaza station; bus lines Q23, Q48.

The wave of red sauce that threatens to cover Queens crests at Park Side.

A southern Italian citadel for years, Park Side revels in gutsy, soulful food without a risotto in sight. And on a weekday night it's packed like a jar of peppers.

You may wait a while before you're seated, reservations or not. But the perpetual-motion maitre d' makes sure no chair is empty a moment longer than it takes to change the tablecloth and rearrange the pepper and salt. Efficiency, practicality and not losing sight of the goal typify Park Side.

A special starter of eggplant, roasted peppers, grilled asparagus and the like is light, fresh and very good. Or you could veer toward a husky shrimp cocktail, fat and glossy Portobello mushrooms, or an ample seafood salad. The rounds of fried zucchini are a crisp opener, worth nibbling while you peruse the rest of the back-to-basics menu. Only with designated specials does Park Side divert from the tested and true.

Pastas are ample, familiar and fine. They prepare an expert linguini with white clam sauce and an uncompromising rendition of linguini or fedelini with olive oil and garlic. Ravioli are hearty, whether filled with ricotta or porcini mushrooms. The scarlet sauce is first-rate.

The skill with the straightforward extends to steak alla pizzaiola, a fibrous, flavorful sirloin awash in crimson. Park Side also is the right spot for veal alla Parmigiana. The meat is tender, the sauce has a touch of sweetness, and the cheese melts on cue. You're tempted to ask for a loaf of bread and just down a hero.

Veal piccata, with a cloudy, lemony sauce, is, in contrast, light and even subtle. Likewise the citric chicken scarpariello, off the bone and on the mild side instead of golden, garlicky and paired with chunks of sausage.

Squid, conch, and shrimp fra diavolo do have a hellish kick, spurred with pepper. The menu mentions the incendiary taste you may impart with Vincent's hot sauce. Anyway, this diavolo is no meek marinara in disguise.

Vegetables with oil and garlic are mandatory with most of Park Side's selections. Recommended are both the generous portion of escarole and the assertive broccoli rabe.

Desserts are surprisingly limited, or at least in great demand. The Italian cheesecake was gone during recent visits. Content yourself with spongy tirami su, the peach cake, or a trembling crème caramel.

Some days, you may step outside and observe a bocce game in progress in the park across the street, the one that must give the restaurant a name as direct as the food.

—Gianotti

PATOUG
220-06 Horace Harding Expwy.
Bayside
(718) 279-3500

HOURS: Sunday–Thursday, 11 a.m.–11 p.m.; Friday, 11 a.m.–2 a.m.; Saturday, 11 a.m.–4 a.m.

PRICES: Entrées $7.20–$23.50; appetizers $2.50–$4. AE, MC, V.
RESERVATIONS: Recommended for weekends, especially after 9 p.m. Saturdays.
ACCESS: Wheelchair-accessible; restrooms equipped for disabled.
KIDS: Children's menu Sundays, 11 a.m.–4 p.m., $4.50 (cartoons on large screen).
ENTERTAINMENT: Belly dancers and live music Friday–Saturday.
PARKING: Valet parking Friday–Saturday.
HOW TO FIND IT: Between 220th Street and Springfield Boulevard; subway line 7 to Main Street/Flushing station, then take bus Q27; or line E to Jamaica Center/Parsons Boulevard station, then take bus Q30.

To bread and wine, Omar Khayyam could add sambuseh and torshi. But the Persian poet never made it to Patoug.

In the ever-active melting pot of Queens cookery, Persian food is one of the newer elements. After you've explored eastern Asia and western Europe, a stop in between is refreshing.

You enter a restaurant whose design does little to suggest the cuisine. The dining room is a neutral, stuccoed affair in off-white. The seating arrangements are in black.

The food immediately transports you. The best way to start at Patoug is with combination platters of appetizers. Hummus, the appetizer of mashed chick-peas, or tahini, sesame paste and garlic, is a vibrant opener, slathered on warm pita bread.

Pair it with torshi, a lively blend of chopped pickled vegetables, or with sambuseh, crunchy, half-moon dumplings packed with ground beef, vegetables and chickpeas. Masto khiar refers to a homemade yogurt finished with chopped cucumber and mint that complements this and many other dishes.

The house's baba ganoush, or baked eggplant sparked with garlic and tahini, continues the series of appealing appetizers. You could make a very good meal of appetizers alone at Patoug, particularly if you try the kashk-bademjian, or cooked eggplant emboldened with onions and a tomatoey sauce, and panir-sabzi, feta cheese matched with vegetables.

Falafel, quarter-size, deep-fried combos of chickpeas and vegetables, are on the dry side, but they're helped by a salad capped with tahini sauce. If the soup of the day is barley, try it: a bracing bowlful, with rice, and a round of lime on top.

They do a lot of char-broiling here, and most of it is excellent. The kebob barg, marinated and skewered striplets of tenderloin, is flavorful and juicy. Jujeh kebob is cuts of Cornish hen seasoned with saffron and lemon, cooked the same way with the same result.

Kebob kobideh is composed of two skewers of well-seasoned ground beef. Shashlik, marinated and neatly charred chunks of lamb, is sturdy competition. The most modest item, of course, is the marinated, boneless chicken breast. The vegetarian shish kebob, with eggplant, onion, tomato, mushrooms and peppers, is recommended either as an entrée or a side dish for the table.

Baghali polo, meltingly tender braised leg of lamb, arrives on a mound of rice. Diners needing a wintry main course should sample one of the khoreshes, the restaurant's hearty stews, also with basmati rice.

Seafood choices are few. But the char-broiled fillet of salmon is moist and tasty. Trout broiled in butter and shrimp Française are respectable alternatives. Shrimp are available on the familiar skewer, too.

For your finale, Turkish coffee is appropriate. But it's the definition of acquired taste. To the uninitiated, the beverage has the character of moistened, sweetened sand.

Baklava, with finely ground nuts, is a standard ending, as is the Persian ice cream, scented with rosewater. Another Persian sweet, faloodeh, has the impact of cold cream and needs more than a couple of shots of lemon juice to cut it. Next time: the cream puffs.

Omar didn't sing too long about desserts.

—Gianotti

PENANG CUISINE MALAYSIA
38-04 Prince St.
Flushing
(718) 321-2877/2078

HOURS: Daily, 11 a.m.–11:45 p.m.
PRICES: Entrées $6.95–$18.95; appetizers $1.60–$6.95.
ACCESS: Dining area wheelchair-accessible, restrooms are not.
RESERVATIONS: Not accepted for weekends.
HOW TO FIND IT: Near 38th Avenue; subway line 7 to Main Street/Flushing station; bus lines Q12, Q15, Q16, Q17

"You have tried the rest, now try the best," exhorts the motto on the paper takeout menu at Penang Cuisine Malaysia. Now plenty of places have mottos like that, usually to be taken with an ample grain of salt. But Penang, named for a Malaysian island, has justifiable reason to boast. It just might really be the best.

I'm an eager adventurer in Maylasian eating and can't lay claim to being an expert. So, thanks to my friend Lorie, I enlisted her friend Zang Toi, the fashion designer, as my walking reference guide to all things Malaysian. Zang said that Penang's food is some of the best food of his homeland in New York, and based on two incredible visits there, I believe him.

Even without knowing a lot about Malaysian food—I had had it three or four times before Penang—I know that this seems like the perfect place to get acquainted with the delights of this earthy, spicy cuisine. Penang is one in a cluster of Malaysian restaurants on this block; if there's a "Little Malaysia" in New York, this is it.

This exciting style of cooking—here, usually by ethnic Chinese who are from Malaysia—is a bit like Chinese cooking but seems even more akin to Indian food with its appealing breads and curries, and to Thai food with its fiery flavors. Curry leaves, coriander, lemongrass, scallions, ginger, fish sauce, garlic and chile pepper abound.

Begin, as Zang suggested we do, with roti canai, which the menu describes as an Indian pancake. It turned out to be a fresh-baked flatbread served with a pungent, chile-fired dipping sauce. You can get it with or without a layer of cooked egg in the middle (Zang likes it with), and with or without onions (Zang prefers without). We've tried it and liked it in all variations. In Malaysia, the egg version is often eaten dipped in sugar at breakfast time.

Other excellent starters included ikin bilis, a heap of crisp, deep-fried anchovies with red and green pepper, and Penang lobak, a type of spring roll. Deep-fried white turnip rolls lavishly strewn with fresh coriander and served with bits of pickled vegetables seemed like a revelation, better than you ever thought turnips could be.

We ordered with abandon and were pleasantly overwhelmed by such taste thrills as stuffed eggplant with chile in broth; squid with both fried and steamed noodles; squid with "Chinese watercress" (a green leafy vegetable that isn't watercress as we know it), and a bowl of asam laksa—thick noodles in a broth that contained lots of greens and red onion. Indian rojak, a combination of jellyfish, shrimp, tofu, shrimp cake and hard-boiled egg, was topped with deep-fried shallots.

We ate a braised and curried beef called redang, a whole steamed snapper with plenty of chile zing, fish head cooked with greens in a white coconut broth, jumbo shrimp in a wine casserole, watercress with preserved bean curd, baby-oyster omelet. Kang kung, a leafy green vegetable that in Malaysia would be thrown to the animals, made a delicious vegetable side dish. Curried fish with tamarind-based curry and okra—ladyfingers in Maylaysian parlance—was smashing.

Hainanese chicken, steamed in soy and served with pickled cucumbers, was moist and tasty, but curried chicken "with potato" disappointed us, because there really did seem to be no more than one small potato. Chicken rice, Zang's favorite, is a byproduct of Hainanese chicken. To some, this beloved dish is perhaps the best test of a Malaysian kitchen's abilities. Coconut milk and broth from cooking a plump chicken are added slowly to the sautéed rice as it cooks and expands, and the dish is aromatic with the scents of ginger, garlic and deep-black soy sauce.

A few beers are available, and if you want to do as Malaysians do, choose Guinness stout, a preferred drink in hot countries. Fresh coconut juice is also refreshing and lighter than you might expect. A dessert pancake liberally scattered with peanuts was wonderful, but Malaysians dote on a shaved ice dish with colorful syrups, kernels of corn, red beans, peanuts, coconut and jiggly squares of green gelatin. In English they call it "ABC." Stir together and lap it up. To my Malaysian friends, the only big difference is the prices; here ABC costs $1.80 and back home, they said wistfully, you could buy it for about a dime.

RICHARD'S PLACE
200-05 Linden Blvd.
St. Albans
(718) 723-0041

HOURS: Dinner Wednesday–Thursday, 4:30–10 p.m.; Friday–Saturday, 4:30–11 p.m.; Sunday, 1–8 p.m. Lunch Monday–Saturday, noon–4:30 p.m.
PRICES: Entrées $8–$10.95; appetizers $2.95. Lunch $5.25–$5.75.
ACCESS: Dining area/restrooms wheelchair-accessible.
RESERVATIONS: Recommended for groups of 4 or more.
KIDS: Any menu item half-price.
HOW TO FIND IT: At 200th Street; subway line E to Jamaica Center/Parsons Boulevard station, then bus line Q4.

How do I know that Richard Jones, owner of Richard's Place, is a chef par excellence?

It's not because Jones, 42, went to New York Tech's Culinary School. It's not because he can turn out an elegant filet mignon with mushrooms as well as a mean plate of fried catfish. And it's not because he grew up learning the tricks of the chef trade from his father, Sam, who owned restaurants in Aiken, S.C., and Augusta, Ga.

No, it is Jones' well-seasoned black-iron pots and pans that are the telling clue. Sure, there's other evidence, but black iron, which is my own preference for frying chicken and fish, is seldom found in restaurant kitchens; nothing holds the heat so well and so evenly. A peek at those reassuring iron pots and pans made me think I was about to be treated to some cooking that tasted like home, and I wasn't wrong.

Richard's is housed in the L-shaped corner storefront that once was Minnie T's, home of the world's best coconut cake. (Gracious, unflappable Rhonda Jones, Richard's wife, works the front of the house while he cooks.) Chicken and waffles, another Minnie T trademark, are still on the menu, and the crisp-fried chicken is flawless.

But that's getting ahead of the story. To start, instead, at the beginning, order lacy, ambrosial oyster-corn fritters served with delicious remoulade sauce. Yes, even southern cooks know about balsamic vinegar now, and Richard's tumble of greens is dressed with a vinaigrette that relies on it. Somehow, though, I prefer to go without salad for one night if it's a choice between it and gratifyingly zippy chicken wings.

If you're lucky, the breadbasket will include not only well-made cornbread (slightly sweet, but not cloyingly so) but dandy light rolls, too—like the ones you'd make yourself for Sunday dinner, if only you had time.

Most entrées come with four vegetables instead of the usual two, and since I always pine for extras, I'm delighted. You also have a choice between vegetable dishes that may include pork for seasoning and vegetable dishes that are strictly vegetarian; Jones does a good job with them either way. Fresh green beans were great seasoned with a bit of pork, but they also were first-rate sautéed. Sweet potatoes always seem too sweet to me when sugar is added, but other eaters at my table liked them just fine. Collard greens were slightly sweet, too, perhaps more from the bright bits of carrot cooked with them than from sugar. Black-eyed peas were cooked into submission (I hate it when beans and peas are al dente), and there was macaroni and cheese (always a vegetable in southern cooking). Perhaps very best of all was the sautéed cabbage, well seasoned with onion and gussied up with bits of carrot.

Smothered pork chops were tender beneath a cozy brown gravy, and blackened catfish was tasty and moist. When snapper was a special it was lightly coated in fine-ground white cornmeal, true southern-style. Country chicken fricasseed to tenderness with peppers and onions was a better choice than baked chicken, which seemed bland by comparison. But barbecued chicken in a sauce with a fair amount of tang was a winner.

Apple and peach cobblers were both family-size portions; two adults could share one serving, easy. Intriguing, not-too-sweet pumpkin cheesecake in a short crust (that means with plenty of shortening) was good to the last crumb. Bread pudding, Jones' signature dish, was tops, but for me the ultra-sweet strawberry sauce on the plate with it was overkill.

Sweetened, homemade iced tea and lemonade were poured freely, so we had seconds and even thirds and fourths. Coffee was fresh and hot. I'd like to have some of it with breakfast, along with the grits and home fries that hold sway earlier in the day.

On two occasions, service was somewhat slow, though the wait staff seemed efficient. Because of the large takeout business, I think, the kitchen gets backed up. For food of this caliber, though, I'm ready to wait and sip lemonade.

SCALA BRAZIL RODIZIO
35-48 31st St.
Astoria
(718) 472-2323

HOURS: Daily, noon–midnight.
PRICES: Fixed price, $12.95. AE, DS, MC, V.
ACCESS: Wheelchair-accessible; restrooms equipped for disabled.
RESERVATIONS: Recommended for Friday–Sunday.
KIDS: No children's menu but will accommodate.
HOW TO FIND IT: At 36th Avenue; subway line N to 36th/Washington Avenues station; bus lines Q66, Q102.

In Brazil, well-traveled friends tell me, it costs at least $35 to go to a churrascaria. That's an all-you-can-eat barbecue, with meats galore.

Lucky for you and me, we live closer to Astoria than to Rio de Janeiro, and at New York's first churrascaria, beneath the El in Astoria, the tariff is an unbelievable $12.95. Don't ask me how the food can be good at that price, but I swear it is.

Through the window of Scala Brazil, which is next door to a related nightclub, you can see luscious chunks of meat grilling on a rotisserie. The fragrance of roasting meat as you walk through the door is blissful.

First, help yourself from the buffet, but don't take too much or you'll never have room for all the meat later. On the long buffet, you'll find several types of soup—black bean, white bean with cow's feet one day, a thin caldo verde another. (Add a spoonful or two of rice to the soups as thickening.) There's usually feijoada, the lusty stew of black beans and meat, with traditional accompaniments on the side: fluffy fariofa, or manioc flour, for thickening; slices of orange; chopped-up kale with brown beans.

Wait, that's not all. There's a stack of beautifully grilled eggplant, zucchini and red onions, a veritable vat of creamy potato salad, crisp green salad. And you can go back for seconds, or even thirds.

If you're in luck, cachaca, the clear and potent spirit distilled from sugarcane, will be on hand for making caipirinha, $5 each. Caipirinha is pronounced kuy-per-REEN-yah, or something like that.

"Strong hands," said one waiter with a proud grin when we asked him the secret of this favorite Brazilian cocktail. The strength comes in when someone in the kitchen squeezes lots of lime wedges into a glass, packing them down over a bit of sugar, and then adds that delicious cachaca. If there is no cachaca, as was the case on one of our visits, you could try having the drink with vodka ($4), but it's really not the same. Instead, you might have beer, wine from a limited selection or guarana, the Brazilian soft drink.

I could have made a hearty supper with food from the buffet. (And vegetarians might want to do just that, helping themselves to plenty of rice and beans, the ones cooked without meat, and a surfeit of salad and grilled vegetables.) But next come the waiters—on weekends, wearing gaucho pants and red neckerchiefs— bringing platters of good french fries (add a sprinkle of salt), mellow sautéed bananas, crisp sticks of cassava and irresistible squares of crusty fried polenta. The polenta goes especially well with tangy fresh salsa from the bowl on the table. And, yes, you can ask for more of any of these side dishes, too.

The waiters are good about explaining the various cuts of meat as they are borne to the tables on skewers. Some of them were cuts unfamiliar to us, and local butchers might get a few tips from these folks. A waiter shaved meat off the larger roasts at the table, catching juices in a soup bowl. When everyone at one table had been served, he was off to the next group of diners. But very soon, was back, brandishing yet another spectacular piece of meat.

One night we were offered eight or more meat dishes, another night, seven. The first round often is pieces of succulent roasted chicken. Then there were Italian-style fennel sausages, pieces of juicy pork loin, slightly chewy but flavorful beef ribs, luscious filet, then another cut of beef that came from "behind" the filet, grilled chicken hearts, more beef, more chicken, more sausages. This was definitely meat, meat and more meat. The edges of the roasts were appetizingly browned, almost caramelized. And the aroma was so enticing. Who can resist just another bite or two, and maybe some fresh bananas? The idea of a dance hall next door is a good one; you could either work off the meat extravaganza by dancing, or you could dance until you're famished.

It is possible to order seafood dishes, and we tried two. Muqueca de peixe, a fish stew made with coconut sauce and cassava flour purée was mild but tasty, but shrimp "Stroganoff," made with mushrooms and cognac seemed fussy and overly sauced when compared to the simple goodness of the barbecued meats.

Strong coffee in demitasse cups is the right ending, but if you must have a dessert, still-warm rice pudding smothered in whipped cream was better than coconut pudding with prune sauce.

As for me, maybe just another sliver of that scrumptious pork roast. And how can I say no to one more carving of juicy beef filet?

SHIN JUNG
136-33 37th Ave.
Flushing
(718) 460-5026

HOURS: Monday–Saturday, 11 a.m.–11 p.m.; Sunday, 11 a.m.–9 p.m.
PRICES: $6.95–$15.95, except for some $27.95 specials that can be shared. AE, MC, V.
ACCESS: Main level wheelchair-accessible.
RESERVATIONS: Taken only for larger parties.
HOW TO FIND IT: Near Northern Boulevard; subway line 7 to Main Street/Flushing station; bus lines Q12, Q15, Q17.

"You'll know it," my pal Allan said. He was talking about the Korean restaurant he'd discovered, the one that looked like a barn or country house.

That is how Shin Jung looked from the outside. Inside, it was positively dripping with chandeliers, not found in most barns. Shin Jung was, to be sure, a Korean barbecue, true to its location in the heart of a Korean barbecue strip of Flushing. But we also encountered never-before-tasted Korean dishes.

"Soju," we said to the waitress, "what is that?" Korean Scotch, she said. I like to live dangerously, so we ordered some. It came chilled in a handsome green bottle, almost like a miniature Bombay gin bottle, and it was a clear liquid not the least like Scotch, more like vodka, though not so potent, distilled from sweet potatoes. Everybody wanted some, after all.

And so it went at Shin Jung—we kept encountering new taste thrills. As you sip soju or some sake, an array of small bowls will appear: blocks of tofu in a zesty sauce of hot pepper, scallion and garlic; a clear, subtle aspic soaking up a peppery, sesame-scallion sauce; lightly pickled, delicate stems of broccoli; a heap of crisp, julienned, vinegared daikon; spinach with sesame, and, of course, pungent pickled cabbage, or kimchi.

There is no listing for appetizers, but pa jeon would do just fine. It's a huge, delicious Korean pancake of eggs, scallion and seafood served with a garlicky, soy-based dipping sauce. As other possible starters, consider the page-long listing of noodle and rice dishes. We liked duk mandoo gook, well-flavored, pork-stuffed dumplings in a broth with some sliced rice cakes (a bit slippery to cut with chopsticks, so use your soup spoon). Bibim bab, a popular Korean dish of minced beef, rice, cellophane noodles, vegetables, fried egg and, of course, a generous dollop of chile sauce, was top-notch here. It's all mixed together at the table, and it won't hurt to add kimchi. Yooke jang, another popular soup, was wonderfully spicy, filled with shredded beef, scallions and fiddlehead-type ferns.

For the barbecue grill, we chose thin strips of sliced, marinated rib-eye steak, plain short ribs and o jing a gui, meaty strips of squid marinated in a peppery garlic sauce. And if you like cows' feet, order tender, savory ujok moochim (prepared, not to grill).

The menu described boyang chungol as goat meat and vegetables in spicy broth, but in reality this homey dish—$27.95 but easily split four ways—was somewhat akin to the southern cooking of this country. The goat was long-simmered and pulled into shreds, and the vegetable in the tasty broth was wild sesame leaves, or perilla, reminiscent of collard greens.

Even oranges, the only dessert, were prime—plump, cold and bursting with juice. They were perfect with a mug of gentle corn-and-barley tea.

SILVER POND SEAFOOD RESTAURANT
56-50 Main St.
Flushing
(718) 463-2888

HOURS: Daily, 8:30 a.m.–2 a.m.
PRICES: Entrées $8.35–$26.95; Beijing duck $34.75; soups $7.25–$15.75; shark's-fin soup $46.95; appetizers $3.25–$19.95 (for combination plate). AE.
ACCESS: Not wheelchair-accessible.
RESERVATIONS: Recommended.
HOW TO FIND IT: Near Booth Memorial Avenue; subway line 7 to Main Street station, then Q44 bus; bus line Q44 (on Main Street).

This transformed '50s diner has been a glitzy staple on Main Street for years. It's fast, brusque, crowded, lively. And, for all the bluntness and debates with staff, worth visiting for vivid food.

The restaurant is packed with contented families. Tables carry bottles of Coke and Sprite. There's much animation. You feel as if you've crashed a party. When the eating starts, the fun does. And the focus is on the food.

Some of it is on display. Silver Pond has a series of tanks with carp, crabs and lobsters—the aquarium of the condemned. They're routinely plucked out with a net, occasionally dropped on the rug, and periodicallty displayed or waved for inspection before execution. That last gesture is for the shellfish, the finfish having been carried off in plastic containers.

All of them depart valiantly and in a worthy cause. The crabs, in particular, are sweet and right, whether they're small or large, steamed with ginger and scallions or finished in vibrant black bean sauce. Lobster is available in these preparations, too. Devotees of abalone may find it available braised with oyster sauce, sliced with vegetables or duck feet or sea cucumber.

Deep-fried fresh oysters arrive as puffy pillows, crackling outside, tender and moist within. An entrée dubbed "smoked sable with salad" is a husky portion of flaky, smoky, white meat that's more like tilefish than the Sunday morning staple. The salad, thickly dressed, adds nothing. Sable "sizzling" with black bean sauce competes with vigor.

By comparison, shrimp get the least imaginative treatment. A pasty production of prawns with honey walnuts is dullness defined. You're better off with the baked salted jumbo shrimps, or the shrimps with macadamia nuts.

Baked chicken in salt is among Silver Pond's top entrées, juicy, crisp and pleasantly saline. The straightforward roasted chicken and the steamed chicken with ham and Chinese broccoli also are winners.

Likewise, the fried, boneless squab, complemented by a singular lemon sauce. The flavorful, almost gamey squab also may be had sautéed with straw mushrooms, or simply well-roasted.

But Silver Pond's big bird is Beijing duck, one of the best versions in the city. It comes in two delicious courses. The first is the fragile, lacquered skin on steamed buns that have been dabbed with hoisin, using a butterflied scallion as the brush. That's followed by a stir-fry of the fine meat and vegetables. All that's missing is a soup made from the bones.

The house's soups are uniformly first-rate, whether you're lured to the basic or the exotic. Stewed bird's-nest and braised superior shark's fin are pricey and distinctive.

Mellow corn soup with minced chicken and the ample seafood and bean curd soup are commendable rivals. And the hot and sour is a model of the genre, with bite and spark. The West Lake beef, egg drop and Chinese parsley number would be improved by subtracting the meat.

Thin pork chops, with chili and spiced salt, are chewy but tasty. The pork chop with pepper and black bean sauce elicits the same reaction. Sweet and sour pork is apt to send you back to the days of John Foster Dulles, but has more verve than usual.

Any of the bean-curd dishes should be considered, especially the fried, stuffed bean curd with minced shrimp, and the braised bean curd with black mushrooms and other vegetables.

To end at the beginning, crunchy rice paper egg rolls are good starters. Fried shrimp are satisfying, roast pork routine, and fried squid papery. You'll like the steamed bun, steamed shrimp dumplings and fried meat dumplings.

Quartered oranges arrive at the end of your meal. Your bill arrives only when you ask for it.

—Gianotti

SPOLINI'S

116-25 Metropolitan Ave.
Kew Gardens
(718) 805-5852

HOURS: Dinner Monday–Thursday, 4–10 p.m.; Friday–Saturday, 4–11 p.m.; Sunday, 4–9 p.m. Lunch Monday–Friday, noon–4 p.m.
PRICES: Entrées $11.50-$38; pasta $11.50–$17.75; appetizers $4.25–$17.75. Lunch $5.75–$19.
RESERVATIONS: Recommended for weekends.
ACCESS: One step at entrance; dining area wheelchair-accessible, restrooms are not.
PARKING: Valet parking.
HOW TO FIND IT: Near 116th Street; subway line E to Union Turnpike/Kew Gardens stations, then take bus Q10 or Q37; bus lines Q10, Q37, Q54.

Family-style Italian restaurants, which suit this decade the way garlic does tomatoes, have become as abundant as the platters they serve.

Spolini's, a Queens mainstay, is a model of the genre, from the portable blackboard of specials to the large placard listing the heavyweight regulars. The prices are fair and the food is good. No one leaves hungry. Most carry leftovers.

Part of the sidewalk in front of Spolini's is cordoned off, as if to ensure you know where you're headed, or to control a crowd. There's also a sign for valet parking, which in this neighborhood of tight street space becomes a genuine plus for those who haven't arrived by bus. Inside, Spolini's is a room of faux-marble-top tables just large enough to hold a few of the platters the kitchen sends out.

Stuffed artichokes are a generous and well-seasoned starter, with tender leaves and a heart to match. You get two, each the size of a pair of clenched fists. Before that, however, you'll be nibbling on rounds of gratis, well-done bruschetta. Pace yourself.

Stuffed mushrooms are plump, seven to an order, with a lively breading. The baked clams are small and tasty, though the oreganata on top occasionally in singed. Eggplant rollatine and fried eggplant both are flavorful and to the point. Likewise, the fried peppers and fried zucchini.

The house's seafood salad is $17. But the plate could feed three contented visitors. The combination of shrimp, squid and conch has a light, lemony edge.

Pastas are essential at Spolini's, and most of them are of the rustic, no-nonsense variety. The linguine with white clam sauce, for example, almost could pass for a rich cousin of oil and garlic. There must be a head of the mellow, whole cloves amid the minced shellfish and al dente pasta. You, and your health-care provider, will enjoy it. Eat here and you'll never even consider taking one of those garlic pills.

About as much garlic is in the hearty, soulful penne tossed with broccoli rabe and olive oil. Add some crushed hot pepper, and you're set. Rigatoni alla vodka may be a special, and it's a robust, reliable version.

The combination of veal scaloppine and fried eggplant in a light red sauce is enough for tonight's dinner and tomorrow's lunch. The elemental veal Parmigiana could last yu till the next day's meals, too.

Veal pizzaiola veers toward neutrality, and could be mistaken for a marinara in disguise. The steak pizzaiola is a better choice, anyway. You can do without the chewy veal finished with lemon and white wine.

Chicken scarpariello, alive with garlic, is on the bone, golden, herbaceous, excellent. This dish has an many renditions as there are chefs. The one at Spolini's keeps to the natural flavors, and doesn't include sausage.

A whole red snapper, broiled and then glossed with a dressing of garlic, olive oil and herbs, is among the lighter entrées, and definitely among the best. The fish is snowy, moist and inviting.

Sautéed escarole, spinach and broccoli are first-rate accompaniments to any of the entrées. The escarole with olive oil and garlic is homeyness defined.

The sole dessert that merits your attention and the calories is the ricotta cheesecake. The rest is pretty much the standard Bindi line of frozen finales, imported from Italy. They look pretty, but invariably they taste as if they've traveled long and hard. Better a sweet, if not from the kitchen, then at least from a local bakery.

But after the first three courses at Spolini's, you won't have any room left. They must know that.

—Gianotti

STICK TO YOUR RIBS TEXAS BARBECUE
5-16 51st Ave.
Long Island City
(718) 937-3030

HOURS: Monday–Friday, 11 a.m.–9 p.m.; Saturday, noon–9 p.m. Closed Sunday.
PRICES: Entrées $12–$15; appetizers $3–$6; lunch $7–$10.
ACCESS: Wheelchair-accessible; restrooms equipped for disabled.
PARKING: Lot adjoining restaurant accessible after 5 p.m.
HOW TO FIND IT: Between 5th Street and Vernon Boulevard; subway line 7 to Vernon Boulevard/Jackson Avenue station; bus line Q103 or B61.

There's Sonny Bryan's barbecue pit in Dallas. And, now, there's Stick to Your Ribs in Long Island City.

You'd feel right reaching this unadorned, authentic spot for Texas beef while riding on horseback, after seeing a rerun of "The Searchers." If John Wayne knew that Robert Pearson's great barbecue would be his reward, he'd have found Natalie Wood a half hour earlier.

This kind of barbecue, intense and true, doesn't just happen in any joint. Deep in the heart of L.I.C., Stick to Your Ribs is a tiny place along a street that needs repaving in a neighborhood where residences are outnumbered by factories and warehouses.

You'll recognize it by the Lone Star flag without and the Lone Star beer within.

And perhaps by the small white, plastic table and chairs for those visitors immune to car fumes who insist on dining al fresco. Inside, the scene is minimalist. Stick to Your Ribs seats about 20 people, depending on girth.

Ten plain, butcher-block tables offer a view of the slicing and chopping. A ristra of chiles rests atop the refrigerator, illuminated by a Bud sign. You can check the time on the neon-rimmed, Texas Barbecue clock. The walls are tiled, and decorated with writings about the Stick to Your Ribs phenomenon, here and that other untamed outpost, Connecticut. A basket of Wet-Naps is near the door.

If you're waiting for a takeout order to feed the troops, it's likely you'll have a conversation with one of the folks operating the slow-cook machinery toward the rear of the restaurant. After all, at the core of this establishment is the pit. It works overtime, cooking barbecue for up to 18 hours a day. Stick to Your Ribs burns oak, hickory and any competition.

The menu is blunt. The eatery extols outstanding beef brisket, chopped beef and barbecued pork shoulder; immortalizes ribs of beef, lamb and pork; and adds barbecued chicken, two kinds of chili, cornbread, some coleslaw, potatoes, beans, a couple of burgers.

Most of the stuff is terrific. The barbecued Texas beef is brisket in its glory—tender, rosy, with a memorable flavor that's accented by a range of sauces. They are: mild, medium, madness and mean. Usually, medium will do. But after "mean" is a dash and the phrase "as hot as you like—just ask!"

Raising the heat is simple. Keeping flavor isn't. Stick to Your Ribs can do both. Barbecued pork shoulder, lush and irresistible, is a good way to satisfy any curiosity about degrees of fieriness. Still, jolts above medium start to call too much attention to themselves instead of the barbecue.

Chopped barbecued beef, barbecued chicken and barbecued pork all are woodsy, smoky stars akin to Sloppy Joes in peak form. They're generously sauced and guarantee that you'll leave with a pound or two of take-out. The sandwiches are on a crusty roll. They need no more embellishments. But the coleslaw and sweetish salad shouldn't be ignored.

North Carolina chopped pork expands the Stick to Your Ribs repertoire. It's lean, vinegary, sweet-sour, white rather than the unflinching red of Texas. While pleasing, it's not so vivid a reminder of trips south.

Hamburgers and cheeseburgers compete with those of a first-class diner. The hearty "Chili New England Style With Beans" tastes grand, and provides an afterglow. But the whole barbecued chicken veers toward dryness, something you could ignore because of the strong, smoky character. Barbecued sausage also could be juicier, and trails the rest.

With this food, you'll be content having beer. It costs $2 for Lone Star, $1.25 for Bud. The differences between them are, well, subtle. Texas beef doesn't require Pilsner Urquell, anyway. Those who ended up here because they got lost probably will have a Corona, for $2.25. No limes were spotted during recent visits.

None of the predicted "specials" were, either. The menu says that whole pig, wild boar, alligator, venison, buffalo and rattlesnake are en route. You can have a slab of dense spoon pudding or a basic brownie while contemplating these prospects.

But you won't linger, even though the seats are more comfortable than Sonny Bryan's old school desks. Don't forget takeout. This newcomer has made Texas portable for city slickers.

Stick to Your Ribs does. Get on the IRT, pilgrim.

—*Gianotti*

TANDOOR
95-25 Queens Blvd.
Rego Park
(718) 997-6800

HOURS: Dinner Sunday–Thursday, 5:30–11 p.m.; Friday–Saturday, 5:30–11:30 p.m. Lunch daily, noon–3 p.m.
PRICES: Entrées $11.95–$19.95. Lunch weekdays $6.99, weekends $9.99. AE, MC, V.
RESERVATIONS: Recommended.
ACCESS: Dining area wheelchair-accessible; restrooms downstairs.
KIDS: No menu but will accommodate.
PARKING: At rear of restaurant for dinner only.
HOW TO FIND IT: Between 62nd Drive and 63rd Road; subway line R to 63rd Drive station; bus line Q60.

Tandoor is a first-class passage to India: the Taj of local restaurants. Big, bright, standing out along the boulevard, the place should lure diners who've reveled in vindaloos, those nibbling papadam the first time and anyone in a low-flying plane.

Tandoor has a mid-block locale on a site best remembered for a free-standing Howard Johnson's in the '60s. Pass through the ornate door and you'll find a two-story space with an airy, atrium effect and a waterfall plunging against a geometric, marble backdrop. And many tables offer window views of the chef working at the tandoor, the barrel-shaped, high-temperature oven.

The breads he bakes are terrific. Try tasty onion kulcha and alu paratha, an unleavened, whole-wheat disc packed with potatoes. Pudina paratha, accented with mint, and keema naan, with minced meat, are excellent. Poori arrives as a fragile, deep-fried, whole-wheat balloon. Papadam is a subtly spiced lentil wafer.

You'll enjoy the crunchy vegetable fritters, or pakoras, and samosas, triangular pastries holding a hearty combination of potatoes and peas. The two are included on a fine hors d'oeuvres platter that has a cut of aromatic, minced-lamb sausage and batter-fried chicken.

Crab Goa, a sauté of crabmeat with tomatoes, onions and mint, is respectable. So is macchle Amritsari, or nuggets of tilefish, marinated, floured and finished in the oven. An entrée of tilefish masala, flavored with ginger, garlic, tomato and onion, stays moist and true.

The tandoori mixed grill, with the familiar, reddened chicken, plus sausage and cubed lamb, excels. The tandoori special dinner adds lamb cooked in cream and modest spices, skewered chicken and deftly prepared vegetables.

Tandoor's vegetarian specialties are delectable, exotic and healthful, whether you're devoted to chickpeas and diced potatoes, superbly seasoned and fried lentils, savory baked eggplant, or with marvelous biryani, the classic basmati rice shaded with saffron and flecked with raisins and nuts.

The kitchen can expertly turn up the BTUs whenever you like. Ask them to ignite the rogan josh, the crimson combo of lamb, red chiles, cumin, cardamom and cinnamon. Lamb or beef vindaloo, a zesty, tart preparation, is best hot, too. Boti kabab bhuna, or roasted, cubed leg of lamb, competes with these. So does beef jalfrazie, sautéed with tomatoes, onions and mushrooms. Lighter, but creamy and just as good are chicken tikka sagwala, or diced meat finished with spinach and herbs.

Desserts are led by syrupy sweet gulab jammun, or a slowly fried milk sweet shaped into burnished, mellow balls; kulfi, the rosy Indian ice cream, and kheer, a spin on rice pudding.

You'll receive the royal treatment throughout. And leave feeling as if you've hit the jackpot.

—Gianotti

TERESA'S
70-34 Austin St.
Forest Hills
(718) 520-2909

HOURS: Daily, 7 a.m.–11 p.m.
PRICES: Dinner $8–$10; lunch specials $6–$8; breakfast $4–$5. AE, MC, V.
RESERVATIONS: Recommended.
ACCESS: Dining area wheelchair-accessible, restrooms are not.
HOW TO FIND IT: Near Continental Avenue; subway line E to 71st Avenue/Continental Avenue station; bus lines Q23, Q60.

With your personal index of leading economic indicators trailing Washington's, with your finances tied more to credit card rates than to the prime, you know why a third branch of Teresa's has opened.

This snappy newcomer is the offspring of the Teresa's on the Lower East Side and in Brooklyn Heights. The restaurants specialize in hearty Polish cooking at a homey cost. You can get out of Teresa's for about $10, often less, and be content. Or spend more and take care of tomorrow's meals, too.

And you can do it morning, noon and night. They're ready with eggs and babka toast for breakfast, goulash and kielbasa for lunch and dinner, pierogi and blintzes all day long. Somebody may even order a cheeseburger. The heavy-duty consumption will occur in a bright, cream-shaded establishment that's full of honey-toned wood accents.

Given the frequency with which soups are ordered, it's a prudent move to go with the no-tablecloth look. Depending on the day you're here, the choices run from Ukrainian borscht to pea, cabbage, tomato, pickle, and white borscht. Daily, you may have chicken soup, mushroom-barley, tripe, vegetable and cold red borscht while it's summer.

The cool soup is very good, invigorating stuff. Mushroom-barley, of course, will brace you for a snowstorm. But the one to try is tripe, which is husky, tender and true.

Pierogi, the marvelous little packets of dough, hold meat, cheese, potato, sauerkraut with mushrooms or a combo of these. You can have them either boiled or fried. Any way is the right way. But the favorites are fried potato, and cheese, with a side order of sour cream. You should not leave Teresa's until you've eaten at least two.

Equally essential are potato pancakes. These are big, gilded ovals, as close to greaseless as they ought to be. Fluffy and excellent. Another mandatory dish is apple fritters. Thinly sliced apples are battered and quickly fried, then capped with a drift of powdered sugar. The fritters are terrific at any point during the meal.

Veal-stuffed cabbage will ensure neither you nor anyone you're with will feel compelled to have a midnight snack. The familiar entrée is given its humble due. It's preferable to the veal goulash, which is on the fatty side.

Boiled beef in white horseradish sauce should have more bite in the sauce instead of requiring it for the chewy meat. But the roast pork is a generous serving. The juicy roast chicken is understandably popular. Broiled salmon: flaky and moist. And it's hard to dine here without sampling the kielbasa, the smoky sausage that pairs so well with the house's gutsy, stewed sauerkraut. It's available fried or boiled.

You have a choice of two vegetables with the main courses. Boiled or mashed potatoes, a refreshing cucumber salad threaded with dill, plain carrots and that zesty kraut are among them. So's kasha, the buckwheat groats that translate into soul food at countless tables.

Teresa's has a quintet of domestic bottled beers, six imports. The temptation is to stay with Zywiec, the Polish beer. It's light and easygoing. Molsen Golden and Budweiser are on draft.

Sweets at Teresa's are uncomplicated affairs. Rice pudding is more soothing than flavorful and the babka is a bit dry. But the apple cake with whipped cream is thick and genuinely fruity.

The best finale is a blintz, ultrathin, enclosing creamy cheese, blueberries, apples, cherries, or a combination of fruit and cheese. In keeping with the price point, Teresa's has them in half-orders, too, for $3.25.

With that approach, it's definitely the right restaurant for tough times.

—*Gianotti*

UNCLE GEORGE'S
33-19 Broadway
Astoria
(718) 626-0593

HOURS: Daily, 24 hours.
PRICES: Entrées $4–$12; appetizers $2–$5; salads $4–$6.
ACCESS: Dining area/restrooms wheelchair-accessible.
KIDS: Half portions available.
HOW TO FIND IT: At 34th Street; subway line N to Broadway; bus line Q102.

Don't look for a sign that says Uncle George's outside this restaurant.
Look for a sign that says:

E
N
Y
X
T
H
Z

In other words, it will look like Greek to you. It is Greek. (And that Z is really more like a double Z.) Does that really mean Uncle George's? Beats me.

But you'll know you're on the right street corner by the clusters of hungry people standing in the street waiting for tables to turn over, by the lamb, pig and chickens turning on spits in the window. Meat skewered on a pole and ready for roasting is carried without ceremony from the cold locker at the back to the ever-glowing coals at the front. To some, this may not seem like an appetizing sight.

But it becomes more appealing by the minute, as the meat browns and sizzles and sends clouds of delicious roasting-pork aroma into the air to mingle with cigarette smoke and lively chatter.

The motto at Uncle George's Greek Tavern is "always open," a reassuring thought. If a yearning for succulent roasted lamb and orzo flavored with its juices should hit you in the middle of the night, you know where to go.

But as a prelude to the meat course, try a hit of tomato-onion salad with slabs of feta and a hefty sprinkling of oregano, and maybe some skordalia (cold, garlicky mashed potatoes) and taramasalata, the carp-roe spread. Both had more distinction than too-thick tzaziki, the yogurt-based dip, which could have used more garlic. Greek beer or tart Greek rosé wine, here served in a tin carafe that's like a giant measuring cup, went well with everything.

We liked meat entrées best. You can't beat those hunks of juicy pork with crispy browned edges. Lamb was a fine choice, too. Beef "stew," chunks of meat served with okra, was not as moist as the lamb.

As for vegetable side dishes, you'll never go wrong with lemon-roasted potatoes sprinkled with oregano. Our group of eaters liked the okra, though to some it would seem overcooked. Escarole, which came with fish dishes, was stewed well past bright green to the shade kitchen manufacturers always call avocado. But with a squeeze of fresh lemon juice, it still tasted good. Red snapper was beautifully crisped on the outside, moist within.

From the red-and-white-checked oilcloth tablecloths to the unceremonious service, this is a no-frills joint. But the prices ($6 for chicken, $8 for lamb, $10 for pig, all with vegetables) make it a splendid place for the day before payday.

So eat your meat and potatoes and repair elsewhere in the neighborhood for dessert and strong Greek coffee.

ABOUT THE AUTHOR

Sylvia Carter left Iowa when she was several days old and moved to Missouri, where she was raised on a farm just west of the Mississsippi. Her father Charlie planted potatoes on the day she was born and always said maybe that's why he could hardly plant enough to keep her in them. She ate lots of catfish, picked gallons of strawberries and milked a Guernsey cow named Goldie. Her mother, Frances Elizabeth Smith Carter, made legendary doughnuts and angel food cakes, and her grandmother Girtha Pearl Johnson Smith churned butter and made the best pie crusts. Somehow, these were the things that made her a restaurant writer. But first, she got a bachelor of journalism degree from the University of Missouri and did general assignment reporting at the *Detroit Free Press* (where she won 1/54 of a Pulitzer Prize), the *New York Daily News* and *Newsday*. She has worked at *Newsday* long enough to qualify for either binoculars or a clock as a 25th anniversary gift and thinks she will probably pick the binoculars.

INDEX